Get the eBook FREE!

(PDF, ePub, Kindle, and liveBook all included)

We believe that once you buy a book from us, you should be
able to read it in any format we have available. To get electronic
versions of this book at no additional cost to you, purchase and
then register this book at the Manning website.

Go to https://www.manning.com/freebook and follow the
instructions to complete your pBook registration.

That's it!
Thanks from Manning!

Microservices in .NET Core

Microservices in .NET Core

WITH EXAMPLES IN NANCY

CHRISTIAN HORSDAL GAMMELGAARD

MANNING

SHELTER ISLAND

For online information and ordering of this and other Manning books, please visit
www.manning.com. The publisher offers discounts on this book when ordered in quantity.
For more information, please contact

Special Sales Department
Manning Publications Co.
20 Baldwin Road
PO Box 761
Shelter Island, NY 11964
Email: orders@manning.com

♺ Recognizing the importance of preserving what has been written, it is Manning's policy to have
the books we publish printed on acid-free paper, and we exert our best efforts to that end.
Recognizing also our responsibility to conserve the resources of our planet, Manning books are
printed on paper that is at least 15 percent recycled and processed without the use of elemental
chlorine.

Manning Publications Co.
20 Baldwin Road
PO Box 761
Shelter Island, NY 11964

Development editor: Dan Maharry
Technical Development Editor: Michael Lund
Project editors: Tiffany Taylor
and Janet Vail
Copyeditor: Tiffany Taylor
Proofreaders: Katie Tennant
and Melody Dolab
Technical proofreader: Karsten Strøbaek
Typesetter: Gordan Salinovic
Cover designer: Marija Tudor

ISBN 9781617293375
Printed in the United States of America
1 2 3 4 5 6 7 8 9 10 – EBM – 22 21 20 19 18 17

brief contents

contents

preface

When I first talked to Manning about writing a book, we discussed a book about Nancy. Part of me was excited to write about Nancy again, because it's an awesome web framework, but my first book was about Nancy, and a different part of me wanted this book to be something more. I felt that Nancy deserves not only to be explained and shown off, but also to be put into a context that shows *why* Nancy is such a nice web framework to work with. For me, the thing that makes Nancy so nice is that it's so easy to work with. It's a framework that gets out of your way and lets you just write the stuff that you set out to write. At the same time, it's a powerful framework that grows along with your needs. After some contemplation and some back-and-forth with Manning, it became clear that the context I wanted to put Nancy into was *microservices*. Microservices allow for the lightweight, fast way of working that I've come to appreciate over the years. They also accentuate the need for lightweight, yet powerful technologies—just like Nancy. At this point, the different ideas for what this book should be started to fall into place: I wanted to write a book that was more about designing and implementing microservices than about any specific technology, while at the same time showcasing some great, lightweight .NET technologies. That's the book you're about to read, and I hope that you'll not only learn how to be successful with microservices, but also learn the value of carefully choosing libraries and frameworks that value simplicity, that get out of your way, and that are a pleasure to work with.

acknowledgments

Writing a book takes time—a lot of time. So the first thank you is to my wife, Jane Horsdal Gammelgaard, for supporting me all the way through. You're awesome, Jane.

I would like to thank my editor, Dan Maharry, who, through great suggestions, gentle nudges, the occasional shove, and a relentless focus on creating a high-quality product, pushed me to write a much better book than I would have otherwise. A big thank you also goes to my technical editor, Michael Lund, for his thorough code reviews and suggestions for improvements, and for ripping my line of reasoning apart whenever it wasn't clear. A special thanks to Karsten Strøbæk for his in-depth technical proofreading.

I can't thank enough the amazing group of technical peer reviewers: Andy Kirsch, Brian Rasmussen, Cemre Mengu, Guy Matthew LaCrosse, James McGinn, Jeff Smith, Jim McGinn, Matt R. Cole, Morten Herman Langkjær, Nestor Narvaez, Nick McGinness, Ronnie Hegelund, Samuel Bosch, and Shahid Iqbal. They suggested topics and other ways of presenting topics and caught typos and mistakes in code and terminology. Each pass through the review process and each piece of feedback provided through the forum discussions helped shape the book.

Finally, I want to thank the people at Manning who made this book possible: publisher Marjan Bace, acquisitions editor Greg Wild, and everyone on the editorial and production teams, including Tiffany Taylor, Katie Tennant, Melody Dolab, and Gordan Salinovic.

about this book

Microservices in .NET Core is a practical introduction to writing microservices in .NET using lightweight and easy-to-use technologies, like the awesome Nancy web framework and the powerful OWIN (Open Web Interface for .NET) middleware. I've tried to present the material in a way that will enable you to use what you learn right away. To that end, I've tried to tell you why I build things the way I do, as well as show you exactly how to build them.

The Nancy web framework, used throughout this book, was started by Andreas Håkansson, who still leads the project. Andreas was soon joined by Steven Robbins, and the two of them made Nancy great. Today Nancy is carried forward by Andreas, Steven, the Nancy Minions (Kristian Hellang, Jonathan Channon, Damian Hickey, Phillip Haydon, and myself), and the broader community. The full list of Nancy contributors can be found at http://nancyfx.org/contribs.html.

OWIN is an open standard for the interface between web servers and web applications. The work on OWIN was started in late 2010 by Ryan Riley, Benjamin van der Veen, Mauricio Scheffer, and Scott Koon. Since then, a broad community has contributed to the OWIN standard specification—through a Google group in the early days, and now through the OWIN GitHub repository (https://github.com/owin/owin)—and to implementing OWIN.

Who should read this book

Microservices in .NET Core is a developers' book first, but architects and others can benefit from it, too. I wrote it keeping in mind .NET developers who want to get started writing distributed server-side systems in general and microservices in particular, which means that the focus is on what a developer needs to know and do to write the code for a system of microservices. Working knowledge of C# and a bit of HTTP knowledge is assumed.

How this book is organized

Microservices in .NET Core has 12 chapters spread across four parts:

Part 1 gives a quick introduction to microservices, answering what they are and why they're interesting. This part also introduces Nancy and OWIN, the main technologies used throughout the book.

- Chapter 1 introduces microservices—what they are and why they matter. It introduces the six characteristics of microservices that I use to guide the design and implementation of microservices. At the end of the chapter, we say hello to Nancy and OWIN.
- Chapter 2 is a comprehensive example of coding a microservice using Nancy and OWIN, along with the Polly library and .NET Core. At the end of the chapter, we have a complete, albeit simple, microservice.

Part 2 covers how to split a system into microservices and how to implement functionality in a system of microservices.

- Chapter 3 covers how to identify microservices and decide what to put into each microservice. This chapter is about the design of a system of microservices as a whole.
- Chapter 4 shows how to design and implement the collaboration between microservices. This chapter discusses the different ways microservices can collaborate and shows how to implement those collaborations.
- Chapter 5 discusses where data should be stored in a system of microservices and how some of the data may be replicated across several microservices.
- Chapter 6 explains and demonstrates the implementation of some important techniques for making microservice systems robust.
- Chapter 7 takes a thorough look at testing a microservice system, including testing the complete system, testing each microservice, and testing the code inside the microservices.

Part 3 shows how to speed up development of new microservices by building a solid microservice platform tailored to the needs of your particular system. Such a platform provides implementations of a bunch of important concerns that cut across the entire system of microservices, such as logging, monitoring, and security. In this part you'll build such a platform and see how it's used to create new microservices quickly.

- Chapter 8 gives an in-depth introduction to OWIN, walks through building OWIN middleware, and shows how OWIN middleware is well suited for handling many crosscutting concerns.

- Chapter 9 explains the importance of monitoring and logging in a microservice system. Building on the OWIN knowledge from chapter 8, you'll build OWIN middleware implementing monitoring support and middleware that aids good logging from your microservices.
- Chapter 10 discusses security in a microservice system. The highly distributed nature of a microservice system poses some security concerns that we discuss in this chapter. I'll also walk you through using OWIN middleware to implement security features in your microservices.
- Chapter 11 builds on top of chapters 9 and 10 to create a microservice platform. The platform is built by taking the OWIN middleware from the previous chapters and packaging it in NuGet packages ready to be shared across microservices. The chapter includes an example of creating a new microservice using the platform.

Part 4 consists of chapter 12, which rounds off the book with some approaches to creating end-user applications for a microservices system. The chapter also shows how to build a small application on top of some of the microservices from earlier chapters.

Together, the 12 chapters will teach you how to design and code microservices using a lightweight, no-nonsense, .NET-based technology stack.

Code conventions and downloads

Most chapters in this book have sample code. All of this can be found in the download for this book on Manning's site at https://www.manning.com/books/microservices-in-net-core, or in the Git repository on GitHub found at https://github.com/horsdal/microservices-in-dotnetcore.

The code is based on .NET Core, so to run it, you need to install .NET Core, the dotnet command-line tool, and a suitable IDE. You can find information on how to set these up in appendix A.

Throughout the book, I use a number of third-party open source libraries, particularly the Nancy web framework. .NET Core is a big shift from "traditional" .NET, so existing libraries need to be ported and thoroughly tested before they can claim full .NET Core support. At the time of writing .NET Core has just reached the 1.0.0 release, so not all libraries have been tested on .NET Core. For this reason, the book uses pre-release versions of libraries—Nancy, for instance, is used in a pre-release version of Nancy 2.0. If, when you read the book, there are stable releases for .NET core of the different libraries (for example, if the stable Nancy 2.0 is out), I recommend using those as you code along with the examples.

In the GitHub repository, at https://github.com/horsdal/microservices-in-dotnetcore, the master branch contains the code as it appears in the book. As stable releases of libraries for .NET Core come out, I plan to create a current branch and keep a copy of the code there that I will keep mostly up-to-date with the latest versions of libraries for a few years after publication of this book.

This book contains many examples of source code, both in numbered listings and inline with normal text. In both cases, source code is formatted in a `fixed-width font like this` to separate it from ordinary text. Sometimes code is also in bold to highlight code that has changed from previous steps in the chapter, such as when a new feature adds to an existing line of code.

In many cases, the original source code has been reformatted; I've added line breaks and reworked indentation to accommodate the available page space in the book. In rare cases, even this was not enough, and listings include line-continuation markers (➥). Additionally, comments in the source code have often been removed from the listings when the code is described in the text. Code annotations accompany many of the listings, highlighting important concepts.

Author Online

Purchase of *Microservices in .NET Core* includes free access to a private web forum run by Manning Publications where you can make comments about the book, ask technical questions, and receive help from the author and from other users. To access the forum and subscribe to it, point your web browser to https://www.manning.com/books/microservices-in-net-core. This page provides information on how to get on the forum once you are registered, what kind of help is available, and the rules of conduct on the forum. It also provides links to the source code for the examples in the book, errata, and other downloads.

Manning's commitment to our readers is to provide a venue where a meaningful dialog between individual readers and between readers and the authors can take place. It is not a commitment to any specific amount of participation on the part of the authors, whose contribution to the forum remains voluntary (and unpaid). We suggest you try asking the author challenging questions lest his interest strays!

The Author Online forum and the archives of previous discussions will be accessible from the publisher's website as long as the book is in print.

About the author

Christian is an independent consultant with many years of experience building web and distributed systems on .NET as well as other platforms. He is part of the Nancy maintainer team and is a Microsoft MVP for .NET.

about the cover illustration

The figure on the cover of *Microservices in .NET Core* is captioned "Emperor of China in his Robes, in 1700." The illustration is taken from publisher Thomas Jefferys' *A Collection of the Dresses of Different Nations, Ancient and Modern* (four volumes), London, published between 1757 and 1772. The title page states that these are hand-colored copperplate engravings, heightened with gum arabic. Thomas Jefferys (1719–1771) was called "Geographer to King George III." He was an English cartographer who was the leading map supplier of his day. He engraved and printed maps for government and other official bodies and produced a wide range of commercial maps and atlases, especially of North America. His work as a mapmaker sparked an interest in local dress customs of the lands he surveyed and mapped, which are brilliantly displayed in this collection.

Fascination with faraway lands and travel for pleasure were relatively new phenomena in the late 18th century and collections such as this one were popular, introducing both the tourist as well as the armchair traveler to the inhabitants of other countries. The diversity of the drawings in Jefferys' volumes speaks vividly of the uniqueness and individuality of the world's nations some 200 years ago. Dress codes have changed since then and the diversity by region and country, so rich at the time, has faded away. It is now often hard to tell the inhabitant of one continent from another. Perhaps, trying to view it optimistically, we have traded a cultural and visual diversity for a more varied personal life. Or a more varied and interesting intellectual and technical life.

At a time when it is hard to tell one computer book from another, Manning celebrates the inventiveness and initiative of the computer business with book covers based on the rich diversity of regional life of two centuries ago, brought back to life by Jeffreys' pictures.

Part 1

Getting started with microservices

This first part explains what microservices are and why you should care. I'll begin by discussing six characteristics you can use to recognize and guide your design of microservices. Along the way, we'll look at the benefits and costs of microservices.

Toward the end of chapter 1, I'll give you a whirlwind tour of the technology stack used throughout the book; the stack consists of .NET Core, the Nancy web framework, and OWIN. Chapter 2 moves on to an example of building your first microservice. You'll also see more of Nancy's strengths.

Microservices at a glance

This chapter covers

- Understanding microservices and their core characteristics
- Examining the benefits and drawbacks of microservices
- An example of microservices working in concert to serve a user request
- Using the Nancy web framework for a simple application

In this chapter, I'll explain what microservices are and demonstrate why they're interesting. We'll also look at the six characteristics of a microservice. Finally, I'll introduce you to the two most important technologies we'll use in this book: the .NET-based Nancy web framework and the OWIN middleware pipeline.

1.1 What is a microservice?

A *microservice* is a service with one, and only one, very narrowly focused capability that a remote API exposes to the rest of the system. For example, think of a system for managing a warehouse. If you broke down its capabilities, you might come up with the following list:

3

- Receive stock arriving at the warehouse
- Determine where new stock should be stored
- Calculate placement routes inside the warehouse for putting stock into the right storage units
- Assign placement routes to warehouse employees
- Receive orders
- Calculate pick routes in the warehouse for a set of orders
- Assign pick routes to warehouse employees

Let's consider how the first of these capabilities—receive stock arriving at the warehouse—would be implemented as a microservice. We'll call it the *Receive Stock microservice*.

1 A request to receive and log new stock arrives over HTTP. This might come from another microservice or perhaps from a web page that a foreman uses to register stock arrivals. The Receive Stock microservice has to register the new stock in its own data store.

2 A response is sent back from the Receive Stock microservice to acknowledge that the stock has been received.

Figure 1.1 shows the Receive Stock microservice receiving a request from another collaborating microservice.

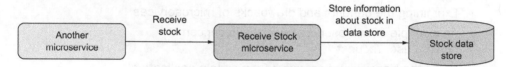

Figure 1.1   The Receive Stock microservice exposes an API to be used when new stock arrives. Other microservices can call that API.

Each little capability in the system is implemented as an individual microservice. Every microservice in a system

- Runs in its own separate process
- Can be deployed on its own, independently of the other microservices
- Has its own dedicated data store
- Collaborates with other microservices to complete its own action

It's also important to note that microservices don't need to be written in the same programming language (C#, Java, Erlang, and so on) or for the same platform (IIS, Node, NGINX, and so on) as ones they collaborate with. They just need to know how to communicate with each other. Some may communicate via a service bus or a binary protocol like Thrift, depending on system requirements; but by far the most common scenario is for microservices to communicate over HTTP.

> **NOTE** This book focuses on implementing microservices in .NET using C# and the Nancy web framework. The microservices I'll show you are small, tightly focused Nancy applications that collaborate over HTTP.

1.1.1 What is a microservices architecture?

This book focuses on designing and implementing individual microservices, but it's worth noting that the term *microservices* can also be used to describe an *architectural style* for an entire system consisting of many microservices. Microservices *as an architectural style* is a lightweight form of service-oriented architecture (SOA) where the services are tightly focused on doing one thing each and doing it well. A system with a microservices architecture is a distributed system with a (probably large) number of collaborating microservices.

The microservices architectural style is quickly gaining in popularity for building and maintaining complex server-side software systems, and understandably so: microservices offer a number of potential benefits over both more traditional, service-oriented approaches and monolithic architectures. Microservices, when done well, are malleable, scalable, and resilient, and they allow for a short lead time from the start of implementation to deployment in production. This combination often proves elusive for complex software systems.

1.1.2 Microservice characteristics

I've said that a microservice is *a service with a very narrowly focused capability*, but what exactly does that mean? Well, because the microservices technique is still emerging (as of early 2016), there's still no accepted definition in the industry of precisely what a microservice is.[1] We can, however, look at what generally characterizes a microservice. I've found there to be six core microservice characteristics:

- A microservice is responsible for a single capability.
- A microservice is individually deployable.
- A microservice consists of one or more processes.
- A microservice owns its own data store.
- A small team can maintain a handful of microservices.
- A microservice is replaceable.

This list of characteristics should help you recognize a well-formed microservice when you see one, and it will also help you scope and implement your own microservices. By incorporating these characteristics, you'll be on your way to getting the best from your microservices and producing a *malleable, scalable,* and *resilient* system as a result. Throughout this book, I'll show how these characteristics should drive the design of your microservices and how to write the code that a microservice needs to fulfill them. Now, let's look briefly at each characteristic in turn.

---

[1] For further discussion of what characterizes microservices, I recommend this article on the subject: Martin Fowler and James Lewis, "Microservices: A Definition of This New Architectural Term," March 25, 2014, http://martinfowler.com/articles/microservices.html.

RESPONSIBLE FOR A SINGLE CAPABILITY

A microservice is *responsible for one and only one capability* in the overall system. We can break this statement into two parts:

- A microservice has a single responsibility.
- That responsibility is for a capability.

The Single Responsibility Principle has been stated in several ways. One traditional form is "A class should have only one reason to change."[2] Although this way of putting it specifically mentions a *class*, the principle turns out to apply beyond the context of a class in an object-oriented language. With microservices, we apply the Single Responsibility Principle at the service level.

A more current way of stating the Single Responsibility Principle, also from Uncle Bob, is as follows: "Gather together the things that change for the same reasons. Separate those things that change for different reasons."[3] This way of stating the principle applies to microservices: a microservice should implement exactly one capability. That way, the microservice will have to change only when there's a change to that capability. Furthermore, you should strive to have the microservice fully implement the capability, so that only one microservice has to change when the capability is changed.

There are two types of capabilities in a microservice system:

- A *business capability* is something the system does that contributes to the purpose of the system, like keeping track of users' shopping carts or calculating prices. A good way to tease apart a system's separate business capabilities is to use domain-driven design.
- A *technical capability* is one that several other microservices need to use—integration to some third-party system, for instance. Technical capabilities aren't the main drivers for breaking down a system to microservices; they're only identified when you find several business-capability microservices that need the same technical capability.

> **NOTE** Defining the scope and responsibility of a microservice is covered in chapter 3.

INDIVIDUALLY DEPLOYABLE

A microservice should be *individually deployable*. When you a change a microservice, you should be able to deploy that changed microservice to the production environment without deploying (or touching) any other part of your system. The other microservices in the system should continue running and working during the deployment of the changed microservice, and continue running once the new version is deployed.

Consider an e-commerce site. When a change is made to the Shopping Cart microservice, you should be able to deploy just that microservice, as illustrated in figure 1.2.

---

2   Robert C. Martin, "SRP: The Single Responsibility Principle," http://mng.bz/zQyz.
3   Robert C. Martin, "The Single Responsibility Principle," May 8, 2014, http://mng.bz/RZgU.

Figure 1.2   Other microservices continue to run while the Shopping Cart microservice is being deployed.

Meanwhile, the Price Calculation microservice, the Recommendation microservice, the Product Catalog microservice, and others should continue working and serving user requests.

Being able to deploy each microservice individually is important because in a microservice system, there are many microservices, and each one may collaborate with several others. At the same time, development work is done on some or all of the microservices in parallel. If you had to deploy all or groups of them in lockstep, managing the deployments would quickly become unwieldy, typically resulting in infrequent and big, risky deployments. This is something you should definitely avoid. Instead, you want to be able to deploy small changes to each microservice frequently, resulting in small, low-risk deployments.

To be able to deploy a single microservice while the rest of the system continues to function, the build process must be set up with the following in mind:

- Each microservice must be built into separate artifacts or packages.
- The deployment process must also be set up to support deploying microservices individually while other microservices continue running. For instance, you might use a rolling deployment process where the microservice is deployed to one server at a time, in order to reduce downtime.

The fact that you want to deploy microservices individually affects the way they interact. Changes to a microservice's interface usually must be backward compatible so that other existing microservices can continue to collaborate with the new version the same way they did with the old. Furthermore, the way microservices interact must be robust in the sense that each microservice must expect other services to fail once in a while and must continue working as best it can. One microservice failing—for instance, due to downtime during deployment—must not result in other microservices failing, only in reduced functionality or slightly longer processing time.

NOTE Microservice collaboration and robustness are covered in chapters 4, 5, and 7.

CONSISTS OF ONE OR MORE PROCESSES

A microservice must run in a separate process, or in separate processes, if it's to remain as independent as possible of other microservices in the same system. The same is true if a microservice is to remain individually deployable. Breaking that down, we have two points:

- Each microservice must run in separate processes from other microservices.
- Each microservice can have more than one process.

Consider a Shopping Cart microservice again. If it ran in the same process as a Product Catalog microservice, as shown in figure 1.3, the Shopping Cart code might cause a side effect in the Product Catalog. That would mean a tight, undesirable coupling between the Shopping Cart microservice and the Product Catalog microservice; one might cause downtime or bugs in the other.

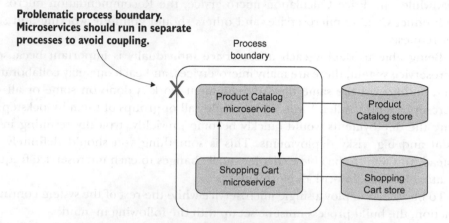

Figure 1.3   Running more than one microservice within a process leads to high coupling.

Now consider deploying a new version of the Shopping Cart microservice. You'd either have to redeploy the Product Catalog microservice too, or you'd need some sort of dynamic code-loading capable of switching out the Shopping Cart code in the running process. The first option goes directly against microservices being individually deployable. The second option is complex and at a minimum puts the Product Catalog microservice at risk of going down due to a deployment to the Shopping Cart microservice.

Speaking of complexity, why should a microservice consist of more than one process? You are, after all, trying make each microservice as simple as possible to handle.

Let's consider a Recommendation microservice. It implements and runs the algorithms that drive recommendations for your e-commerce site. It also has a database that stores the data needed to provide recommendations. The algorithms run in one process, and the database runs in another. Often, a microservice needs two or more processes so it can implement everything (such as data storage and background processing) it needs in order to provide a capability to the system.

OWNS ITS OWN DATA STORE

A microservice owns the data store where it stores the data it needs. This is another consequence of a microservice's scope being a complete capability. Most business capabilities require some data storage. For instance, a Product Catalog microservice needs

All communication with the Product Catalog microservice must go through the public API.

Direct access to the Product Catalog store is not allowed. The Product Catalog microservice owns the Product Catalog store.

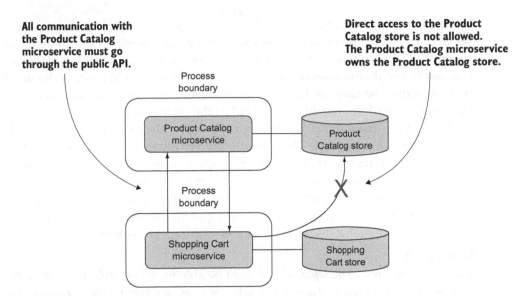

Figure 1.4   One microservice can't access another's data store.

some information about each product to be stored. To keep Product Catalog loosely coupled with other microservices, the data store containing the product information is completely owned by the microservice. The Product Catalog microservice decides how and when the product information is stored. As illustrated in figure 1.4, other microservices, such as Shopping Cart, can only access product information through the interface to Product Catalog and never directly from the Product Catalog data store.

The fact that each microservice owns its own data store makes it possible to use different database technologies for different microservices depending on the needs of each microservice. The Product Catalog microservice, for example, might use SQL Server to store product information; the Shopping Cart microservice might store each user's shopping cart in Redis; and the Recommendations microservice might use an Elasticsearch index to provide recommendations. The database technology chosen for a microservice is part of the implementation and is hidden from the view of other microservices.

This approach allows each microservice to use whichever database is best suited for the job, which can also lead to benefits in terms of development time, performance, and scalability. The obvious downside is the need to administer, maintain, and work with more than one database, if that's how you choose to architect your system. Databases tend to be complicated pieces of technology, and learning to use and run one reliably in production isn't free. When choosing a database for a microservice, you need to consider this trade-off. But one benefit of a microservice owning its own data store is that you can swap out one database for another later.

NOTE   Data ownership, access, and storage are covered in chapter 5.

MAINTAINABLE BY A SMALL TEAM

So far, I haven't talked much about the size of a microservice, even though the *micro* part of the term indicates that microservices are small. I don't think it makes sense to discuss the number of lines of code that a microservice should have, or the number of requirements, use cases, or function points it should implement. All that depends on the complexity of the capability provided by the microservice.

What does make sense, though, is considering the amount of work involved in maintaining a microservice. The following rule of thumb can guide you regarding the size of microservices: *a small team of people—five, perhaps—should be able to maintain at least a handful of microservices*. Here, *maintaining* a microservice means dealing with all aspects of keeping it healthy and fit for use: developing new functionality, factoring out new microservices from ones that have grown too big, running it in production, monitoring it, testing it, fixing bugs, and everything else required.

REPLACEABLE

For a microservice to be *replaceable*, it must be able to be rewritten from scratch within a reasonable time frame. In other words, *the team maintaining the microservice should be able to replace the current implementation with a completely new implementation and do so within the normal pace of their work*. This characteristic is another constraint on the size of a microservice: if a microservice grows too large, it will be expensive to replace; but if it's kept small, rewriting it is realistic.

Why would a team decide to rewrite a microservice? Perhaps the code is a big jumble and no longer easily maintainable. Perhaps it doesn't perform well enough in production. Neither is a desirable situation, but changes in requirements over time can result in a codebase that it makes sense to replace rather than maintain. If the microservice is small enough to be rewritten within a reasonable time frame, it's OK to end up with one of these situations from time to time. The team does the rewrite based on all the knowledge obtained from writing the existing implementation, keeping any new requirements in mind.

Now that you know the characteristics of microservices, let's look at their benefits, costs, and other considerations.

1.2   *Why microservices?*

Building a system from microservices that adhere to the characteristics outlined in the previous section has some appealing benefits: they're malleable, scalable, and resilient, and they allow a short lead time from start of implementation to deployment to production. These benefits are realized because, when done well, microservices

- Enable continuous delivery
- Allow for an efficient developer workflow because they're highly maintainable
- Are robust by design
- Can scale up or down independently of each other

Let's talk more about these points.

1.2.1 Enabling continuous delivery

The microservices architectural style takes continuous delivery into account. It does so by focusing on services that

- Can be developed and modified quickly
- Can be comprehensively tested by automated tests
- Can be deployed independently
- Can be operated efficiently

These properties enable continuous delivery, but this doesn't mean continuous delivery follows from adopting a microservices architecture. The relationship is more complex: practicing continuous delivery becomes easier with microservices than it typically is with more traditional SOA. On the other hand, fully adopting microservices is possible only if you're able to deploy services efficiently and reliably. Continuous delivery and microservices complement each other.

The benefits of continuous delivery are well known. They include increased agility on the business level, reliable releases, risk reduction, and improved product quality.

> **What is continuous delivery?**
>
> *Continuous delivery* is a development practice where the team ensures that the software can always be deployed to production quickly at any time. Deploying to production remains a business decision, but teams that practice continuous delivery prefer to deploy to production often and to deploy newly developed software shortly after it hits source control.
>
> There are two main requirements for continuous delivery. First, the software must always be in a fully functional state. To achieve that, the team needs a keen focus on quality. This leads to a high degree of test automation and to developing in very small increments. Second, the deployment process must be repeatable, reliable, and fast in order to enable frequent production deployments. This part is achieved through full automation of the deployment process and a high degree of insight into the health of the production environment.
>
> Although continuous delivery takes a good deal of technical skill, it's much more a question of process and culture. This level of quality, automation, and insight requires a culture of close collaboration among all parties involved in developing and operating the software, including businesspeople, developers, information security experts, and system administrators. In other words, it requires a DevOps culture where development and operations collaborate and learn from each other.

Continuous delivery goes hand in hand with microservices. Without the ability to deploy individual microservices quickly and cheaply, implementing a system of microservices will quickly become expensive. If microservice deployment isn't automated, the amount of manual work involved in deploying a full system of microservices will be overwhelming.

Along with continuous delivery comes a DevOps culture, which is also a prerequisite for microservices. To succeed with microservices, everybody must be invested in making the services run smoothly in production and in creating a high level of transparency into the health of the production system. This requires the collaboration of people with operations skills, people with development skills, people with security skills, and people with insight into the business domain, among others.

This book doesn't focus on continuous delivery or DevOps, but it does take for granted that the environment in which you develop microservices uses continuous delivery. The services built in this book can be deployed to on-premises data centers or to the cloud using any number of deployment-automation technologies capable of handling .NET. This book covers the implications of continuous delivery and DevOps for individual microservices. In part 3, we'll go into detail about how to build a platform that handles a number of the operational concerns that all microservices must address. In addition, in appendix B, we'll explore the primary options for running the microservices developed throughout the book in a production environment.

1.2.2   *High level of maintainability*

Well-factored and well-implemented microservices are highly maintainable from a couple of perspectives. *From a developer perspective*, several factors play a part in making microservices maintainable:

- Each well-factored microservice provides *a single capability*. Not two—just one.
- A microservice owns its data store. No other services can interfere with a microservice's data store. This, combined with the typical size of the codebase for a microservice, means you can understand a complete service all at once.
- Well-written microservices can (and should) be comprehensibly covered by automated tests.

From an operations perspective, a couple of factors play a role in the maintainability of microservices:

- A small team can maintain a handful of microservices. Microservices must be built to be operated efficiently, which implies that you should be able to easily determine the current health of any microservice.
- Each microservice is individually deployable.

It should follow that issues in production can be discovered in a timely manner and be addressed quickly, such as by scaling out the microservice in question or deploying a new version of the microservice. The characteristic that a microservice owns its own data store also adds to its operational maintainability, because the scope of maintenance on the data store is limited to the owning microservice.

Favor lightweight

Because every microservice handles a single capability, microservices are by nature fairly small both in their scope and in the size of their codebase. The simplicity that follows from this limited scope is a major benefit of microservices.

When developing microservices, it's important to avoid complicating their codebase by using large, complicated frameworks, libraries, or products because you think you may need their functionality in the future. Chances are, this won't be the case, so you should prefer smaller, lightweight technologies that do what the microservice needs right now. Remember, a microservice is replaceable; you can completely rewrite a microservice within a reasonable budget if at some point the technologies you used originally no longer meet your needs.

1.2.3 Robust and scalable

A microservices-based distributed architecture allows you to scale out each service individually based on where bottlenecks occur. Furthermore, microservices favor asynchronous event-based collaboration and stress the importance of fault tolerance wherever synchronous communication is needed. When implemented well, these properties result in highly available, highly scalable systems.

1.3 Costs and downsides of microservices

Significant costs are associated with choosing a microservices architecture, and these costs shouldn't be ignored:

- Microservice systems are distributed systems. The costs associated with distributed systems are well known. They can be harder to reason about and harder to test than monolithic systems, and communication across process boundaries or across networks is orders of magnitude slower than in-process method calls.
- Microservice systems are made up of many microservices, each of which has to be developed, deployed, and managed in production. This means you'll have many deployments and a complex production setup.
- Each microservice is a separate codebase. Consequently, refactorings that move code from one microservice to another are painful. You need to invest in getting the scope of each microservice just right.

Before jumping head first into building a system of microservices, you should consider whether the system you're implementing is sufficiently complex to justify the associated overhead.

Do microservices perform?

One question that always seems to pop up in discussions of whether to use microservices is whether a system built with microservices will be as performant as a system that's not. The argument against is that if the system is built from many collaborating microservices, every user request will involve several microservices, and the collaboration between these microservices will involve remote calls between them. What happens when a user request comes in? Do you chain together a long series of remote calls going from one microservice to the next? Considering that remote calls are orders of magnitude slower than calls inside a process, this sounds slow.

The problem with this argument is the idea that you'd be making roughly the same calls between different parts of the system as you would if everything were in one process. First, the interaction between microservices should be much less fine-grained than calls within a process tend to be. Second, as we'll discuss in chapters 4 and 5, you'll prefer event-based asynchronous collaboration over making synchronous remote calls, and you'll store copies of the same data in several microservices to make sure it's available where it's needed. All in all, these techniques drastically reduce the need to make remote calls while a user is waiting. Moreover, the fine-grained nature of microservices enables you to scale out the specific parts of the system that get congested.

There isn't a simple yes or no answer as to whether microservices perform well. What I can say is that a well-designed microservice system can easily meet the performance requirements of many, if not most, systems.

1.4   Greenfield vs. brownfield

Should you introduce microservices from the get-go on a new project, or are they only relevant for large, existing systems? This question tends to come up in discussions about microservices.

The microservices architectural style has grown out of the fact that many organizations' systems started out small but have grown big over time. Many of these systems consist of a single large application—a monolith that often exposes the well-known disadvantages of big, monolithic systems:

- Coupling is high throughout the codebase.
- There's hidden coupling between subcomponents—coupling the compiler can't see because it's the result of implicit knowledge about how certain strings are formatted, how certain columns in a databases are used, and so on.
- Deploying the application is a lengthy process that may involve several people and system downtime.
- The system has a one-size-fits-all architecture intended to handle the most complex components. If you insist on architectural consistency across the monolith, the least complex parts of the system will be overengineered. This is true of layering, technology choices, chosen patterns, and so on.

The microservices architecture arose as a result of solving these problems in existing monolithic systems. If you repeatedly split subcomponents of a monolith into ever-smaller and more-manageable parts, microservices are eventually created.[4]

On the other hand, new projects are started all the time. Are microservices irrelevant for these greenfield projects? That depends. Here are some questions you need to ask yourself:

- Would this system benefit from the ability to deploy subsystems separately?
- Can you build sufficient deployment automation?
- Are you sufficiently knowledgeable about the domain to properly identify and separate the system's various independent business capabilities?
- Is the system's scope large enough to justify the complexity of a distributed architecture?
- Is the system's scope large enough to justify the cost of building the deployment automation?
- Will the project survive long enough to recover the up-front investment in automation and distribution?

Some greenfield projects meet these criteria and may benefit from adopting a microservices architecture from the outset.

1.5 Code reuse

Adopting a microservices architecture leads to having many services, each of which has a separate codebase that you'll have to maintain. It's tempting to look for code reuse across services in the hope that you can reduce the maintenance effort; but although there's an obvious potential benefit to code reuse, pulling code out of a service and into a reusable library incurs a number of hidden costs:

- The service now has one more dependency that you must understand in order to understand the complete service. This isn't to say that there's more code to comprehend; but by moving code out of the service and into a library, you move the code further away, making simple code navigation slower and refactoring more difficult.
- The code in the new library must be developed and maintained with multiple use cases in mind. This tends to take more effort than developing for just one use case.
- The shared library introduces a form of coupling between the services using it. Updates to the library driven by the needs of service A may not be needed in service B. Should service B update to the new version of the library even though it's not strictly necessary? If you upgrade B, it will have code it doesn't need;

---

[4] Some microservice advocates argue that the correct way to arrive at microservices is to apply the Strangler pattern repeatedly to different subcomponents of the monolith. See Martin Fowler, "MonolithFirst," June 3, 2015, http://martinfowler.com/bliki/MonolithFirst.html.

and, worse, B will run the risk of errors caused by that code. If you don't upgrade, you'll have several versions of the library in production, further complicating maintenance of the library. Both cases incur some complexity, either in service B or in the combined service landscape.

These points apply particularly to business code. Business code should almost never be reused across microservices. That type of reuse leads to harmful coupling between microservices.

With these points in mind, you should be wary of code reuse and only judiciously attempt it. There is, however, a case to be made for reusing infrastructure code that implements technical concerns.

To keep a service small and focused on providing one capability well, you'll often prefer to write a new service from scratch rather than add functionality to an existing service. It's important to do this quickly and painlessly, and this is where code reuse across services is relevant. As we'll explore in detail in part 3 of this book, there are a number of technical concerns that all services need to implement in order to fit well into the overall service landscape. You don't need to write this code for every single service; you can reuse it across services to gain consistency in how these technical aspects are handled and to reduce the effort needed to create a new service.

1.6 Serving a user request: an example of how microservices work in concert

To get a feel for how a microservices architecture works, let's look at an example: a user of an e-commerce website adding an item to their shopping cart. From the viewpoint of the client-side code, an AJAX request is fired to the backend system via an API gateway, and an updated shopping cart along with some price information is returned. This is as simple as the interaction shown in figure 1.5. We'll return to the topic of API gateways in chapter 12.

This is neither surprising nor exciting. The interesting part is the interactions taking place behind the API Gateway microservice to fulfill the request. To add the new item to the user's shopping cart, API Gateway uses a few other microservices. Each microservice is a separate process, and in this example they communicate via HTTP requests.

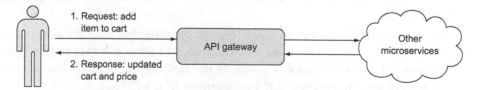

Figure 1.5   When front-end code makes a request to add an item to the shopping cart, it only communicates with the API Gateway microservice. What goes on behind the gateway isn't visible.

1.6.1 Main handling of the user request

All the microservices and their interactions for fulfilling a user request to add an item to their shopping cart are shown in figure 1.6. The request to add an item to the shopping cart is divided into smaller tasks, each of which is handled by a separate microservice:

- The API Gateway microservice is responsible only for a cursory validation of the incoming request. Once it's validated, the work is delegated first to the Shopping Cart microservice and then to the Price Calculation microservice.
- The Shopping Cart microservice uses another microservice—Product Catalog—to look up the necessary information about the item being added to the cart. Shopping Cart then stores the user's shopping cart information in its own data store and returns a representation of the updated shopping cart to API Gateway. For performance and robustness reasons, Shopping Cart will likely cache the responses from Product Catalog.
- The Price Calculation microservice uses the current business rules of the e-commerce website to calculate the total price of the items in the user's shopping cart, taking into account any applicable discounts.

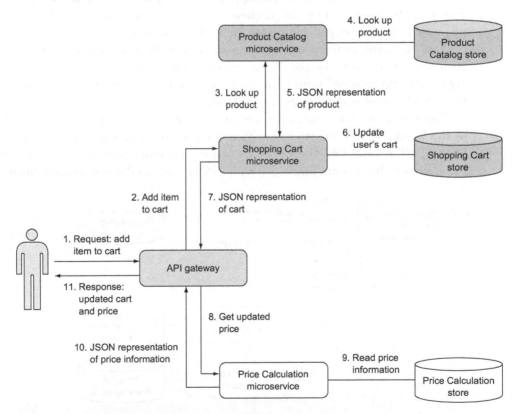

Figure 1.6   The API Gateway microservice is all the client sees, but it's a thin layer in front of a system of microservices. The arrows indicate calls between different parts of the system, and the numbers on the arrows show the sequence of calls.

Each of the microservices collaborating to fulfill the user's request has a single, narrowly focused purpose and knows as little as possible about the other microservices. For example, the Shopping Cart microservice knows nothing about pricing or the Price Calculation microservice, and it knows nothing about how products are stored in the Product Catalog microservice. This is at the core of microservices: each one has a single responsibility.

1.6.2 *Side effects of the user request*

At this e-commerce website, when a user adds an item to their shopping cart, a couple of actions happen in addition to adding the item to the cart:

1 The recommendation engine updates its internal model to reflect the fact that the user has shown a high degree of interest in that particular product.
2 The tracking service records that the user added the item to their cart in the tracking database. This information may be used later for reporting or other business intelligence purposes.

Neither of these actions needs to happen in the context of the user's request; they may as well happen after the request has ended, when the user has received a response and is no longer waiting for the backend system.

You can think of these types of actions as side effects of the user's request. They aren't direct effects of the request to update the user's shopping cart; they're secondary effects that happen because the item was added to the cart. Figure 1.7 zooms in on the side effects of adding an item to the cart.

The trigger for these side effects is an ItemAddedToShoppingCart event published by the Shopping Cart microservice. Two other microservices subscribe to events from Shopping Cart and take the necessary actions as events (such as ItemAddedToShoppingCart events) occur. These two subscribers react to the events asynchronously—

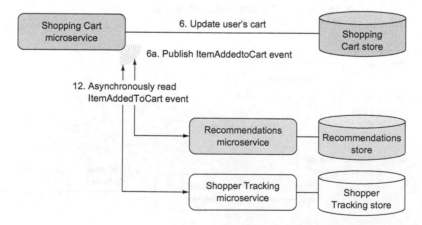

Figure 1.7   The Shopping Cart microservice publishes events, and other subscribing microservices react.

outside the context of the original request—so the side effects may happen in parallel with the main handling of the request or after the main handling has completed.

NOTE Implementing this type of event-feed-based collaboration is covered in chapter 4.

1.6.3 The complete picture

In total, six different microservices are involved in handling the request to add an item to a shopping cart, as shown in figure 1.8. None of these microservices know anything about the internals of the others. Five have their own private data stores dedicated to

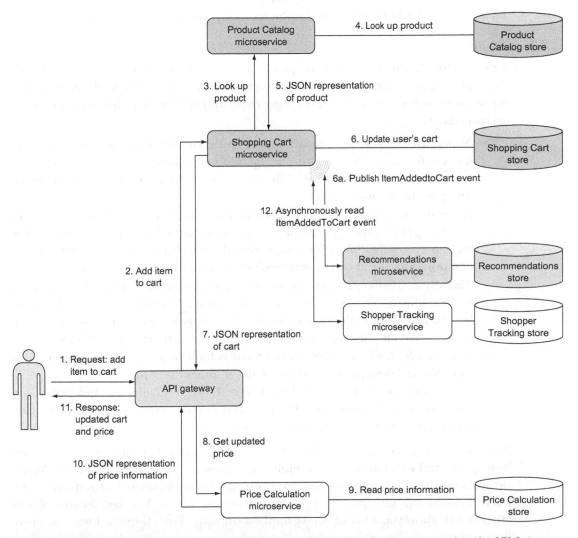

Figure 1.8 When a user adds an item to their shopping cart, the front end makes a request to the API Gateway microservice, which collaborates with other microservices to fulfill the request. During processing, microservices may raise events that other microservices can subscribe to and handle asynchronously.

serving only their purposes. Some of the handling happens synchronously in the context of the user request, and some happens asynchronously.

This is a typical microservice system. Requests are handled through the collaboration of several microservices, each with a single responsibility and each as independent of the others as possible.

Now that we've taken a high-level look at a concrete example of how a microservices system can handle a user request, it's time to take a brief look at a .NET-based technology stack for microservices.

1.7 A .NET microservices technology stack

It's time to say hello to the two technologies used most in this book: Nancy and OWIN.

1.7.1 Nancy

Nancy (http://nancyfx.org/) is an open source, .NET-based web framework built with the explicit goal of giving developers a Super Duper Happy Path to developing web applications and services. The term *Super Duper Happy Path* describes the core values behind Nancy:

- *Nancy just works.* There are sensible defaults for everything, so no (or next to no) configuration or ceremony is required to get started. Applications similarly expand to take advantage of different parts of Nancy. Out of the box, everything works in a logical way.
- *Nancy is easy to customize.* If you hit a bump in the road where Nancy's defaults aren't exactly right for your application, it's easy to customize Nancy to your needs. If the regular customization isn't enough, everything in Nancy—down to the core—is componentized and can be swapped out for your own implementations.
- *Nancy is low ceremony and low friction.* When you're building a Nancy application, the framework gets out of your way. The APIs are designed to be flexible and to let you write your code the way you want. In other words, with Nancy you get to concentrate on your application code rather than on dealing with Nancy.
- *Nancy applications are testable.* Nancy itself is built in a test-driven fashion. Likewise, Nancy allows an easy test-driven-development flow for writing Nancy applications. Not only are Nancy's APIs designed with testability in mind, but Nancy also comes with a companion library (Nancy.Testing) specifically aimed at making it easy to write tests for Nancy applications.

Because of these core values and the Super Duper Happy Path they support, Nancy is my preferred web framework for building microservices on .NET. You'll use Nancy throughout the book, and as I walk you through the complexities of implementing microservices, I'll also show you many features of Nancy. The last section of this chapter will show you a bit of Nancy application code. First, though, I want to introduce OWIN.

1.7.2 OWIN

The *Open Web Interface for .NET* (OWIN,
http://owin.org) is an open standard that defines
an interface between .NET web servers and .NET
web applications. OWIN decouples the web server
and the web application from each other. An
OWIN-compliant web server receiving HTTP
requests from the network delegates the handling
of those requests to the web application through
the standardized OWIN interface. The web server
has no knowledge of the specifics of the web application. All it knows, and all it cares about, is that the
web application can receive requests through the
OWIN interface. Likewise, the web application has
no knowledge of the web server. It only knows that
requests come in through the OWIN interface.

As illustrated in figure 1.9, this is achieved using
an adapter that implements the OWIN interface on
top of the web server, and using an OWIN-compliant
web framework to implement the web application.
All incoming requests are sent through the OWIN
adapter by the web server. The OWIN adapter and
the web framework then communicate through the
OWIN interface. The result is that the web application is decoupled from the web server, lending
some portability to web applications.

Because web servers and web applications only
know about the OWIN interface, you can insert
components between the web server and the web application without making any
changes to either one. These components are called *OWIN middleware*. Figure 1.10
shows an OWIN web server with request-logging OWIN middleware and an OWIN web
application on top. The web server can't know that it isn't communicating directly
with the web application; the OWIN middleware uses the exact same interface, so it
looks like an application to the web server and like a web server to the application.

In figure 1.10, the stack includes only one piece of middleware, but there's no reason you couldn't have more. One piece of middleware can delegate to another piece
of middleware as well as to an application. As long as all the pieces use the OWIN interface, you can compose the stack with as many pieces of middleware as you like.

Nancy is OWIN-compliant, so the microservices you build with Nancy work as OWIN
applications in the OWIN pipeline. In this book, you'll use middleware to take care of
a number of cross-cutting technical concerns that don't fit nicely with application
code. In part 3, we'll dive into implementing support for monitoring, performance

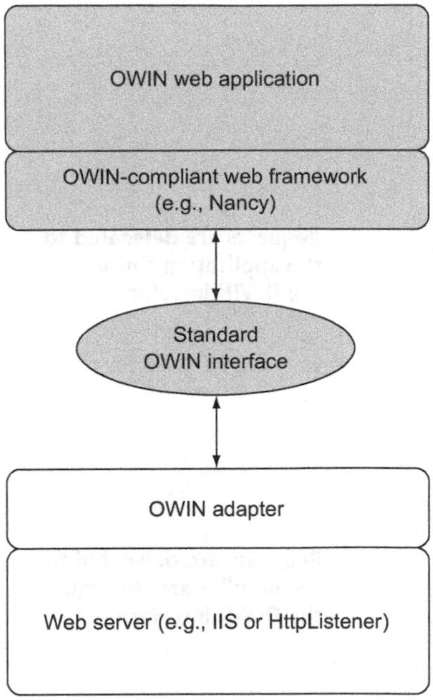

**Figure 1.9 A web application
implemented on top of OWIN
communicates with the web server
through the standardized OWIN
interface. The server can implement
the OWIN interface directly or can
come with an adapter that translates
between the OWIN interface and the
web server's native interface.**

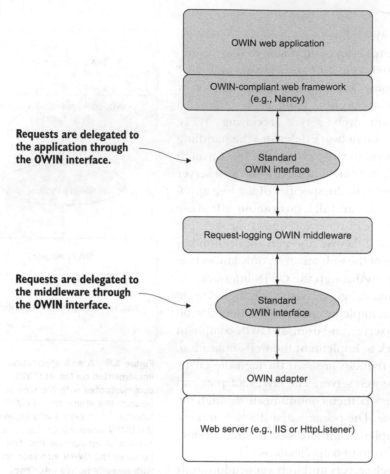

Figure 1.10   An OWIN web server with OWIN middleware and an OWIN web application on top. The web server delegates incoming requests to the layers above: in this case, the request-logging middleware, which writes a log message about the request and then delegates to the web application. To the web server, the middleware looks like an OWIN-compliant application; and to the application, the middleware looks like an OWIN-compliant web server.

logging, request logging, and security as pieces of middleware that can be reused across all your microservices.

You can gain two primary benefits from using middleware: cross-cutting technical concerns are separated nicely from the application logic, and the middleware can be reused so you can easily build new microservices without having to spend time rebuilding the same monitoring, logging, and security code.

1.7.3   *Setting up a development environment*

Before you can start coding your first microservice, you need to have the right tools. To follow along with the examples in this book, you'll need a development environment for creating ASP.NET Core applications. Developing ASP.NET applications used to be synonymous with using Visual Studio, but with the cross-platform Core version of ASP.NET, other options are available:

- If you're on Windows, the most common IDE to use is probably still Visual Studio 2015 with the Web Tools Extension for ASP.NET Core plug-in.
- If you're on Linux, OS X, or Windows, you can use Visual Studio Code, the ATOM editor with the OmniSharp plug-in, or JetBrains Rider.

All of these—Visual Studio 2015, Visual Studio Code, ATOM with the OmniSharp plug-in, and JetBrains Rider—support developing and running ASP.NET Core applications. They all give you a nice C# editor with IntelliSense and refactoring support. They're all aware of ASP.NET Core, and they can all launch ASP.NET Core applications. They're also all free—even Visual Studio in its Community Edition.

TIP At the time of writing, only Visual Studio and Visual Studio Code allow you to debug ASP.NET Core applications.

Once you have an IDE installed, you need to get a version of the ASP.NET Core command-line tool. To do so, follow the instructions for installing .NET Core at http://dot.net. This gives you a command-line tool called `dotnet` that you'll use to perform a number of different tasks involved with microservices, including restoring NuGet packages, building, creating NuGet packages, and running microservices.

In addition to an IDE and `dotnet`, you'll also need a tool for making HTTP requests. I recommend Postman, but Fiddler and curl are also good and popular tools. You can use any of these to follow along with the examples in this book.

NOTE In appendix A, you'll find download, installation, and quick usage information for Visual Studio, Visual Code, Atom with OmniSharp, JetBrains Rider, and Postman. Now is the time to set up the tools of your choice—you'll need them throughout the book.

1.8 A simple microservices example

Once you have a development environment up and running, it's time for a Hello World–style microservices example. You'll use Nancy to create a microservice that has only a single API endpoint. Typically, a microservice has more than one endpoint, but one is enough for this example. The endpoint responds with the current UTC date and time in either JSON or XML format, depending on the request headers. This is illustrated in figure 1.11. You'll also add a piece of OWIN middleware that logs every incoming request to the console.

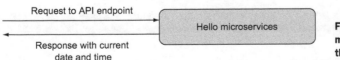

Figure 1.11 A Hello World–style microservice that responds with the current date and time

NOTE When I talk about an *API endpoint*, an *HTTP endpoint*, or just an *endpoint*, I mean a URL where one of your microservices reacts to HTTP requests.

To implement this example, you'll follow these four steps:

1 Create an empty ASP.NET Core application.
2 Add Nancy to the application.
3 Add a Nancy module with an implementation of the endpoint.
4 Add OWIN middleware that logs every request to the console.

The following sections will go through each step in detail.

1.8.1 Creating an empty ASP.NET Core application

The first thing you need to do is create an empty ASP.NET Core application called *HelloMicroservices*. If you chose to install Visual Studio, you can create the project by selecting File > New > Project from the menu. In the New Project dialog box, choose ASP.NET Web Application, and then choose Empty under ASP.NET Core Templates.

If you chose to install either Visual Studio Code or ATOM and followed the instructions in appendix A, you also installed the Yeoman scaffolding tool. You can use Yeoman to create an empty ASP.NET Core application by using the command yo aspnet in a shell and then choosing Empty Application from the menu.

Once you've created your empty ASP.NET Core application and named it Hello-Microservices, you should have a project that contains these files:

- Hellomicroservices\Program.cs
- Hellomicroservices\Startup.cs
- Hellomicroservices\project.json

There are other files in the project, but these are the one you'll be concerned with.

This is a complete application, ready to run. It will respond to any HTTP request with the string "Hello World". You can start the application from the command line by going to the folder containing the project.json file and typing the command dotnet run.

The application runs on localhost port 5000 (note that if you choose to run it from inside Visual Studio, you may get another port). If you go to http://localhost:5000 in a browser, you'll get the Hello World response.

1.8.2 Adding Nancy to the project

You can add Nancy to the project as a NuGet package by adding Nancy to the dependencies section in the project.json file that's part of your empty application. You'll also need the Microsoft.AspNetCore.Owin package, so go ahead and add that too. The dependencies section of project.json should look similar to the following listing.

> **Listing 1.1 dependencies section of project.json**

```
"dependencies": {
    "Microsoft.NETCore.App": {
        "version": "1.0.0",
```

```
    "type": "platform"
  },
  "Microsoft.AspNetCore.Server.IISIntegration": "1.0.0",
  "Microsoft.AspNetCore.Server.Kestrel": "1.0.0",
  "Microsoft.AspNetCore.Owin": "1.0.0",
  "Nancy": "2.0.0-barneyrubble"
},
```

When you save the project.json file in Visual Studio, Visual Studio Code, or ATOM with OmniSharp, the IDE will perform a package restore, which means it will download any new NuGet packages specified in dependencies. Once the package restore is done, Nancy will be part of the project.

Now that you've added the Nancy NuGet package, you need to tell ASP.NET Core to use Nancy. You do so in the Startup.cs file, which is already part of the project. There's already some code in Startup.cs; replace it with the code in the next listing, which first tells ASP.NET Core to use OWIN and then adds Nancy to the OWIN pipeline.

Listing 1.2   Configuring ASP.NET Core in Startup.cs

```
namespace Hellomicroservices
{
  using Microsoft.AspNetCore.Builder;
  using Nancy.Owin;

  public class Startup
  {
    public void Configure(IApplicationBuilder app)   ◄─── ASP.NET Core calls this method
    {                                                      during application startup.
      app.UseOwin(buildFunc =>                         ◄─── Configures ASP.NET Core
        buildFunc.UseNancy()    ◄───                        to use OWIN. buildFunc
      );                                                    can be used to set up
    }                             Adds Nancy to the OWIN     the OWIN pipeline.
  }                               pipeline.
}                                 This allows Nancy to handle
                                  incoming HTTP requests.
```

At this point, you have an ASP.NET Core application with Nancy added; but the application can't handle any requests yet, because you haven't set up any routes in Nancy. If you restart the application and again go to http://localhost:5000 in a browser, you'll get a 404 Not Found response. Let's fix that.

1.8.3   *Adding a Nancy module with an implementation of the endpoint*

Now you'll add a Nancy module with an implementation of the single API endpoint. A *Nancy module* is a class that inherits from NancyModule; it's used to declare which endpoints the application can handle and to implement the behavior for each endpoint. Nancy automatically discovers all classes that inherit from NancyModule on startup and registers all routes declared in the Nancy modules. Declaring routes in a Nancy module is done using Nancy's internal DSL for dealing with HTTP. You can add a Nancy module by creating a file called CurrentDateTimeModule.cs and adding the following code to it.

> **Listing 1.3   Nancy module**

```
namespace Hellomicroservices
{
  using System;
  using Nancy;

  public class CurrentDateTimeModule        ⟵  Declares a Nancy
     : NancyModule                              module
  {
    public CurrentDateTimeModule()            Declares a route and route handler. Sets
    {                                         requests to / to return the current date
      Get("/", _ => DateTime.UtcNow);    ⟵   and time as JSON or XML.
    }
  }
}
```

In this module, you declare a route for the path / with the expression Get("/", …?). You also tell Nancy that any HTTP GET request to / should be handled by the lambda _ ? DateTime.UtcNow;. Every time a request to / comes in, the response is the current UTC date and time.

> **NOTE** By convention, I use _ as the name of lambda parameters that aren't used on the right side of the lambda arrow.

You can now rerun the application and again point your browser to http://local-host:5000. Your browser will hit the route on your Nancy module and show an error page. Why? Because Nancy can't find a view for the / route. This is OK. The intention of this little application isn't to serve HTML to a browser, but to serve JSON or XML data. To test that your application can do that, use Postman or a similar tool to make an HTTP GET request to the root of your application with an Accept header with the value application/json. The test in Postman is shown in figure 1.12.

On the wire, this is the request:

```
                     HTTP method (GET), path (/), and
                     protocol (HTTP/I.l) used in the request    List of request headers. In
Host to which the                                               this case, there's only an
request is made    GET / HTTP/1.1          ⟵                    Accept header with the
                   Host: localhost:5000                         value application/json.
                   Accept: application/json   ⟵
```

The response from this request is the current UTC data and time, serialized as JSON:

```
HTTP/1.1 200 OK
Content-Type: application/json; charset=utf-8

"2016-06-06T19:50:09.2556094Z"
```

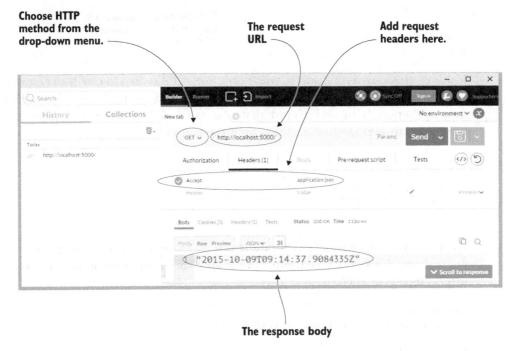

Choose HTTP method from the drop-down menu.

The request URL

Add request headers here.

The response body

Figure 1.12 Postman makes it easy to send HTTP requests and control the request details, such as the headers and HTTP method.

If you change the Accept header in the preceding request to application/xml, the response will be serialized as XML. Nancy supports both JSON and XML serialization and takes the Accept header into account when serializing the response. You've now implemented your first API endpoint with Nancy.

1.8.4 Adding OWIN middleware

Now that you have a minimal Nancy application up and running, you can use a piece of OWIN middleware to add some simple request logging. Your application already has an OWIN pipeline, albeit a short one. It contains only one component: Nancy. The code in listing 1.4, which goes in the Startup class, adds to the pipeline a component that writes "Got request" to the console every time a request comes in. It then passes the request to the next component in the pipeline: Nancy.

Listing 1.4 OWIN middleware that writes a string

```
app.UseOwin(buildFunc =>
{
  buildFunc(next => env =>
  {
    System.Console.WriteLine("Got request");
```

Adds a piece of middleware (a lambda expression) to the OWIN pipeline

The middleware writes a string to standard out once for each incoming request.

```
    return next(env);
  });
  buildFunc.UseNancy();
});
```

Calls the next middleware in the OWIN pipeline and passes all the request data to it

If this code seems a little odd to you, don't worry; I'll return to OWIN in chapters 9, 10, and 11 and explain how it works and how to use its strengths in microservices. For now, it's enough to understand that you can build up an OWIN pipeline in the `Startup` class and that the middleware is the lambda:

```
next => env =>
  {
    System.Console.WriteLine("Got request");
    return next(env);
  }
```

With the request-logging OWIN middleware in place, the console output of your little microservice looks like this, if you run the application and then make a few requests to http://localhost:5000:

```
PS> dotnet run
Application started. Press Ctrl+C to shut down.
Got request
Got request
Got request
Got request
Got request
Got request
```

> **NOTE** Throughout the book, you'll use OWIN middleware to take care of cross-cutting concerns like request logging and monitoring.

This completes the example. With only a little code, you've created your first, simple microservice with a single endpoint that can provide the current UTC date and time as either JSON or XML. Furthermore, the microservice has rudimentary request logging in the form of writing out text to the console every time a request comes in.

1.9 Summary

- *Microservices* is an overloaded term used both for the microservices architectural style and for individual microservices in a system of microservices.
- The microservices architectural style is a special form of SOA, where each service is small and provides one and only one business capability.
- A microservice is a service with a single, tightly focused capability.
- I'll refer to six characteristics of a microservice in this book. A microservice
  - Is responsible for providing a single capability.
  - Is individually deployable. You must be able to deploy every microservice on its own without touching any other part of the system.

- Runs in one or more processes, separate from other microservices.
- Owns and stores the data belonging to the capability it provides in a data store that the microservice itself has access to.
- Is small enough that a small team of around five people can develop and maintain a handful or more of them.
- Is replaceable. The team should be able to rewrite a microservice from scratch in a short period of time if, for instance, the codebase has become a mess.

- Microservices go hand in hand with continuous delivery:

- Having small, individually deployable microservices makes continuous delivery easier.

- Being able to deploy automatically, quickly, and reliably simplifies deploying and maintaining a system of microservices.

- A system built with microservices allows for scalability and resilience.

- A system built with microservices is malleable: it can be easily changed according to your business needs. Each microservice by itself is highly maintainable, and even creating new microservices to provide new capabilities can be done quickly.

- Microservices collaborate to provide functionality to the end user.

- A microservice exposes a remote public API that other microservices may use.

- A microservice can expose a feed of events that other microservices can subscribe to. Events are handled asynchronously in the subscribers but still allow subscribers to react to events quickly.

- Nancy is a lightweight .NET web framework that's easy to get started with.

- Nancy modules are used to set up endpoints in Nancy applications.

- OWIN allows you to build a pipeline of middleware that runs on each request and is well situated for handling cross-cutting concerns.

- Most microservices don't serve HTML from their endpoints, but rather data in the form of JSON or XML. Applications like Postman and Fiddler are good for testing such endpoints.

A basic shopping
cart microservice

This chapter covers

- A nearly complete implementation of the Shopping Cart microservice
- Creating HTTP endpoints with Nancy
- Implementing a request from one microservice to another
- Implementing a simple event feed for a microservice with Nancy

In chapter 1, we looked at how microservices work and how they can be characterized. You also set up a simple technology stack—C#/Nancy/OWIN—that lets you create microservices easily, and you saw a basic Shopping Cart microservice. In this chapter, you'll implement four main parts of this microservice using Nancy:

- A basic HTTP-based API allowing clients to retrieve a cart, delete it, and add items to it. Each of these methods will be visible as an HTTP endpoint, such as http://myservice/add/{item_number}.

- A call from one service to another for more information. In this case, the Shopping Cart microservice will ask the Product Catalog microservice for pricing information based on the `item_number` of the item being added to the cart.
- An event feed that the service will use to publish events to the rest of the system. By creating an event feed for the shopping cart, you'll make it possible for other services (such as the recommendation engine) to update their own data and improve their capabilities.
- The domain logic for implementing the behavior of the shopping cart.

To keep things simple, you won't do a complete implementation of this microservice in this chapter. We'll look at the following topics and complete the microservice during the course of the book:

- The Shopping Cart microservice should have its own data store, but you won't implement it or the data access code to get data in and out of it. Chapter 5 covers this in full.
- Any production-ready microservice should include support for monitoring and logging. If a microservice doesn't provide regular insight into its health, it becomes difficult to keep the overall system running steadily. But these functions don't directly provide a business capability, so I've left logging and monitoring capabilities to be discussed in chapter 9.

Let's get to it.

> **NOTE** Be sure you've set up your development environment. In appendix A, you'll find download, installation, and quick usage information about IDEs you can use to follow along with the code throughout this book. This chapter has lots of code, so if you haven't already set up a development environment, now is the time to do it.

2.1   *Overview of the Shopping Cart microservice*

In chapter 1, we looked at how an e-commerce site built with microservices might handle a user's request to add an item to their shopping cart. The complete overview of how the request is handled is repeated in figure 2.1.

The Shopping Cart microservice plays a central role when a user wants to add an item to their shopping cart. But it's not the only process in which Shopping Cart plays a role. It's equally important to let the user see their shopping cart and delete an item from it. The Shopping Cart microservice must support those processes through its HTTP API, just as it supports adding an item to a shopping cart. Figure 2.2 shows the interactions between the Shopping Cart microservice and the other microservices in the system.

The Shopping Cart microservice supports three types of synchronous requests:

- Getting a shopping cart
- Adding an item to a shopping cart
- Deleting an item from a shopping cart

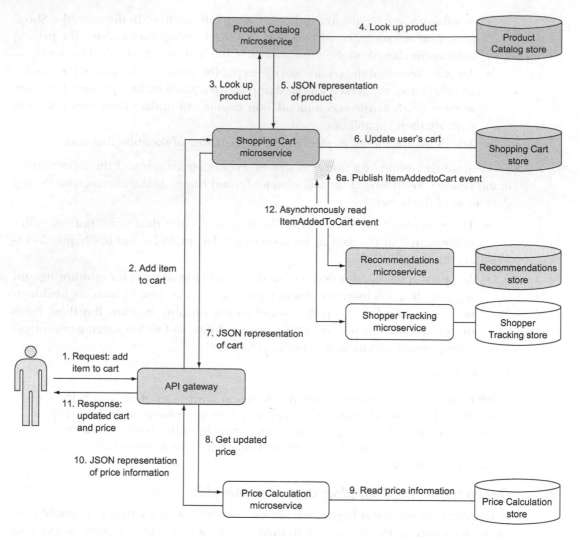

Figure 2.1 The Shopping Cart microservice allows other microservices to get a shopping cart, add items to and delete items from a shopping cart, and subscribe to events from Shopping Cart.

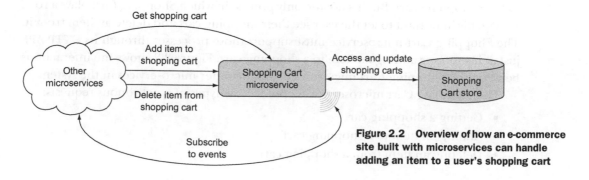

Figure 2.2 Overview of how an e-commerce site built with microservices can handle adding an item to a user's shopping cart

On top of that, it exposes an event feed that other microservices can subscribe to. Now that you've seen an overview of the Shopping Cart microservice's complete functionality, you can start drilling into its implementation.

2.1.1 Components of the Shopping Cart microservice

Let's zoom in and see what this microservice looks like at closer range. As shown in figure 2.3, the Shopping Cart microservice consists of these components:

- A small Shopping Cart domain model that's responsible for implementing any business rules related to shopping carts.
- An HTTP API component that's responsible for handling all incoming HTTP requests. The HTTP API component is divided into two modules: one handles requests from other microservices to do something, and the other exposes an event feed.
- Two data store components: `EventStore` and `ShoppingCartStore`. These data store components are responsible for talking to the data store (`ShoppingCartStore`):
  - `EventStore` handles saving events to and reading them from the data store.
  - `ShoppingCartStore` handles reading and updating shopping carts in the data store. Note that shopping carts and events may be stored in different databases; we'll return to this in chapter 5.
- A `ProductCatalogClient` component that's responsible for communicating with the Product Catalog microservice shown in figure 2.1. Placing that communication in `ProductCatalogClient` serves several purposes:
  - It encapsulates knowledge of the other microservice's API in one place.
  - It encapsulates the details of making an HTTP request.
  - It encapsulates caching results from the other microservice.
  - It encapsulates handling errors from the other microservice.

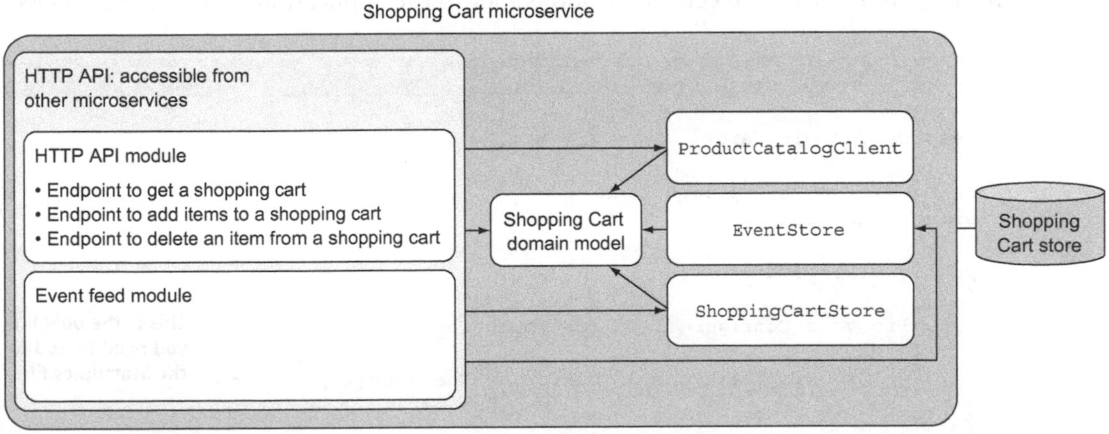

Shopping Cart microservice

Figure 2.3   The Shopping Cart microservice is a small codebase with a few components that provide one focused business capability.

This chapter includes the code for the domain model, the HTTP API, and a basic implementation of `ProductCatalogClient`, but skips `EventStore` and `ShoppingCart-Store` and the data store. In addition, for the sake of brevity, this chapter omits error-handling code. Chapters 4 and 5 go into further detail about how to implement microservice APIs easily with Nancy; chapter 5 also returns to the subject of storing data in a microservice. Chapter 6 dives deeper into how to design robustness into clients such as `ProductCatalogClient`.

2.2 Implementing the Shopping Cart microservice

Now that you understand the Shopping Cart microservice's components, it's time to get into the code.

> ### New technologies used in this chapter
>
> In this chapter, you'll begin using two new technologies:
>
> - `HttpClient` is a .NET Core type for making HTTP requests. It provides an API for creating and sending HTTP requests as well as reading the responses that come back.
> - Polly is a library that makes it easy to implement one of the more common policies for handling remote-call failures. Out of the box, Polly has support for various retry and circuit breaker policies. I'll discuss circuit breakers in chapter 6.

2.2.1 Creating an empty project

The first thing you need to do is set up a Nancy project, just as in chapter 1. Create an empty ASP.NET Core application called `ShoppingCart`, and add the `Nancy` NuGet package to the new project. Then, add Nancy to the application in the `Startup` class.

Listing 2.1 `Startup` class that starts up Nancy

```
namespace ShoppingCart
{
  using Microsoft.AspNet.Builder;
  using Nancy.Owin;

  public class Startup
  {
    public void Configure(IApplicationBuilder app)
    {
      app.UseOwin(buildFunc => buildFunc.UseNancy());      ← This is the only line
    }                                                         you need to add to
  }                                                           the Startup.cs file.
}
```

You now have an empty Nancy application that's ready to go.

2.2.2 *The Shopping Cart microservice's API for other services*

In this section, you'll implement the Shopping Cart microservice's HTTP API, which is highlighted in figure 2.4. This API has three parts, each of which is implemented as an HTTP endpoint:

- An HTTP GET endpoint where other microservices can fetch a user's shopping cart by providing a user ID. The response is a shopping cart serialized as either JSON or XML.
- An HTTP POST endpoint where other microservices can add items to a user's shopping cart. The items to be added are passed to the endpoint as an array of product IDs. The array can be in XML or JSON, and it must be the body of the request.
- An HTTP DELETE endpoint where other microservices can remove items from a user's shopping cart. The items to be deleted are passed in the body of the request as an XML or JSON array of product IDs.

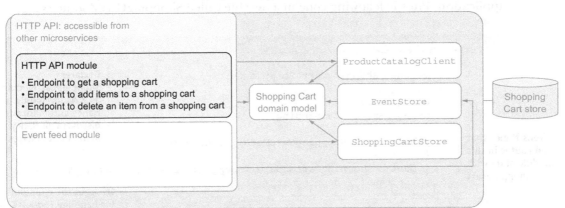

Figure 2.4 Implementing the HTTP API component

The following three sections each implement one of the endpoints.

GETTING A SHOPPING CART

The first part of the HTTP API that you'll implement is the endpoint that lets other microservices fetch a user's shopping cart. Figure 2.5 shows how other microservices can use an endpoint to get a shopping cart.

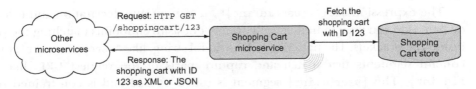

Figure 2.5   Other microservices can use an endpoint on Shopping Cart to get a shopping cart in XML or JSON format.

The endpoint accepts HTTP GET requests. Its URL includes the ID of the user whose shopping cart the other microservice wants, and the body of the response is an XML or JSON serialization of that shopping cart. The request should include an Accept header indicating whether the response body should be XML or JSON.

For example, the API gateway in figure 2.1 may need the shopping cart for a user with ID 123. To get that, it sends this HTTP request:

```
HTTP GET /shoppingcart/123 HTTP/1.1
Host: shoppingcart.my.company.com
Accept: application/json
```

This is a request to shoppingcart/123 on the Shopping Cart microservice, and the 123 part of the URL is the user ID.

To handle such requests, you need to add to the ShoppingCart project a new Nancy module called ShoppingCartModule. As mentioned in chapter 1, a Nancy module is a class that inherits from NancyModule and is used to implement endpoints in a Nancy application. Put the following code in a new file called ShoppingCartModule.cs.

Listing 2.2   Endpoint to access a shopping cart by user ID

```
namespace ShoppingCart.ShoppingCart
{
    using Nancy;
    using Nancy.ModelBinding;

    public class ShoppingCartModule : NancyModule
    {
        public ShoppingCartModule(IShoppingCartStore shoppingCartStore)
            : base("/shoppingcart")
        {
            Get("/{userid:int}", parameters =>
            {
                var userId = (int) parameters.userid;
                return shoppingCartStore.Get(userId);
            });
        }
    }
}
```

Annotations:
- Tells Nancy that all routes in this module start with /shoppingcart
- Declares ShoppingCartModule as a NancyModule. Nancy automatically discovers all Nancy modules at startup.
- Declares the endpoint for handling requests to /shoppingcart/{userid}, such as /shoppingcart/123
- Sets the user ID to the userid segment of the request URL
- Returns the user's shopping cart. Nancy serializes it to XML or JSON before sending it to the client.

You can already see some important parts of Nancy in action here. Let's break down this code.

The expression Get("/{userid:int}", …?) is a route declaration and is how you declare that you want to handle HTTP GET requests to endpoints matching the pattern inside the brackets. The pattern can be a literal string, like "/shoppingcart"; or it can contain segments that match and capture parts of the request URL, like {userid:int}. The {userid:int} segment is called userid and is constrained to only match integer values.

After the route declaration comes a lambda expression:

```
parameters =>
{
  var userId = (int) parameters.userid;
  return shoppingCartStore.Get(userId);
};
```

This is the route handler, and it's the piece of code that's executed every time the Shopping Cart microservice receives a request to a URL that matches the route declaration. For instance, when the API gateway requests a shopping cart via the URL /shoppingcart/123, this is the code that handles the request.

The route handler takes a single argument, `parameters`, which gives access to all the captured segments of the request URL. The `parameters` object is dynamic and allows you to get the captured segments as if they were properties on the `parameters` object. That's how `parameters.userid` works: the `parameters.userid` type is dynamic, so you have to cast to an `int` before you can use it as an `int`.

The route handler uses a `shoppingCartStore` object that the `ShoppingCartModule` constructor takes as an argument:

```
public ShoppingCartModule(IShoppingCartStore shoppingCartStore)
```

Because the route handle is in the `ShoppingCartModule` constructor, `shoppingCartStore` is in scope in the route handler.

The constructor argument has the type `IShoppingCartStore`, which is an interface. Nancy will automatically find an implementation of `IShoppingCartStore`; and, as long there's no ambiguity, it will provide an instance of `ShoppingCartModule`. I'm leaving out the data-storage code in this chapter, but the code in the code download accompanying this book contains the `IShoppingCart` interface and a dummy implementation of it.

The route handler returns a `ShoppingCart` object that it gets back from `shoppingCartStore`:

```
return shoppingCartStore.Get(userId);
```

The `ShoppingCart` type is specific to the Shopping Cart microservice, so Nancy has no way of knowing about this particular type. But Nancy is liberal in what you can return from a route handler. You can return any object you want, and Nancy will handle it sensibly. In this case, you want to serialize the `ShoppingCart` object and return the data to the caller, and this is exactly what Nancy does.

The following listing shows an example of the response to a request to /shoppingcart/123.

Listing 2.3   Example response from the Shopping Cart microservice

```
HTTP/1.1 200 OK
Content-Type: application/json; charset=utf-8        ◁─── The response body is in JSON.

539                                ◁─── Length of the response body
{
    "userId": 42,
    "items": [                       ◁─── Shopping cart serialized as JSON
        {
            "productcatalogId": 1,
            "productName": "Basic t-shirt",
            "description": "a quiet t-shirt",
            "price": {
                "currency": "eur",
                "amount": 40
            }
        },
        {
            "productcatalogId": 2,
            "productName": "Fancy shirt",
            "description": "a loud t-shirt",
            "price": {
                "currency": "eur",
                "amount": 50
            }
        }
    ]
}
```

As you can see, you can get a lot of functionality up and running with a small amount of code by relying on Nancy.

ADDING ITEMS TO A SHOPPING CART

The second endpoint you need to add to the Shopping Cart microservice lets you add items to a user's shopping cart. Figure 2.6 shows how other microservices can use this endpoint.

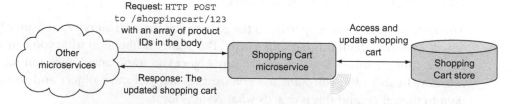

Figure 2.6   Other microservices can add items to a shopping cart with an HTTP POST request that includes an array of product IDs in the request body.

Like the HTTP GET endpoint in the previous section, this new endpoint receives a user ID in the URL. This time, the endpoint accepts HTTP POST requests instead of HTTP GET, and the request should provide a list of items in the body of the request. For example, the following request adds two items to user 123's shopping cart.

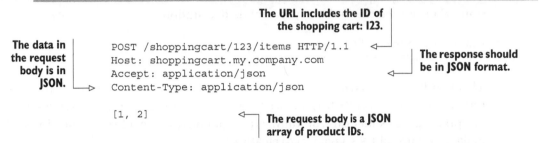

Listing 2.4 Adding two items to a shopping cart

The data in the request body is in JSON.

The URL includes the ID of the shopping cart: 123.

```
POST /shoppingcart/123/items HTTP/1.1
Host: shoppingcart.my.company.com
Accept: application/json
Content-Type: application/json

[1, 2]
```

The response should be in JSON format.

The request body is a JSON array of product IDs.

To handle such requests, you need to add another route declaration to Shopping-CartModule. The new route handler reads the items from the body of the request, looks up the product information for each one, adds them to the correct shopping cart, and returns the updated shopping cart.

The new route declaration is shown in the next listing. Add it to the Shopping-CartModule constructor.

Listing 2.5 Handler for a route to add items to a shopping cart

```
public class ShoppingCartModule : NancyModule
{
  public ShoppingCartModule(
    IShoppingCartStore shoppingCartStore,
    IProductcatalogClient productcatalog,
    IEventStore eventStore)
    : base("/shoppingcart")
  {
    Get("/{userid:int}"], parameters => { ... });

    Post("/{userid:int}/items",
      async (parameters, _) =>
    {
      var productcatalogIds = this.Bind<int[]>();
      var userId = (int) parameters.userid;

      var shoppingCart = shoppingCartStore.Get(userId);
      var shoppingCartItems = await
        productcatalog
        .GetShoppingCartItems(productcatalogIds)
        .ConfigureAwait(false);
      shoppingCart.AddItems(shoppingCartItems, eventStore);
```

Declares an HTTP POST endpoint for /shoppingcart/{userid}/item

Reads and deserializes the array of product IDs in the HTTP request body

Fetches the product information from the Product Catalog microservice

Adds items to the cart

```
        shoppingCartStore.Save(shoppingCart);          ⟵  Saves the updated cart
                                                            to the data store
      return shoppingCart;                      ⟵
    });                                    ⌐  Returns the updated cart
  }
}
```

Two new Nancy capabilities are at play here. First, the new route handler is asynchronous. You can see this in the async lambda declaration:

```
Post("/{userid:int}/items",
  async (parameters, _) =>
```

This handler is declared asynchronous because it makes a remote call to the Product Catalog microservice. Performing that external call asynchronously saves resources in Shopping Cart. Nancy can run fully asynchronously, which allows application code to make good use of C#'s async/await feature.

Second, the body of the request contains a JSON array of product IDs. These are the items that should be added to the shopping cart. The route handler uses Nancy's model binding to read these into a C# array:

```
var productcatalogIds = this.Bind<int[]>();
```

Nancy's model binding supports any serializable C# object. You'd often use a more structured object than a flat JSON array to send data into an endpoint, and reading that would be just as easy as in this case. The type parameter in this.Bind<int[]>() would just need to be changed to a type other than int[]. Out of the box, Nancy supports binding to JSON and XML data; but as you'll see in chapter 4, adding other formats is straightforward.

The new route handler uses two objects that aren't already present in Shopping-CartModule. You once again rely on Nancy to provide them through constructor arguments. Nancy's dependency injection automatically provides the dependencies when instantiating the modules.

Listing 2.6   Adding module dependencies as constructor arguments

```
public ShoppingCartModule(
    IShoppingCartStore shoppingCartStore,        Only used to pass into the
    IProductcatalogClient productCatalog,        AddItems call, where it
    IEventStore eventStore)             ⟵        will be used later
```

Other microservices can now add items to shopping carts. They should similarly be allowed to remove items from shopping carts.

async/await at a glance

C# 5 introduced two new keywords, `async` and `await`, to allow methods to run asynchronously easily. A basic `async` method looks like this:

Declares method as async

```
public async Task<int> WaitForANumber()
{
  await Task.Delay(1000)
    .ConfigureAwait(false);
  return 10;
}
```

Yields the current thread until the task completes

Allows execution to be resumed with a different thread context

Because the method is async, the return value is automatically wrapped in a Task.

When you call this method, the thread of execution continues as usual until `await`. The `await` keyword works in conjunction with *awaitables*—the most common awaitable is `System.Threading.Tasks.Task<T>`—and asynchronously waits until the awaitable completes. This means two things happen when execution reaches `await`:

- The remainder of the method is queued up for execution when the awaitable—in this case, the `Task` returned from `Task.Delay(1000)`—completes. When the awaitable completes, the rest of the method is executed, possibly on a new thread but with same state as before the `await` reestablished.
- The current thread of execution returns from the `async` method and continues in the caller.

The `ConfigureAwait(false)` call in the preceding code snippet tells the `Task` not to save the current thread context. As a consequence, the thread context isn't reestablished when method execution resumes. Because the code doesn't rely on the thread context, it can skip that saving and reestablishing.

In server-side code, like microservices, many requests require some I/O, such as calling a data store or another microservice. If you can execute the I/O asynchronously instead of blocking a thread while waiting for the I/O to complete, you save resources on your servers. In some situations, you may also gain some performance, but that isn't the general case. I use `async/await` and `Tasks` a lot in this book to save resources on the server and gain scalability.

REMOVING ITEMS FROM A SHOPPING CART

The third and last endpoint is an HTTP DELETE endpoint that, as shown in figure 2.7, lets other microservices remove items from shopping carts. You should now have the hang of adding endpoints to Nancy modules. You need to implement an HTTP DELETE endpoint that takes an array of product IDs and removes those products from the cart. Add the following code to the `ShoppingCartModule` constructor.

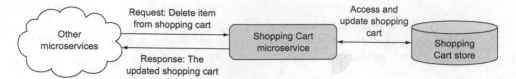

Figure 2.7   Other microservices can remove items from a shopping cart with an HTTP `DELETE`
request by providing an array of product IDs in the request body.

Listing 2.7   Endpoint for removing items from a shopping cart

```
public class ShoppingCartModule : NancyModule
{
  public ShoppingCartModule(
    IShoppingCartStore shoppingCartStore,
    IProductCatalogClient productCatalog,
    IEventStore eventStore)
    : base("/shoppingcart")
  {
    Get("/{userid:int}"], parameters => { ... });

    Post("/{userid:int}/items",
      async (parameters, _) => { ... });

    Delete("/{userid:int}/items", parameters =>
    {
      var productCatalogIds = this.Bind<int[]>();
      var userId = (int)parameters.userid;

      var shoppingCart = shoppingCartStore.Get(userId);
      shoppingCart.RemoveItems(productCatalogIds, eventStore);
      shoppingCartStore.Save(shoppingCart);

      return shoppingCart;
    });
  }
}
```

> **Using the same route template for two route declarations is fine if they use different HTTP methods.**

> **The eventStore will be used later in the RemoveItems method.**

This completes `ShoppingCartModule`, which ends up at less than 50 lines of code.
That's why I consider Nancy a lightweight framework.

2.2.3   *Fetching product information*

Now that the API exposed by the Shopping Cart microservice is implemented, let's
switch gears and look at how the product information is fetched from the Product Catalog microservice. Figure 2.8 highlights `ProductCatalogClient`, which you'll implement in this section.

The Product Catalog microservice and the Shopping Cart microservice are
separate microservices running in separate processes, perhaps even on separate
servers. Product Catalog exposes an HTTP API that Shopping Cart uses. Product

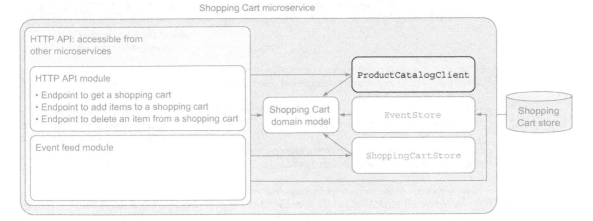

Figure 2.8 ProductCatalogClient

catalog information is fetched in HTTP GET requests to an endpoint on the Product Catalog microservice.

You need to follow these three steps to implement the HTTP request to the Product Catalog microservice:

1. Implement the HTTP GET request.
2. Parse the response from the endpoint at the Product Catalog microservice, and translate it to the domain of the Shopping Cart microservice.
3. Implement a policy for handling failed requests to the Product Catalog microservice.

The subsequent sections walk you through these steps.

IMPLEMENTING THE HTTP GET

The Product Catalog microservice exposes an endpoint at the path /products. The endpoint accepts an array of product IDs as a query string parameter and returns the product information for each of those products. For example, the following request fetches the information for product IDs 1 and 2:

```
HTTP GET /products?productIds=[1,2] HTTP/1.1
Host: productcatalog.my.company.com
Accept: application/json
```

You'll use the HttpClient type to perform the HTTP request. Instead of a real Product Catalog microservice, the implementation uses a microservice made with *Apiary* (https://apiary.io). Apiary is an online service that, among other things, lets you easily create endpoints that return hardcoded responses. In this case, I created an endpoint that returns hardcoded product information. Using that fake endpoint, the following code makes the HTTP GET request to the Product Catalog microservice.

Listing 2.8   HTTP GET request to the Product Catalog microservice

> URL of the fake Product
> Catalog microservice

```
private static string productCatalogBaseUrl =
    @"http://private-05cc8-chapter2productcatalogmicroservice
    ➥ .apiary-mock.com";
    private static string getProductPathTemplate =
        "/products?productIds=[{0}]";

    private static async Task<HttpResponseMessage>
        RequestProductFromProductCatalogue(int[] productCatalogueIds)
    {
        var productsResource = string.Format(
          getProductPathTemplate, string.Join(",", productCatalogueIds));
        using (var httpClient = new HttpClient())
        {
            httpClient.BaseAddress = new Uri(productCatalogueBaseUrl);
            return await
                httpClient.GetAsync(productsResource).ConfigureAwait(false);
        }
    }
}
```

> Adds the product IDs as a
> query string parameter to the
> path of the /products endpoint

> Creates a client for making
> the HTTP GET request

> Tells HttpClient to perform the
> HTTP GET asynchronously

This is pretty straightforward. The only thing to note is that by executing the HTTP GET request asynchronously, the current thread is freed up to handle other things in Shopping Cart while the request is processed in Product Catalog. This is good practice because it preserves resources in the Shopping Cart microservice, making it a bit less resource intensive and more scalable.

2.2.4   *Parsing the product response*

The Product Catalog microservice returns product information as a JSON array. The array includes an entry for each requested product, as shown next.

Listing 2.9   Returning a JSON list of products

```
HTTP/1.1 200 OK
Content-Type: application/json; charset=utf-8

543
[
  {
    "productId": "1",
    "productName": "Basic t-shirt",
    "productDescription": "a quiet t-shirt",
    "price": { "amount" : 40, "currency": "eur" },
    "attributes" : [
    {
```

```
      "sizes": [ "s", "m", "l"],
      "colors": ["red", "blue", "green"]
    }]
  },
  {
    "productId": "2",
    "productName": "Fancy shirt",
    "productDescription": "a loud t-shirt",
    "price": { "amount" : 50, "currency": "eur" },
    "attributes" : [
    {
      "sizes": [ "s", "m", "l", "xl"],
      "colors": ["ALL", "Batique"]
    }]
  }
]
```

This JSON must be deserialized, and the information required to create a list of Shop-pingCart items needs to be read from it. The array returned from Product Catalog is formatted by the microservice's API. To avoid tight coupling between microservices, only the ProductCatalogClient class knows anything about the API of the Product Catalog microservice. That means ProductCatalogClient is responsible for translating the data received from the microservice into types for the ShoppingCart project. In this case, you need a list of ShoppingCartItem objects. The following listing shows the code for deserializing and translating the response data.

Listing 2.10   Extracting data from the response

```
private static async Task<IEnumerable<ShoppingCartItem>>
    ConvertToShoppingCartItems(HttpResponseMessage response)
  {
    response.EnsureSuccessStatusCode();
    var products =
      JsonConvert.DeserializeObject<List<ProductCatalogueProduct>>(
        await response.Content.ReadAsStringAsync().ConfigureAwait(false));  ⟵── Uses Json.NET to deserialize
    return                                                                       the JSON from the Product
      products                                                                   Catalog microservice
        .Select(p => new ShoppingCartItem(          ⟵──┐
          int.Parse(p.ProductId),                        Creates a ShoppingCartItem for
          p.ProductName,                                 each product in the response
          p.ProductDescription,
          p.Price
        ));
  }

  private class ProductCatalogProduct          ⟵──┐ Uses a private
  {                                                   class to represent
    public string ProductId { get; set; }           the product data
    public string ProductName { get; set; }
    public string ProductDescription { get; set; }
    public Money Price { get; set; }
  }
```

If you compare listings 2.9 and 2.10, you may notice that there are more properties in the response than in the ProductCatalogProduct class. This is because the Shopping Cart microservice doesn't need all the information, so there's no reason to read the remaining properties. Doing so would only introduce unnecessary coupling. I'll return to this topic in chapters 4, 5, and 7.

The following listing combines the code that requests the product information and the code that parses the response. This method makes the HTTP GET request and translates the response to the domain of Shopping Cart.

Listing 2.11   Fetching products and converting them to shopping cart items

```
private async Task<IEnumerable<ShoppingCartItem>>
    GetItemsFromCatalogueService(int[] productCatalogueIds)
{
  var response = await
    RequestProductFromProductCatalogue(productCatalogueIds)
    .ConfigureAwait(false);
  return await ConvertToShoppingCartItems(response)
    .ConfigureAwait(false);
}
```

The ProductCatalogClient is almost finished. The only part missing is the code that handles an HTTP request failure.

2.2.5   *Adding a failure-handling policy*

Remote calls can fail. Not only *can* they fail, but when running a distributed system at scale, remote calls often *do* fail. You may not expect the call from Shopping Cart to Product Catalog to fail often, but in an entire system of microservices, there will often be a failing remote call somewhere in the system.

Remote calls fail for many reasons: the network can fail, the call could be malformed, the remote microservice might have a bug, the server where the call is handled may fail during processing, or the remote microservice might be in the middle of a redeploy. In a system of microservices, you must expect failures and design a level of resilience around every place remote calls are made. This is an important topic, and I'll go into more detail in chapter 6.

The level of resilience needed around a particular remote call depends on the business requirements for the microservice making the call. The call to the Product Catalog microservice from the Shopping Cart microservice is important; without the product information, the user can't add items to their shopping cart, which means the e-commerce site can't sell the items to the user. On the other hand, product information doesn't change often, so you could cache it in Shopping Cart and only request it from Product Catalog when the cache doesn't already contain the information. Caching is a good strategy:

- It makes Shopping Cart more resilient to failures in Product Catalog.
- The Shopping Cart microservice will perform better when the product information is present in the cache.
- Fewer calls made from the Shopping Cart microservice mean less stress is put on the Product Catalog microservice.

For now, you won't implement caching; we'll return to the subject of caching for the sake of robustness in chapter 6.

Even with caching in place, some calls from Shopping Cart to Product Catalog are still made. For these calls, you may decide that the best strategy for handling failed calls is to retry the call a couple of times and then give up and fail to add any items to the shopping cart. For this chapter, you'll implement a simple retry policy for handling failing requests. You'll use the Polly library, which you'll install in the `Shopping-Cart` project as a NuGet Package.

> **NOTE** Polly and failure-handling strategies are described in much more detail in chapter 6.

Using a Polly policy involves these two steps:

1 Declare the policy.
2 Use the policy to execute the remote call.

As you can see in the following listing, Polly's API makes both these steps easy.

Listing 2.12 Microservice error-handling policy

```
private static Policy exponentialRetryPolicy =
  Policy
    .Handle<Exception>()                              Uses Polly's fluent API to
    .WaitAndRetryAsync(                               set up a retry policy with
      3,                                              an exponential back-off
      attempt => TimeSpan.FromMilliseconds(100 * Math.Pow(2, attempt)));

public async Task<IEnumerable<ShoppingCartItem>>
  GetShoppingCartItems(int[] productCatalogIds) =>
    exponentialRetryPolicy
      .ExecuteAsync(async () =>
        await GetItemsFromcatalogService(productCatalogIds)     Wraps calls to the Product
          .ConfigureAwait(false));                             Catalog microservice in
                                                               the retry policy
```

This policy around the call to the Product Catalog microservice is simple: in case of failure, retry the call at most three times. And for each failure, double the amount of waiting time before making the next attempt.

This completes the implementation of `ProductCatalogClient`. Even though in has fewer than 100 lines of code, it does a lot: it builds up the HTTP GET request and executes it. It parses the response from Product Catalog and translates it into the shopping cart domain. And it contains the retry policy used for these calls. Next, let's tackle the event feed.

2.2.6   *Implementing a basic event feed*

The Shopping Cart microservice can now store shopping carts and add items to them. The items include product information from the Product Catalog microservice. Shopping Cart also has an API for other microservices that allows them to add items to or delete items from shopping carts and read the contents of a shopping cart.

The piece missing is the event feed. Shopping Cart needs to publish events about changes to shopping carts, and other microservices can subscribe to these events and react to them as required. In the case of items being added to a shopping cart, figure 2.9 (repeated from chapter 1) illustrates how the Recommendations microservice and the Shopper Tracking microservice base part of their functionality on events from the Shopping Cart microservice.

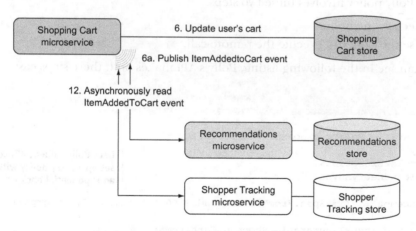

Figure 2.9   The Shopping Cart microservice publishes events about changes to shopping carts to an event feed. The Recommendations and Shopper Tracking microservices subscribe to these events and react as events arrive.

In this section, you'll implement the EventFeed and Shopping Cart domain model components highlighted in figure 2.10. (Chapter 4 returns to the implementation of event feeds and event subscribers.) The domain model is responsible for raising events, and EventFeed allows other microservices to read the events that the Shopping Cart microservice has published.

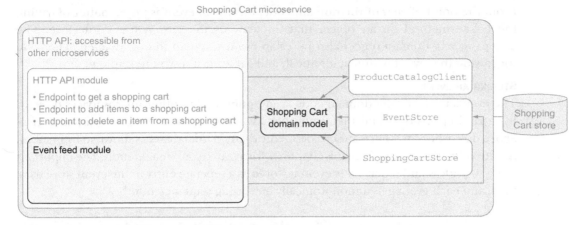

Figure 2.10   The Shopping Cart microservice event feed publishes events to the rest of the e-commerce system.

Implementing the event feed involves these steps:

- *Raise events.* The code in the Shopping Cart domain model raises events when something significant (according to the business rules) happens. Significant events are when items are added to or removed from a shopping cart.
- *Store events.* The events raised by the Shopping Cart domain model are stored in the microservice's data store.
- *Publish events.* Implementing an event feed allows other microservices to subscribe by polling.

We'll work through each of these in turn.

RAISING AN EVENT

In order to be published, events must first be raised. It's usually the domain code in a microservice that raises events, and that's the case in the Shopping Cart microservice. When items are added to a shopping cart, the `ShoppingCart` domain object raises an event by calling the `Raise` method on `IEventStore` and providing the data for the event.

> **Listing 2.13   Raising events**

```
public void AddItems(
     IEnumerable<ShoppingCartItem> shoppingCartItems,
     IEventStore eventStore)
{
  foreach (var item in shoppingCartItems)
    if (this.items.Add(item))
      eventStore.Raise(                          ⟵  Raises an event through the
        "ShoppingCartItemAdded",                     eventStore for each item.
        new { UserId, item });
}
```

From the point of view of the domain code, raising an event is just a matter of calling the `Raise` method on an object that implements the `IEventStore` interface. The `ShoppingCart` domain object also raises an event when an item is deleted. The code for raising that event is almost identical, and I'll leave it to you to implement it.

STORING AN EVENT

The events raised by the domain code aren't published to other microservices directly. Instead, they're stored and then published asynchronously. In other words, all `Event-Store` does when an event is raised is store the event in a database, as shown in listing 2.14. As with other database code in this chapter, I'll leave it to your imagination. The important thing to understand is that every event is stored as a separate entry in the event store database, and each event gets a monotonically increasing sequence number.

Listing 2.14   Storing event data in a database

```
public void Raise(string eventName, object content)
{
  var seqNumber = database.NextSequenceNumber();        ⟵┐ Gets a sequence
  database.Add(                                            │ number for the event
    new Event(
      seqNumber,
      DateTimeOffset.UtcNow,
      eventName,
      content));
}
```

`EventStore` stores every incoming event and keeps track of the order in which they arrive. We'll return to the subject of event stores in chapter 5, where we'll look more at implementing them.

A SIMPLE EVENT FEED

Once events are stored, they're ready to be published—in a sense, they *are* published. Even though one microservice *subscribes* to events from another microservice, an event feed works by having subscribers ask for new events periodically. Because subscribers are responsible for asking for new events, all you need to do in the Shopping Cart microservice is add an HTTP endpoint that allows subscribers to request events. A subscriber can, for example, issue the following request to get all events newer than event number 100:

```
GET /events?start=100 HTTP/1.1
Host: shoppingcart.my.company.com
Accept: application/json
```

Or, if the subscriber wants to limit the number of incoming events per call, it can add an end argument to the request:

```
GET /events?start=100&end=200 HTTP/1.1
Host: shoppingcart.my.company.com
Accept: application/json
```

Place the implementation of this /events endpoint in a new Nancy module, as shown in the following listing. The endpoint takes an optional starting point and an optional ending point, allowing other microservices to request ranges of events.

Listing 2.15 Exposing events to other microservices

```
namespace ShoppingCart.EventFeed
{
  using Nancy;

  public class EventsFeedModule : NancyModule
  {
    public EventsFeedModule(IEventStore eventStore) : base("/events")
    {
      Get("/", _ =>
      {
        long firstEventSequenceNumber, lastEventSequenceNumber;
        if (!long.TryParse(this.Request.Query.start.Value,         ◄─┐
          out firstEventSequenceNumber))                             │
          firstEventSequenceNumber = 0;                              │  Reads the start
        if (!long.TryParse(this.Request.Query.end.Value,          ◄─┤  and end values
          out lastEventSequenceNumber))                              │  from a query
          lastEventSequenceNumber = long.MaxValue;                   │  string parameter

        return
          eventStore.GetEvents(             ◄─┐  Returns the raw list of events.
            firstEventSequenceNumber,          │  Nancy takes care of serializing the
            lastEventSequenceNumber);          │  events into the response body.
      });
    }
  }
}
```

EventsModule mostly uses Nancy features that you've already encountered. The only new bit is that the start and end values are read from query string parameters. As with segments in the URL path, Nancy provides easy access to query string parameters through a dynamic object: Request.Query.

EventsFeedModule uses the event store to filter out events between the start and end values from the client. Although filtering is probably best done at the database level, the following simple implementation illustrates it well.

Listing 2.16 Filtering events based on the start and end points

```
public IEnumerable<Event> GetEvents(
  long firstEventSequenceNumber,
  long lastEventSequenceNumber) =>
    database
      .Where(e =>
        e.SequenceNumber >= firstEventSequenceNumber &&
        e.SequenceNumber <= lastEventSequenceNumber)
      .OrderBy(e => e.SequenceNumber);
```

With the /events endpoint in place, microservices that want to subscribe to events from the Shopping Cart microservice can do so by polling the endpoint. Subscribers can—and should—use the start and end query string parameters to make sure they only get new events. If Shopping Cart is down when a subscriber polls, the subscriber can ask for the same events again later. Likewise, if a subscriber goes down for a while, it can catch up with events from Shopping Cart by asking for events starting from the last event it saw. As mentioned, this isn't a full-fledged implementation of an event feed, but it gets you to the point that microservices can subscribe to events, and the code is simple.

You've now completed the version 1 implementation of your first microservice. As you can see, a microservice is small and has a narrow focus: it provides just one business capability. You can also see that microservice code tends to be simple and easy to understand. This is why you can expect to create new microservices and replace existing ones quickly.

2.3 Running the code

Now that all the code for the Shopping Cart microservice is in place, you can run it the same way you ran the example in chapter 1: from within Visual Studio, or from the command line with dotnet. You can test out all the endpoints with Postman or a similar tool. When you first try to fetch a shopping cart with an HTTP GET to /shoppingcart/123, the cart will be empty. Try adding some items to it with an HTTP POST to /shoppingcart/123/items and then fetching it again; the response should contain the added items. You can also look at the event feed at /events, and you should see events for each added item.

> **WARNING** I haven't shown implementations of EventStore or Shopping-CartStore. If you haven't created your own implementations of these, your microservice won't work.

2.4 Summary

- Implementing a complete microservice doesn't take much code. The Shopping Cart microservice has only the following:
  - Two short Nancy modules
  - A simple ShoppingCart domain class
  - A client class for calling the Product Catalog microservice
  - Two straightforward data access classes: ShoppingCartDataStore and Event-Store (not shown in this chapter)
- Nancy makes it simple to implement HTTP APIs. The route-definition API that Nancy provides makes it easy to add endpoints to a microservice. Just add a route definition and a handler—like Get("/hello", _ ? "world")—to the constructor of a Nancy module, and Nancy will automatically discover it and route requests to the handler.

- Nancy automatically handles serializing response data and deserializing request data. In the application code, you can return any serializable object from a handler, or you can use model binding to have request data deserialized.
- Out of the box, Nancy supports XML and JSON for both request and response data.
- You should always expect that other microservices may be down. To prevent errors from propagating, each remote call should be wrapped in a policy for handling failure.
- The Polly library is useful for implementing failure-handling policies and wrapping them around remote calls.
- Implementing a basic event feed is simple and enables other microservices to react to events. The poor man's event feed implemented in this chapter is just a short Nancy module.
- Domain model code is usually responsible for raising events, which are then stored in an event store and published through an event feed.

Part 2

Building microservices

In this part of the book, you'll learn how to design and code a microservice. The assorted diverse topics all go into designing and coding good, maintainable, reliable microservices:

- Chapter 3 explains how to slice and dice a system into a cohesive set of microservices.
- Chapter 4 shows you how microservices can collaborate to provide functionality for end users. You'll also be introduced to three categories of collaboration and when to use each of them.
- Chapter 5 explores where the data goes in a microservice system and which microservices should take responsibility for which data.
- Chapter 6 teaches you some simple techniques to make a microservice system more robust than it would otherwise be. Using these techniques, you can create a system that keeps running in the face of network failures and individual microservice crashes.
- Chapter 7 turns to testing. You'll learn how to create an effective automated test suite for a microservice system, all the way from broad system-level tests to narrowly focused unit tests.

By the end of part 2, you'll know how to design microservices and how to use .NET Core and Nancy to code them.

Identifying and scoping microservices

This chapter covers

- Scoping microservices for business capability
- Scoping microservices to support technical capabilities
- Managing when scoping microservices is difficult
- Carving out new microservices from existing ones

To succeed with microservices, it's important to be good at scoping each microservice appropriately. If your microservices are too big, the turnaround on creating new features and implementing bug fixes becomes too long. If they're too small, the coupling between microservices tends to grow. If they're the right size but have the wrong boundaries, coupling also tends to grow, and higher coupling leads to longer turnaround. In other words, if you aren't able to scope your microservices correctly, you'll lose much of the benefit microservices offer. In this chapter, I'll teach you how to find a good scope for each microservice so they stay loosely coupled.

The primary driver in identifying and scoping microservices is business capabilities; the secondary driver is supporting technical capabilities. Following these two drivers leads to microservices that align nicely with the list of microservice characteristics from chapter 1:

- A microservice is responsible for a single capability.
- A microservice is individually deployable.
- A microservice consists of one or more processes.
- A microservice owns its own data store.
- A small team can maintain a handful of microservices.
- A microservice is replaceable.

Of these characteristics, the first two and last two can only be realized if the microservice's scope is good. There are also implementation-level concerns that come into play, but getting the scope wrong will prevent the service from adhering to those four characteristics.

3.1 The primary driver for scoping microservices: business capabilities

Each microservice should implement exactly one capability. For example, a Shopping Cart microservice should keep track of the items in the user's shopping cart. The primary way to identify capabilities for microservices is to analyze the business problem and determine the business capabilities. Each business capability should be implemented by a separate microservice.

3.1.1 What is a business capability?

A *business capability* is something an organization does that contributes to business goals. For instance, handling a shopping cart on an e-commerce website is a business capability that contributes to the broader business goal of allowing users to purchase items. A given business will have a number of business capabilities that together make the overall business function.

When mapping a business capability to a microservice, the microservice models the business capability. In some cases, the microservice implements the entire business capability and automates it completely. In other cases, the microservice implements only part of the business capability and thus only partly automates it. In both cases, the scope of the microservice is the business capability.

> ### Business capabilities and bounded contexts
> *Domain-driven design* is an approach to designing software systems that's based on modeling the business domain. An important step is identifying the language used by domain experts to talk about the domain. It turns out that the language used by domain experts isn't consistent in all cases.

(continued)

In different parts of a domain, different things are in focus, so a given word like *customer* may have different focuses in different parts of the domain. For instance, for a company selling photocopiers, a *customer* in the sales department may be a company that buys a number of photocopiers and may be primarily represented by a procurement officer. In the customer service department, a *customer* may be an end user having trouble with a photocopier. When modeling the domain of the photocopier company, the word *customer* means different things in different parts of the model.

A *bounded context* in domain-driven design is a part of a larger domain within which words mean the same things. Bounded contexts are related to but different from business capabilities. A bounded context defines an area of a domain within which the language is consistent. Business capabilities, on the other hand, are about what the business needs to get done. Within one bounded context, the business may need to get several things done. Each of these things is likely a business capability.

3.1.2 Identifying business capabilities

A good understanding of the domain will enable you to understand how the business functions. Understanding how the business functions means you can identify the business capabilities that make up the business and the processes involved in delivering the capabilities. In other words, the way to identify business capabilities is to learn about the business's domain. You can gain this type of knowledge by talking with the people who know the business domain best: business analysts, the end users of your software, and so on—all the people directly involved in the day-to-day work that drives the business.

A business's organization usually reflects its domain. Different parts of the domain are handled by different groups of people, and each group is responsible for delivering certain business capabilities; so, this organization can give you hints about how the microservices should be scoped. For one thing, a microservice's responsibility should probably lie within the purview of only one group. If it crosses the boundary between two groups, it's probably too widely scoped and will be difficult to keep cohesive, leading to low maintainability. These observations are in line with what is known as *Conway's Law.*[1]

> *Any organization that designs a system (defined broadly) will produce a design whose structure is a copy of the organization's communication structure.*

Sometimes you may uncover parts of the domain where the organization and the domain are at odds. In such situations, there are two approaches you can take, both of which respect Conway's Law. You can accept that the system can't fully reflect the domain, and implement a few microservices that aren't well aligned with the domain but are well aligned with the organization; or you can change the organization to reflect the domain. Both approaches can be problematic. The first risks building

---

[1] Melvin Conway, "How Do Committees Invent?" *Datamation Magazine* (April 1968).

microservices that are poorly scoped and that might become highly coupled. The second involves moving people and responsibilities between groups. Those kinds of changes can be difficult. Your choice should be a pragmatic one, based on an assessment of which approach will be least troublesome.

To get a better understanding of what business capabilities are, it's time to look at an example.

3.1.3   *Example: point-of-sale system*

The example we'll explore in this chapter is a point-of-sale system, illustrated in figure 3.1. I'll briefly introduce the domain, and then we'll look at how to identify business capabilities within it. Finally, we'll consider in more detail the scope of one of the microservices in the system.

This point-of-sale system is used in all the stores of a large chain. Cashiers at the stores interact with the system through a thin GUI client—it could be a tablet application, a web application, or a purpose-built till (or register, if you prefer). The GUI client is just a thin layer in front of the backend. The backend is where all the business logic (the business capabilities) is implemented, and it will be our focus.

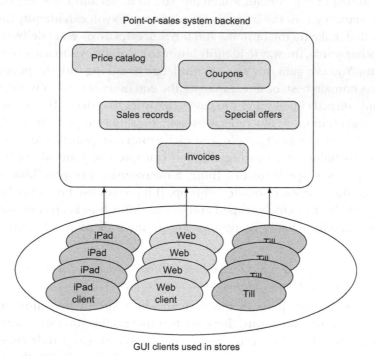

Figure 3.1   A point-of-sale system for a large chain of stores, consisting of a backend that implements all the business capabilities in the system and thin GUI clients used by cashiers in the stores. Microservices in the backend implement the business capabilities.

The system offers cashiers a variety of functions:

- Scan products and add them to the invoice
- Prepare an invoice
- Charge a credit card via a card reader attached to the client
- Register a cash payment
- Accept coupons
- Print a receipt
- Send an electronic receipt to the customer
- Search in the product catalog
- Scan one or more products to show prices and special offers related to the products

These functions are things the system does for the cashier, but they don't directly match the business capabilities that drive the point-of-sale system.

IDENTIFYING BUSINESS CAPABILITIES IN THE POINT-OF-SALE DOMAIN

To identify the business capabilities that drive the point-of-sale system, you need to look beyond the list of functions. You must determine what needs to go on behind the scenes to support the functionality.

Starting with the "Search in the product catalog" function, an obvious business capability is maintaining a product catalog. This is the first candidate for a business capability that could be the scope of a microservice. Such a Product Catalog microservice would be responsible for providing access to the current product catalog. The product catalog needs to be updated every so often, but the chain of stores uses another system to handle that functionality. The Product Catalog microservice would need to reflect the changes made in that other system, so the scope of the Product Catalog microservice would include receiving updates to the product catalog.

The next business capability you might identify is applying special offers to invoices. Special offers give the customer a discounted price when they buy a bundle of products. A bundle may consist of a certain number of the same product at a discounted price (for example, three for the price of two) or may be a combination of different products (say, buy A and get 10% off B). In either case, the invoice the cashier gets from the point-of-sale GUI client must take any applicable special offers into account automatically. This business capability is the second candidate to be the scope for a microservice. A Special Offers microservice would be responsible for deciding when a special offer applies and what the discount for the customer should be.

Looking over the list of functionality again, notice that the system should allow cashiers to "Scan one or more products to show prices and special offers related to the products." This indicates that there's more to the Special Offers business capability than just applying special offers to invoices: it also includes the ability to look up special offers based on products.

If you continued the hunt for business capabilities in the point-of-sale system, you might end up with this list:

- Product Catalog
- Price Catalog
- Price Calculation
- Special Offers
- Coupons
- Sales Records
- Invoice
- Payment

Figure 3.2 shows a map from functionalities to business capabilities. The map is a logical one, in the sense that it shows which business capabilities are needed to implement each function, but it doesn't indicate any direct technical dependencies. For instance, the arrow from Prepare Invoice to Coupons doesn't indicate a direct call from some Prepare Invoice code in a client to a Coupons microservice. Rather, the arrow indicates that in order to prepare an invoice, coupons need to be taken into account, so the Prepare Invoice function depends on the Coupons business capability.

I find creating this kind of map to be enlightening, because it forces me to think explicitly about how each function is attained and also what each business capability

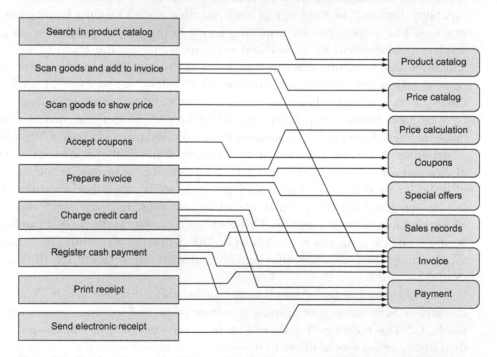

Figure 3.2   The functions on the left depend on the business capabilities on the right. Each arrow indicates a dependency between a function and a capability.

must do. Finding the business capabilities in real domains can be hard work and often requires a good deal of iterating. The list of business capabilities isn't a static list made at the start of development; rather, it's an emergent list that grows and changes over time as your understanding of the domain and the business grows and deepens.

Now that we've gone through the first iteration of identifying business capabilities, let's take a closer look at one of these capabilities and how it defines the scope of a microservice.

THE SPECIAL OFFERS MICROSERVICE

The Special Offers microservice is based on the Special Offers business capability. To narrow the scope of this microservice, we'll dive deeper into this business capability and identify the processes involved, illustrated in figure 3.3. Each process delivers part of the business capability.

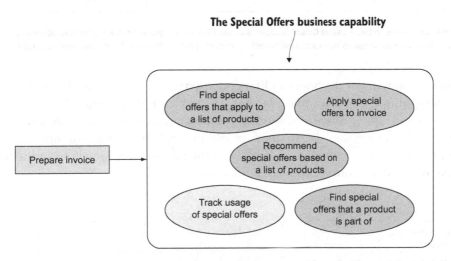

Figure 3.3   The Special Offers business capability includes a number of different processes.

The Special Offers business capability is broken down into five processes. Four of these are oriented toward the point-of-sale GUI clients. The fifth—tracking the use of special offers—is oriented toward the business itself, which has an interest in which special offers customers are taking advantage of.

Implementing the business capability as a microservice means you need to do the following:

- Expose the four client-oriented processes as API endpoints that other microservices can call.
- Implement the usage-tracking process through an event feed. The business-intelligence parts of the point-of-sale system can subscribe to these events and use them to track which special offers are used by customers.

The components of the Special Offers microservice are shown in figure 3.4.

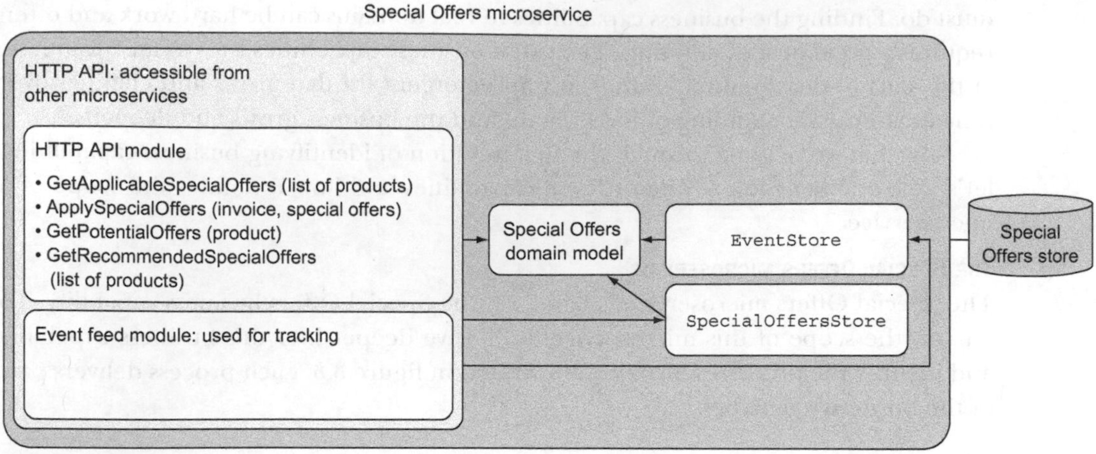

Special Offers microservice

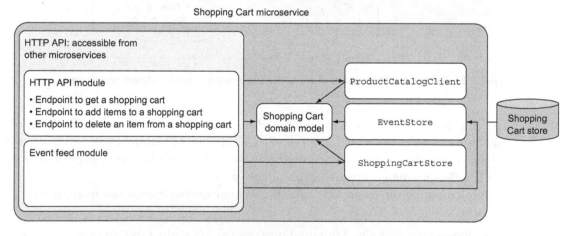

Figure 3.4   The processes in the Special Offers business capability are reflected in the implementation of the Special Offers microservice. The processes are exposed to other microservices through the microservice's HTTP API.

The components of the Special Offers microservice are similar to the components of the Shopping Cart microservice in chapter 2, which is shown again in figure 3.5. This is no coincidence. These are the components microservices typically consist of: an HTTP API that exposes the business capability implemented by the microservice, an event feed, a domain model implementing the business logic involved in the business capability, a data store component, and a database.

Shopping Cart microservice

Figure 3.5   The components of the Shopping Cart microservice from chapter 2 are similar to the components of the Special Offers microservice.

3.2 The secondary driver for scoping microservices: supporting technical capabilities

The secondary way to identify scopes for microservices is to look at supporting techni-cal capabilities. A *supporting technical capability* is something that doesn't directly con-tribute to a business goal but supports other microservices, such as integrating with another system or scheduling an event to happen some time in the future.

3.2.1 What is a technical capability?

Supporting technical capabilities are a secondary driver in scoping microservices because they don't directly contribute to the system's business goals. They exist to sim-plify and support the other microservices that implement business capabilities.

Remember, one characteristic of a good microservice is that it's replaceable; but if a microservice that implements a business capability also implements a complex tech-nical capability, it may grow too large and too complex to be replaceable. In such cases, you should consider implementing the technical capability in a separate micros-ervice that supports the original one. Before discussing how and when to identify sup-porting technical capabilities, a couple of examples would probably be helpful.

3.2.2 Examples of supporting technical capabilities

To give you a feel for what I mean by supporting technical capabilities, let's consider two examples: an integration with another system, and the ability to send notifications to customers.

INTEGRATING WITH AN EXTERNAL PRODUCT CATALOG SYSTEM

In the example point-of-sale system, you identified the product catalog as a business capability. I also mentioned that product information is maintained in another sys-tem, external to the microservice-based point-of-sale system. That other system is an Enterprise Resource Planning (ERP) system. This implies that the Product Catalog microservice must integrate with the ERP system, as illustrated in figure 3.6. The inte-gration can be handled in a separate microservice.

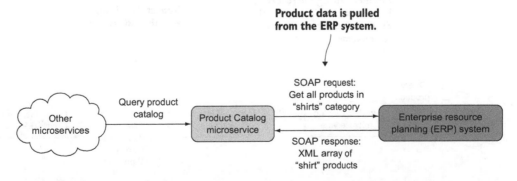

Figure 3.6   Product data flows from the ERP system to the Product Catalog microservice. The protocol used to get product information from the ERP system is defined by the ERP system. It could expose a SOAP web service for fetching the information, or it might export product information to a proprietary file format.

Let's assume that you aren't in a position to make changes to the ERP system, so the integration must be implemented using whatever interface the ERP system has. It might use a SOAP web service to fetch product information, or it might export all the product information to a proprietary file format. In either case, the integration must happen on the ERP system's terms. Depending on the interface the ERP system exposes, this may be a smaller or larger task. In any case, it's a task primarily concerned with the technicalities of integrating with some other system, and it has the potential to be at least somewhat complex. The purpose of this integration is to support the Product Catalog microservice.

You'll take the integration out of the Product Catalog microservice and implement it in a separate ERP Integration microservice that's responsible solely for that one integration, as illustrated in figure 3.7. You'll do this for two reasons:

- By moving the technical complexities of the integration to a separate microservice, you keep the scope of the Product Catalog microservice narrow and focused.
- By using a separate microservice to deal with how the ERP data is formatted and organized, you keep the ERP system's view of what a product is separate from the point-of-sale system. Remember that in different parts of a large domain, there are different views of what terms mean. It's unlikely that the Product Catalog microservice and the ERP system agree on how the product entity is modeled. A translation between the two views is needed and is best done by the new microservice. In domain-driven-design terms, the new microservice acts as an *anti-corruption layer*.

NOTE The anti-corruption layer is a concept borrowed from domain-driven design. It can be used when two systems interact; it protects the domain model in one system from being polluted with language or concepts from the model in the other system.

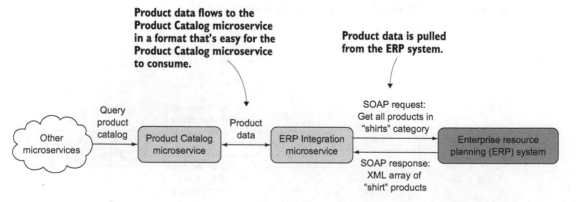

Figure 3.7 The ERP Integration microservice supports the Product Catalog microservice by handling the integration with the ERP system. It translates between the way the ERP system exposes product data and the way the Product Catalog microservice consumes it.

An added benefit of placing the integration in a separate microservice is that it's a good place to address any reliability issues related to integration. If the ERP system is unreliable, the place to handle that is in the ERP Integration microservice. If the ERP system is slow, the ERP Integration microservice can deal with that. Over time, you can tweak the policies used in the ERP Integration microservice to address any reliability issues with the ERP system without touching the Product Catalog microservice at all. This integration with the ERP system is an example of a supporting technical capability, and the ERP Integration microservice is an example of a microservice implementing that capability.

SENDING NOTIFICATIONS TO CUSTOMERS

Now let's consider extending the point-of-sale system with the ability to send notifications about new special offers to registered customers via email, SMS, or push notification to a mobile app. You can put this capability into one or more separate microservices.

At the moment, the point-of-sale system doesn't know who the customers are. To drive better customer engagement and customer loyalty, the company decides to start a small loyalty program where customers can sign up to be notified about special offers. The customer loyalty program is a new business capability and will be the responsibility of a new Loyalty Program microservice. Figure 3.8 shows this microservice, which is responsible for notifying registered customers every time a new special offer is available.

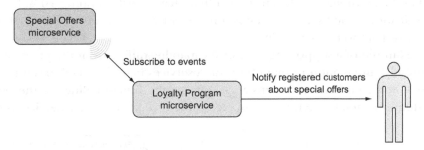

Figure 3.8   The Loyalty Program microservice subscribes to events from the Special Offers microservice and notifies registered customers when new offers are available.

As part of the registration process, customers can choose to be notified by email, SMS, or, if they have the company's mobile app, push notification. This introduces some complexity in the Loyalty Program microservice in that it must not only choose which type of notification to use but also deal with how each one works. As a first step, you'll introduce a supporting technical microservice for each notification type. This is shown in figure 3.9.

This is better. The Loyalty Program microservice doesn't have to implement all the details of dealing with each type of notification, which keeps the microservice's

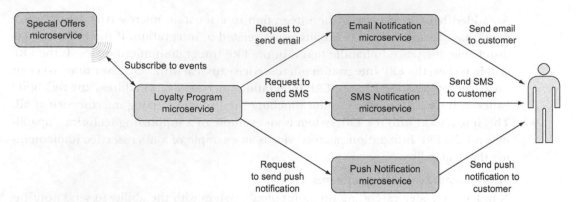

Figure 3.9   To avoid bogging down the Loyalty Program microservice in technical details for handling each type of notification, you'll introduce three supporting technical microservices, one for each type of notification.

scope narrow and focused. The situation isn't perfect, though: the microservice still has to decide which of the supporting technical microservices to call for each registered customer.

This leads you to introducing one more microservice, which acts as a front for the three microservices handling the three types of notifications. This new Notifications microservice is depicted in figure 3.10 and is responsible for choosing which type of notification to use each time a customer needs to be notified. This isn't really a business capability, although it's less technical than dealing with sending SMSs. I consider the Notifications microservice a supporting technical microservice rather than one implementing a business capability.

This example of a supporting technical capability differs from the previous example of the ERP integration in that other microservices may also need to send notifications to specific customers. For instance, one of the functionalities of the point-of-sales system is to send the customer an electronic receipt. The microservice in charge

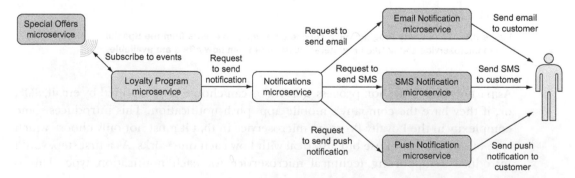

Figure 3.10   To remove more complexity from the Loyalty Program microservice, you'll introduce a Notifications microservice that's responsible for choosing a type of notification based on customer preferences. Introducing this microservice has the added benefit of making notifications easier to use from other microservices.

of that business capability can also take advantage of the Notifications microservice. Part of the motivation for moving this supporting technical capability to separate microservices is that you can reuse the implementation.

3.2.3 *Identifying technical capabilities*

When you introduce supporting technical microservices, your goal is to simplify the microservices that implement business capabilities. Sometimes—such as with sending notifications—you identify a technical capability that several microservices need, and you turn that into a microservice of its own, so other microservices can share the implementation. Other times—as with the ERP integration—you identify a technical capability that unduly complicates a microservice and turn that capability into a microservice of its own. In both cases, the microservices implementing business capabilities are left with one less technical concern to take care of.

When deciding to implement a technical capability in a separate microservice, be careful that you don't violate the microservice characteristic of being individually deployable. It makes sense to implement a technical capability in a separate microservice only if that microservice can be deployed and redeployed independently of any other microservices. Likewise, deploying the microservices that are supported by the microservice providing the technical capability must not force you to redeploy the microservice implementing the technical capability.

Identifying business capabilities and microservices based on business capabilities is a strategic exercise, but identifying technical supporting capabilities that could be implemented by separate microservices is an opportunistic exercise. The question of whether a supporting technical capability should be implemented in its own microservice is about what will be easiest in the long run. You should ask these questions:

- If the supporting technical capability stays in a microservice scoped to a business capability, is there a risk that the microservice will no longer be replaceable with reasonable effort?
- Is the supporting technical capability implemented in several microservices scoped to business capabilities?
- Will a microservice implementing the supporting capability be individually deployable?
- Will all microservices scoped to business capabilities still be individually deployable if the supporting technical capability is implemented in a separate microservice?

If your answer is "Yes" to the last two questions and to at least one of the others, you have a good candidate for a microservice scope.

3.3 *What to do when the correct scope isn't clear*

At this point, you may be thinking that scoping microservices correctly is difficult: you need to get the business capabilities just right, which requires a deep understanding of the business domain, and you also have to judge the complexity of supporting technical capabilities correctly. And you're right: it *is* difficult, and you *will* find yourself in situations where the right scoping for your microservices isn't clear.

This lack of clarity can have several causes, including the following:

- *Insufficient understanding of the business domain*—Analyzing a business domain and building up a deep knowledge of that domain is difficult and time consuming. You'll sometimes need to make decisions about the scope of microservices before you've been able to develop sufficient understanding of the business to be certain you're making the correct decisions.
- *Confusion in the business domain*—It's not only the development side that can be unclear about the business domain. Sometimes the business side is also unclear about how the business domain should be approached. Maybe the business is moving into new markets and must learn a new domain along the way. Other times, the existing business market is changing because of what competitors are doing or what the business itself is doing. Either way, on both the business side and the development side, the business domain is ever-changing, and your understanding of it is emergent.
- *Incomplete knowledge of the details of a technical capability*—You may not have access to all the information about what it takes to implement a technical capability. For instance, you may need to integrate with a badly documented system, in which case you'll only know how to implement the integration once you're finished.
- *Inability to estimate the complexity of a technical capability*—If you haven't previously implemented a similar technical capability, it can be difficult to estimate how complex the implementation of that capability will be.

None of these problems means you've failed. They're all situations that occur time and again. The trick is to know how to move forward in spite of the lack of clarity. In this section, I'll discuss what to do when you're in doubt.

3.3.1 *Starting a bit bigger*

When in doubt about the scope of a microservice, it's best to err on the side of making the microservice's scope bigger than it would be ideally. This may sound weird—I've talked a lot about creating small, narrowly focused microservices and about the benefits that come from keeping microservices small. And it's true that significant benefits can be gained from keeping microservices small and narrowly focused. But you must also look at what happens if you err on the side of too narrow a scope.

Consider the Special Offers microservice discussed earlier in this chapter. It implements the Special Offers business capability in a point-of-sale system and includes five different business processes, as illustrated in figure 3.3 and reproduced on the left side of figure 3.11. If you were uncertain about the boundaries of the Special Offers business capability and chose to err on the side of too small a scope, you might split the business capability as shown on the right side of figure 3.11.

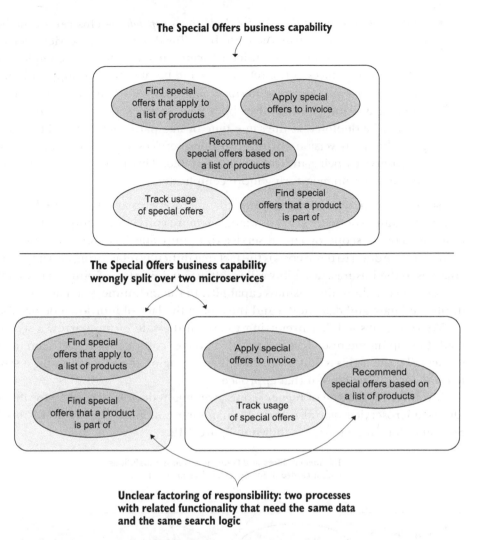

Figure 3.11 If you make the scope of a microservice too small, you'll find that a single business capability becomes split over several highly coupled parts.

If you base the scope of your microservices on only part of the Special Offers business capability, you'll incur some significant costs:

- *Data and data-model duplication between the two microservices*—Both parts of the implementation need to store all the special offers in their data stores.
- *Unclear factoring of responsibility*—One part of the divided business capability can answer whether a given product is part of any special offers, whereas the other part can recommend special offers to customers based on past purchases. These two functions are closely related, and you'll quickly get into a situation where it's unclear in which microservice a piece of code belongs.

- *Obstacles to refactoring the code for the business capability*—This can occur because the code is spread across the code bases for the two microservices. Such cross-code base refactorings are difficult because it's hard to get a complete picture of the consequences of the refactoring and because tooling support is poor.
- *Difficulty deploying the two microservices independently*—After refactoring or implementing a feature that involves both microservices, the two microservices may need to be deployed at the same time or in a particular order. Either way, coupling between versions of the two microservices violates the characteristic of microservices being individually deployable. This makes testing, deployment, and production monitoring more complicated.

These costs are incurred from the time the microservices are first created until you've gained enough experience and knowledge to more correctly identify the business capability and a better scope for a microservice (the entire Special Offers business capability, in this case). Added to those costs is the fact that difficulty refactoring and implementing changes to the business capability will result in you doing less of both, so it will take you longer to learn about the business capability. In the meantime, you pay the cost of the duplicated data and data model and the cost of the lack of individual deployability.

We've established that preferring to err on the side of too narrow a scope easily leads to scoping microservices in a way that creates costly coupling between the microservices. To see if this is better or worse than erring on the side of too big a scope, we need to look at the costs of that approach.

If you err on the side of bigger scopes, you might decide on a scope for the Special Offers microservice that also includes handling coupons. The scope of this bigger Special Offers microservice is shown in figure 3.12.

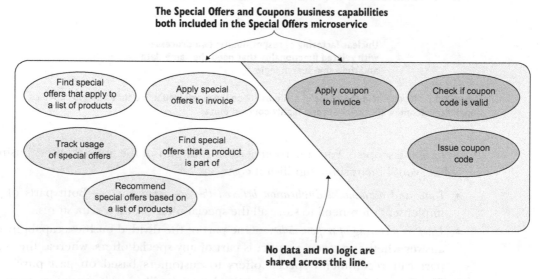

Figure 3.12 If you choose to err on the side of bigger scopes, you might decide to include the handling of coupons in the Special Offers business capability.

There are costs associated with including too much in the scope of a microservice:

- The code base becomes bigger and more complex, which can lead to changes being more expensive.
- The microservice is harder to replace.

These costs are real, but they aren't overwhelming when the scope of the microservice is still fairly small. Beware, though, because these costs grow quickly with the size of each microservice's scope and become overwhelming when the scope is so big that it approaches a monolithic architecture.

Nevertheless, refactoring within one code base is much easier than refactoring across two code bases. This gives you a better chance to experiment and to learn about the business capability through experiments. If you take advantage of this opportunity, you can arrive at a good understanding of both the Special Offers business capability and the Coupons business capability more quickly than if you scoped your microservices too narrowly.

This argument holds true when your microservices are a bit too big, but it falls apart if they're much too big, so don't get lazy and lump several business capabilities together in one microservice. You'll quickly have a large, hard-to-manage code base with many of the drawbacks of a full-on monolith.

All in all, microservices that are slightly bigger than they should ideally be are both less costly and allow for more agility than if they're slightly smaller than they should ideally be. Thus, the rule of thumb is to err on the side of slightly bigger scopes.

Once you accept that you'll sometimes—if not often—be in doubt about the best scope for a microservice and that in such cases you should lean toward a slightly bigger scope, you can also accept that you'll sometimes—if not often—have microservices in your system that are somewhat larger than they should ideally be. This means you should expect to have to carve new microservices out of existing ones from time to time.

3.3.2 Carving out new microservices from existing microservices

When you realize that one of your microservices is too big, you'll need to look at how to carve a new microservice out of it. First you need to identify a good scope for both the existing microservice and the new microservice. To do this, you can use the drivers described earlier in this chapter.

Once you've identified the scopes, you must look at the code to see if the way it's organized aligns with the new scopes. If not, you should begin refactoring toward that alignment. Figure 3.13 illustrates on a high level the refactorings needed to prepare to carve out a new microservice from an existing one. First, everything that will eventually go into the new microservice is moved to its own class library. Then, all communication between code that will stay in the existing microservice and code that will be moved to the new microservice is refactored to go through an interface. This interface will become part of the public HTTP interface of the two microservices once they're split apart.

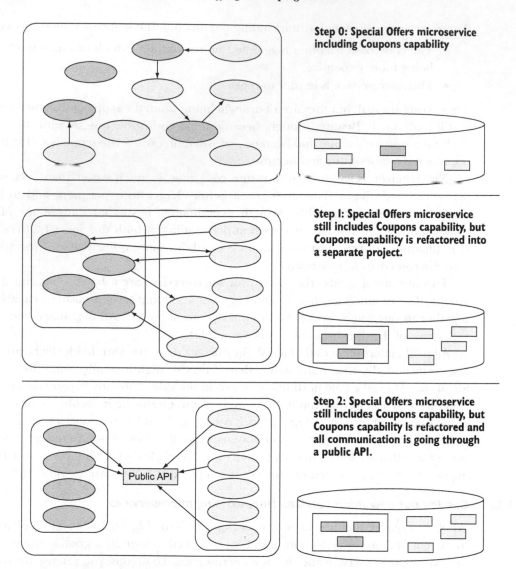

Step 0: Special Offers microservice including Coupons capability

Step 1: Special Offers microservice still includes Coupons capability, but Coupons capability is refactored into a separate project.

Step 2: Special Offers microservice still includes Coupons capability, but Coupons capability is refactored and all communication is going through a public API.

Public API

Figure 3.13   Preparing to carve out a new microservice by refactoring: first move everything belonging to the new microservice into its own project, and then make all communication go through a public API similar to the one the new microservice will end up having.

When you've reached step 2 in figure 3.13, the new microservice can be split out from the old one with a manageable effort. Create a new microservice, move the code that needs to be carved out of the existing microservice over to the new microservice, and change the communication between the two parts to go over HTTP.

3.3.3   *Planning to carve out new microservices later*

Because you consciously err on the side of making your microservices a bit too big when you're in doubt about the scope of a microservice, you have a chance to foresee which microservices will have to be divided at some point. If you know a microservice is likely to be split later, it would be nice if you could plan for that split in a way that will save you one or two of the refactoring steps shown in figure 3.13. It turns out you can often make that kind of plan.

Often you'll be unsure whether a particular function is a separate business capability, so you'll follow the rule of thumb and include it in a larger business capability, implemented within a microservice scoped to that larger business capability. But you can remain conscious of the fact that this area *might* be a separate business capability.

Think about the definition of the Special Offers business capability that includes processes for dealing with coupons. You may well have been in doubt about whether handling coupons was a business capability on its own, so the Special Offers business capability was modeled as including all the processes shown in figure 3.12.

When you first implement a Special Offers microservice scoped to the understanding of the Special Offers business capability illustrated in figure 3.12, you don't know whether the coupons functionality will eventually be moved to a Coupons microservice. You do know, however, that the coupons functionality isn't as closely related to the rest of the microservice as some of the other areas. It's therefore a good idea to put a clear boundary around the coupons code in the form a well-defined public API and to put the coupons code in a separate class library. This is sound software design, and it will also pay off if one day you end up carving out the coupons code to create a new Coupons microservice.

3.4   *Well-scoped microservices adhere to the microservice characteristics*

I've talked about scoping microservices by identifying business capabilities first and supporting technical capabilities second. In this section, I'll discuss how this approach to scoping aligns with these four characteristics of microservices mentioned at the beginning of this chapter:

- A microservice is responsible for a single capability.
- A microservice is individually deployable.
- A small team can maintain a handful of microservices.
- A microservice is replaceable.

NOTE It's important to note that the relationship between the drivers for scoping microservices and the characteristics of microservices goes both ways. The primary and secondary drivers lead toward adhering to the characteristics, but the characteristics also tell you whether you've scoped your microservices well or need to push the drivers further to find better scopes for your microservices.

3.4.1   *Primarily scoping to business capabilities leads to good microservices*

The primary driver for scoping microservices is identifying business capabilities. Let's see how that makes for microservices that adhere to the microservice characteristics.

RESPONSIBLE FOR A SINGLE CAPABILITY

A microservice scoped to a single business capability by definition adheres to the first microservice characteristic: it's responsible for a single capability. As you saw in the examples of identifying supporting technical capabilities, you have to be careful: it's easy to let too much responsibility slip into a microservice scoped to a business capability. You have to be diligent in making sure that what a microservice implements is just one business capability and not a mix of two or more. You also have to be careful about putting supporting technical capabilities in their own microservices. As long as you're diligent, microservices scoped to a single business capability adhere to the first characteristic of microservices.

INDIVIDUALLY DEPLOYABLE

Business capabilities are those that can be performed by largely independent groups within an organization, so the business capabilities themselves must be largely independent. As a result, microservices scoped to business capabilities are largely independent. This doesn't mean there's no interaction between such microservices—there can be a lot of interaction, both through direct calls between services and through events. The point is that the interaction happens through well-defined public interfaces that can be kept backward compatible. If implemented well, the interaction is such that other microservices continue to work even if one has a short outage. This means well-implemented microservices scoped to business capabilities are individually deployable.

REPLACEABLE AND MAINTAINABLE BY A SMALL TEAM

A business capability is something a small group in an organization can handle. This limits its scope and thus also limits the scope of microservices scoped to business capabilities. Again, if you're diligent about making sure a microservice handles only one business capability and that supporting technical capabilities are implemented in their own microservices, the microservices' scope will be small enough that a small team can maintain at least a handful of microservices and a microservice can be replaced fairly quickly if need be.

3.4.2   *Secondarily scoping to supporting technical capabilities leads to good microservices*

The secondary driver for scoping microservices is identifying supporting technical capabilities. Let's see how that makes for microservices that adhere to the microservice characteristics.

RESPONSIBLE FOR A SINGLE CAPABILITY

Just as with microservices scoped to business capabilities, scoping a microservice to a single supporting technical capability by definition means it adheres to the first characteristic of microservices: it's responsible for a single capability.

INDIVIDUALLY DEPLOYABLE

Before you decide to implement a technical capability as a separate supporting technical capability in a separate microservice, you need to ask whether that new microservice will be individually deployable. If the answer is "No," you shouldn't implement it in a separate microservice. Again, by definition, a microservice scoped to a supporting technical capability adheres to the second microservice characteristic.

REPLACEABLE AND MAINTAINABLE BY A SMALL TEAM

Microservices scoped to a supporting technical capability tend to be narrowly and clearly scoped. On the other hand, part of the point of implementing such capabilities in separate microservices is that they can be complex. In other words, microservices scoped to a supporting technical capability tend to be small, which points toward adhering to the microservice characteristics of replaceability and maintainability; but the code inside them may be complex, which makes them harder to maintain and replace.

This is an area where there's a certain back and forth between using supporting technical capabilities to scope microservices on one hand, and the characteristics of microservices on the other. If a supporting technical microservice is becoming so complex that it will be hard to replace, this is a sign that you should probably look closely at the capability and try to find a way to break it down further. As in the example about notification (see section 3.2.2), it's fine to have one supporting technical microservice use others behind the scenes.

3.5 Summary

- The primary driver in scoping microservices is identifying business capabilities. Business capabilities are the things an organization does that contribute to fulfilling business goals.
- You can use techniques from domain-driven design to identify business capabilities. Domain-driven design is a powerful tool for gaining better and deeper understanding of a domain. That kind of understanding enables you to identify business capabilities.
- The secondary driver in scoping microservices is identifying supporting technical capabilities. A supporting technical capability is a technical function needed by one or more microservices scoped to business capabilities.
- Supporting technical capabilities should be moved to their own microservices only if they're sufficiently complex to be a problem in the microservices they would otherwise be part of, and if they can be individually deployed.

- Identifying supporting technical capabilities is an opportunistic form of design. You should only pull a supporting technical capability into a separate microservice if it will be an overall simplification.

- When you're in doubt about the scope of a microservice, lean toward making the scope slightly bigger rather than slightly smaller.

- Because scoping microservices well is difficult, you'll probably be in doubt sometimes. You're also likely to get some of the scopes wrong in your first iteration.

- You must expect to have to carve new microservices out of existing ones from time to time.

- You can use your doubt about scope to organize the code in your microservices so that they lend themselves to carving out new microservices at a later stage.

Microservice collaboration

Each microservice implements a single capability; but to deliver end user functionality, microservices need to collaborate. Microservices can use three main communication styles for collaboration: *commands*, *queries*, and *events*. Each style has its strengths and weaknesses, and understanding the trade-offs between them allows you to pick the appropriate one for each microservice collaboration. When you get the collaboration style right, you can implement loosely coupled microservices with clear boundaries. In this chapter, I'll show you how to implement all three collaboration styles in code.

4.1   *Types of collaboration: commands, queries, and events*

Microservices are fine grained and narrowly scoped. To deliver functionality to an end user, microservices need to collaborate.

As an example, consider the Loyalty Program microservice from the point-of-sale system in chapter 3. The Loyalty Program microservice is responsible for the Loyalty Program business capability. The program is simple: customers can register as users with the loyalty program; once registered, they receive notifications about new special offers and earn loyalty points when they purchase something. Still, the Loyalty Program business capability depends on other business capabilities, and other business capabilities depend on it. As illustrated in figure 4.1, the Loyalty Program microservice needs to collaborate with a number of other microservices.

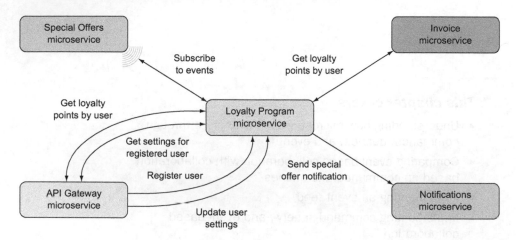

Figure 4.1   The Loyalty Program microservice collaborates with several other microservices. In some cases, the Loyalty Program microservice receives requests from other microservices; at other times, it sends requests to other microservices.

As stated in the list of microservice characteristics in chapter 1, a microservice is responsible for a single capability; and as discussed in chapter 3, that single capability is typically a business capability. End user functionalities—or use cases—often involve several business capabilities, so the microservices implementing these capabilities must collaborate to deliver functionality to the end user.

When two microservices collaborate, there are three main styles:

- *Commands*—Commands are used when one microservice needs another microservice to perform an action. For example, the Loyalty Program microservice sends a command to the Notifications microservice when it needs a notification to be sent to a registered user.
- *Queries*—Queries are used when one microservice needs information from another microservice. Because customers with many loyalty points receive a

discount, the Invoice microservice queries the Loyalty Program microservice for the number of loyalty points a user has.

- *Events*—Events are used when a microservice needs to react to something that happened in another microservice. The Loyalty Program microservice subscribes to events from the Special Offers microservice so that when a new special offer is made available, it can have notifications sent to registered users.

The collaboration between two microservices can use one, two, or all three of these collaboration styles. Each time two microservices need to collaborate, you must decide which style to use. Figure 4.2 shows the collaborations of Loyalty Program again, but this time identifying the collaboration style I chose for each one.

Collaboration based on commands and queries should use relatively coarse-grained commands and queries. The calls made between microservices are remote calls, meaning they cross at least a process boundary and usually also a network. This means calls between microservices are relatively slow. Even though the microservices are fine grained, you must not fall into the trap of thinking of calls from one microservice to another as being like function calls in a microservice.

Furthermore, you should prefer collaboration based on events over collaboration based on commands or queries. Event-based collaboration is more loosely coupled than the other two forms of collaboration because events are handled asynchronously. That means two microservices collaborating through events aren't temporally coupled: the handling of an event doesn't have to happen immediately after the event is raised. Rather, handling can happen when the subscriber is ready to do so. In contrast, commands and queries are synchronous and therefore need to be handled immediately after they're sent.

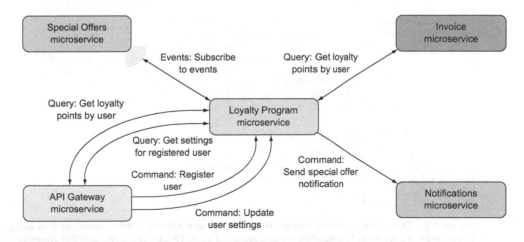

Figure 4.2 The Loyalty Program microservice uses all three collaboration styles: commands, queries, and events.

4.1.1   *Commands and queries: synchronous collaboration*

Commands and queries are both synchronous forms of collaboration. Both are implemented as HTTP requests from one microservice to another. Queries are implemented with HTTP GET requests, whereas commands are implemented with HTTP POST or PUT requests.

The Loyalty Program microservice can answer queries about registered users and can handle commands to create or update registered users. Figure 4.3 shows the command- and query-based collaborations that Loyalty Program takes part in.

Figure 4.3 includes two different queries. "Get loyalty points for registered user" and "Get settings for registered user." You'll handle both of these with the same endpoint that returns a representation of the registered user. The representation includes both the number of loyalty points and the settings. You do this for two reasons: it's simpler than having two endpoints, and it's also cleaner because the Loyalty Program microservice gets to expose just one representation of the registered user instead of having to come up with specialized formats for specialized queries.

Two commands are sent to Loyalty Program in figure 4.3: one to register a new user, and one to update an existing registered user. You'll implement the first with an HTTP POST and the second with an HTTP PUT. This is standard usage of POST and PUT HTTP methods. POST is often used to create a new resource, and PUT is defined in the HTTP specification to update a resource.

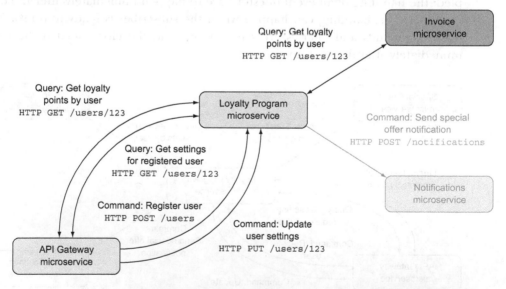

Figure 4.3   The Loyalty Program microservice collaborates with three other microservices using commands and queries. The queries are implemented as HTTP GET requests, and the commands are implemented as HTTP POST or PUT requests. The command collaboration with the Notifications microservice is grayed out because I'm not going to show its implementation—it's done exactly the same way as the other collaborations.

All in all, the Loyalty Program microservice needs to expose three endpoints:

- An HTTP GET endpoint at URLs of the form /users/{userId} that responds with a representation of the user. This endpoint implements both queries in figure 4.3.
- An HTTP POST endpoint at /users/ that expects a representation of a user in the body of the request and then registers that user in the loyalty program.
- An HTTP PUT endpoint at URLs of the form /users/{userId} that expects a representation of a user in the body of the request and then updates an already-registered user.

The Loyalty Program microservice is made up of the same set of standard components you've seen before, as shown in figure 4.4. The endpoints are implemented in the HTTP API component.

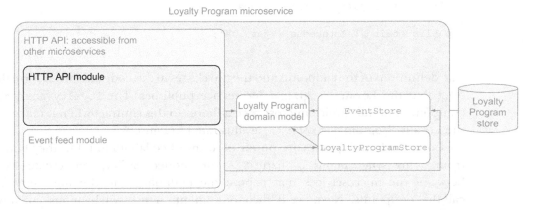

Figure 4.4 The endpoints exposed by the Loyalty Program microservice are implemented in the HTTP API component.

The other sides of these collaborations are microservices that most likely follow the same standard structure, with the addition of a LoyaltyProgramClient component. For instance, the Invoice microservice might be structured as shown in figure 4.5.

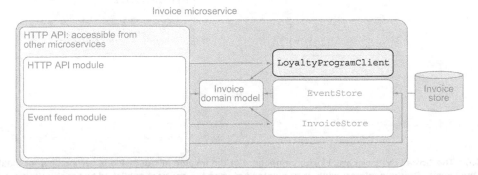

Figure 4.5 The Invoice microservice has a LoyaltyProgramClient component responsible for calling the Loyalty Program microservice.

The representation of a registered user that Loyalty Program will expect to receive in the commands and with which it will respond to queries is a serialization of the following `LoyaltyProgramUser` class.

Listing 4.1 The Loyalty Program microservice's user representation

```
public class LoyaltyProgramUser
{
  public int Id { get; set; }
  public string Name { get; set;  }
  public int LoyaltyPoints { get; set;  }
  public LoyaltyProgramSettings Settings { get; set; }
}

public class LoyaltyProgramSettings
{
  public string[] Interests { get; set; }
}
```

The definitions of the endpoints and the two classes in this code effectively form the contract that the Loyalty Program microservice publishes. The `LoyaltyProgramClient` component in the Invoice microservice adheres to this contract when it makes calls to the Loyalty Program microservice, as illustrated in figure 4.6.

Commands and queries are powerful forms of collaboration, but they both suffer from being synchronous by nature. As mentioned earlier, that creates coupling between the microservices that expose the endpoints and the microservices that call the endpoints. Next, we'll turn our attention to asynchronous collaboration through events.

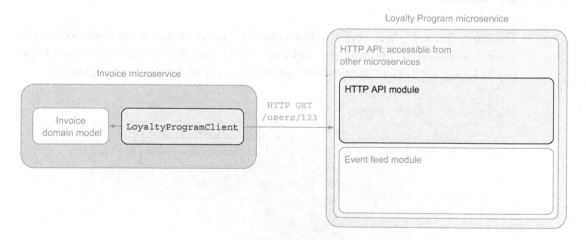

Figure 4.6 The `LoyaltyProgramClient` component in the Invoice microservice is responsible for making calls to the Loyalty Program microservice. It translates between the contract published by Loyalty Program and the domain model of Invoice.

4.1.2 Events: asynchronous collaboration

Collaboration based on events is asynchronous. That is, the microservice that publishes the events doesn't call the microservices that subscribe to the events. Rather, the subscribers poll the microservice that publishes events for new events when they're ready to process them. That polling is what I'll call *subscribing* to an event feed. Although the polling is made out of synchronous requests, the collaboration is asynchronous because publishing events is independent of any subscriber polling for events.

In figure 4.7, you can see the Loyalty Program microservice subscribing to events from the Special Offers microservice. Special Offers can publish events whenever something happens in its domain, such as every time a new special offer becomes active. Publishing an event, in this context, means storing the event in Special Offers. Loyalty Program won't see the event until it makes a call to the event feed on Special Offers. When that happens is entirely up to Loyalty Program. It can happen right after the event is published or at any later point in time.

As with the other types of collaboration, there are two sides to event-based collaboration. One side is the microservice that publishes events through an event feed, and the other is the microservices that subscribe to those events.

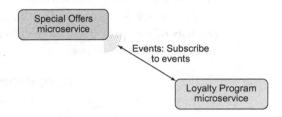

Figure 4.7 The Loyalty Program microservice processes events from the Special Offers microservice when it's convenient for Loyalty Program.

EXPOSING AN EVENT FEED

A microservice can publish events to other microservices via an *event feed*, which is just an HTTP endpoint—at /events, for instance—to which that other microservice can make requests and from which it can get event data. Figure 4.8 shows the components in the Special Offers microservice. Once again, the microservice has the same standard set of components that you've seen several times already. In figure 4.8, the components involved in implementing the event feed are highlighted.

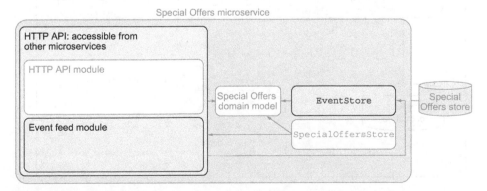

Figure 4.8 The event feed in the Special Offers microservice is exposed to other microservices over HTTP and is based on the event store.

The events published by the Special Offers microservice are stored in its database. The EventStore component has the code that reads events from and writes them to the database. The domain model code can use EventStore to store the events it needs to publish. The Event Feed component is the implementation of the HTTP endpoint that exposes the event to other microservices: that is, the /events endpoint.

The Event Feed component uses EventStore to read events from the database and then returns the events in the body of an HTTP response. Subscribers can use query parameters to control which and how many events are returned.

SUBSCRIBING TO EVENTS

Subscribing to an event feed essentially means you poll the events endpoint of the microservice that you subscribe to. At intervals, you send an HTTP GET request to the /events endpoint to check whether there are any events you haven't processed yet.

Figure 4.9 is an overview of the Loyalty Program microservice, which shows that it consists of two processes. We've already talked about the web process, but the event-subscriber process is new.

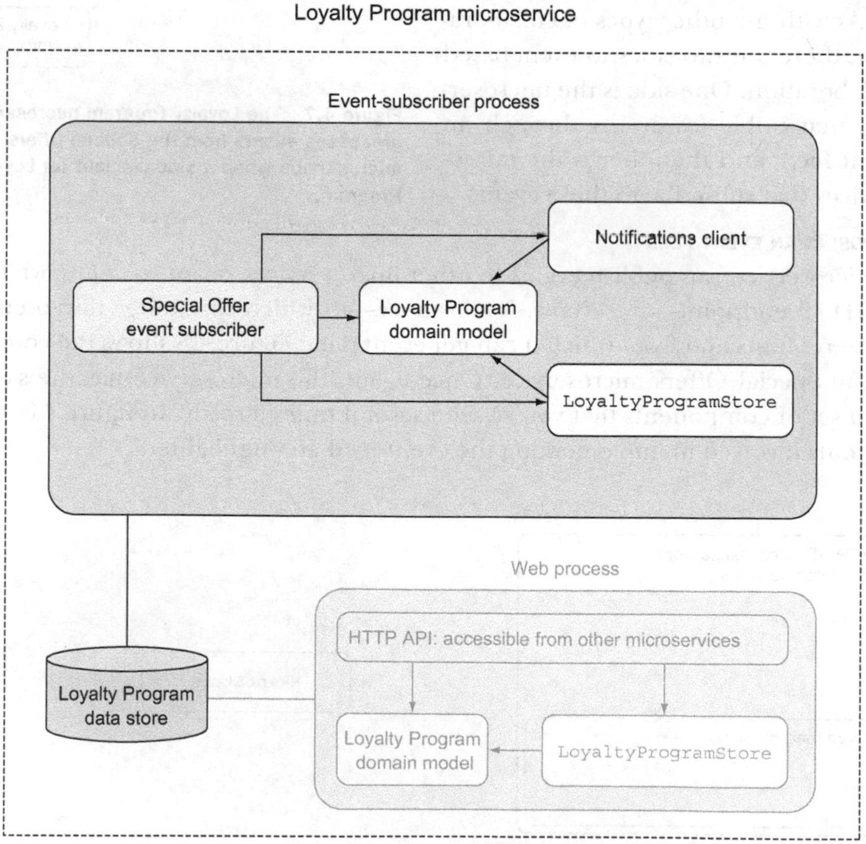

Loyalty Program microservice

Figure 4.9 The event subscription in the Loyalty Program microservice is handled in a event-subscriber process.

The event-subscriber process is a background process that periodically makes requests to the event feed on the Special Offers microservice to get new events. When it gets back new events, it processes them by sending commands to the Notifications microservice to notify registered users about new special offers. The `SpecialOffersSubscriber` component is where the polling of the event feed is implemented, and the `Notifications-Client` component is responsible for sending the command to Notifications.

This is the way you implement event subscriptions: microservices that need to subscribe to events have a subscriber process with a component that polls the event feed. When new events are returned from the event feed, the subscriber process handles the events based on business rules.

Events over queues

An alternative to publishing events over an event feed is to use a queue technology, like RabbitMQ or Service Bus for Windows Server. In this approach, microservices that publish events push them to a queue, and subscribers read them from the queue. Events must be routed from the publisher to the subscribers, and how that's done depends on the choice of queue technology. As with the event-feed approach, the microservice subscribing to events has an event-subscriber process that reads events from the queue and processes them.

This is a perfectly viable approach to implementing event-based collaboration between microservices. But this book uses HTTP-based event feeds for event-based collaboration because it's a simple yet robust and scalable solution.

4.1.3 Data formats

So far, we've focused on exchanging data in JSON format. I've mentioned in passing that XML is supported equally by all the endpoints you've implemented with Nancy. (Nancy comes with JSON and XML serialization and deserialization out of the box.) These two options cover most situations, but there are reasons you might want something else:

- If you need to exchange a lot of data, a more compact format may be needed. Text-based formats such as JSON and XML are a lot more verbose than binary formats like protocol buffers.
- If you need a more structured format than JSON that's still human readable, you may want to use YAML.
- If your company uses proprietary data formatting, you may need to support that format.

In all these cases, you need endpoints capable of receiving data in another format than XML or JSON, and they also need to be able to respond in that other format. As an example, a request to register a user with the Loyalty Program microservice using YAML in the request body looks like this:

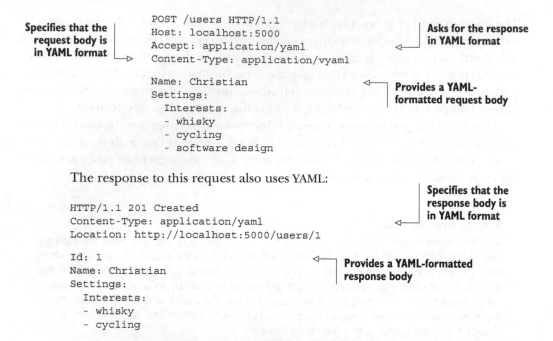

The response to this request also uses YAML:

```
HTTP/1.1 201 Created
Content-Type: application/yaml
Location: http://localhost:5000/users/1

Id: 1
Name: Christian
Settings:
  Interests:
  - whisky
  - cycling
```

Both the preceding request and response have YAML-formatted bodies, and both specify that the body is YAML in the Content-Type header. The request uses the Accept header to ask for the response in YAML. This example shows how microservices can communicate using different data formats and how they can use HTTP headers to tell which formats are used.

4.2   *Implementing collaboration*

This section will show you how to code the collaborations you saw earlier in figure 4.2. I'll use the Loyalty Program microservice as a starting point, but I'll also go into some of its collaborators—the API Gateway microservice, the Invoice microservice, and the Special Offers microservice—in order to show both ends of the collaborations.

Three steps are involved in implementing the collaboration:

1 Set up a project for Loyalty Program. Just as you've done before, you'll create an empty ASP.NET 5 application and add Nancy to it. The only difference this time is that you'll add a little Nancy configuration code.

2 Implement the command- and query-based collaborations shown in figure 4.2. You'll implement all the commands and queries that Loyalty Program can handle, as well as the code in collaborating microservices that use them.

3 Implement the event-based collaboration shown in figure 4.2. You'll start with the event feed in Special Offers and then move on to implement the subscription in Loyalty Program. In the process, you'll add an extra project—and an extra process—to Loyalty Program. After these steps, you'll have implemented all the collaborations of Loyalty Program.

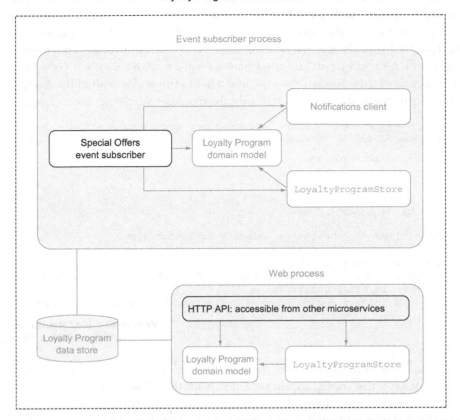

Figure 4.10 The Loyalty Program microservice has a web process that follows the structure you've seen before and an event-subscriber process that handles the subscription to events from the Special Offers microservice. I'll only show the code for the highlighted components in this chapter.

The Loyalty Program microservice consists of a web process that has the same structure you've seen before. This is illustrated at the bottom of figure 4.10. Later, when you implement the event-based collaboration, you'll add another process that I call the *event-subscriber process*. This process is shown at the top of figure 4.10.

In the interest of focusing on the collaboration, I won't show all the code in the Loyalty Program microservice. Rather, I'll include the code for the HTTP API in the web process, and the special offer event subscriber in the event-subscriber process.

4.2.1 Setting up a project for Loyalty Program

The first thing to do in implementing the Loyalty Program microservice is to create an empty ASP.NET 5 application and add Nancy to it as a NuGet package. You've already done this a couple of times—in chapters 1 and 2—so I won't go over the details again here.

This time around, there's one more piece of setup to do: you'll override how Nancy handles responses with a 404 Not Found status code. By default, Nancy puts the HTML for an error page in the body of a 404 Not Found response; but because the clients of the Loyalty Program microservice aren't web browsers but other microservices, you don't need an error page. I'd rather have a response with a 404 Not Found status code and an empty body. Toward this end, add a file to the project called Bootstrapper.cs. In this file, put the following class that inherits from `DefaultNancyBootstrapper`.

Listing 4.2   Nancy bootstrapper

```
namespace LoyaltyProgram
{
  using System;
  using Nancy;
  using Nancy.Bootstrapper;

  public class Bootstrapper : DefaultNancyBootstrapper
  {
    protected override
      Func<ITypeCatalog, NancyInternalConfiguration> InternalConfiguration =>
        NancyInternalConfiguration
          .WithOverrides(builder => builder.StatusCodeHandlers.Clear());    ◁─┐
  }                                                                          │
}                                     Remove all default status-code handlers │
                                         so they don't alter the responses.   ┘
```

Nancy will automatically discover this class at startup, call the `InternalConfiguration` getter, and use the configuration returned from that. You reuse the default configuration except that you clear all `StatusCodeHandlers`, which means you're removing everything that might alter a response because of its status code.

The Nancy bootstrapper

Nancy uses the bootstrapper during application startup to configure both the framework itself and the application. Nancy allows applications to reconfigure the entire framework, and you *can* swap any part of Nancy for your own implementation in your bootstrapper. In this regard, Nancy is open and flexible. In many cases, you don't need to configure the framework—Nancy has sensible defaults—and when you do, you rarely need to swap out entire pieces of Nancy.

To create a bootstrapper, all you have to do is create a class that implements the `INancyBootstrapper` interface, and Nancy will discover it and use it. You won't usually implement that interface directly, because although the interface itself is simple, a fully functional implementation of it isn't. Instead of implementing `INancyBootstrapper` directly, you can take advantage of the default bootstrapper that Nancy comes with out of the box (`DefaultNancyBootstrapper`) and extend it. That class has a number of virtual methods that you can override to hook into different parts of Nancy. There are, for instance, methods to configure the dependency injection container that Nancy uses, methods to set up specialized serialization and deserialization, methods to add error handlers, and more.

(continued)
You'll use the Nancy bootstrapper several times throughout the book, but for the most part you'll rely happily on Nancy's defaults. If an application doesn't have a Nancy bootstrapper, Nancy uses the default one: `DefaultNancyBootstrapper`.

4.2.2 Implementing commands and queries

You now have a web project ready to host the implementations of the endpoints exposed by the Loyalty Program microservice. As listed earlier, these are the endpoints:

- An HTTP GET endpoint at URLs of the form /users/{userId} that responds with a representation of the user. This endpoint implements both queries in figure 4.3.
- An HTTP POST endpoint at /users/ that expects a representation of a user in the body of the request and then registers that user in the loyalty program
- An HTTP PUT endpoint at URLs of the form /users/{userId} that expects a representation of a user in the body of the request and then updates an already-registered user.

You'll implement the command endpoints first and then the query endpoint.

4.2.3 Implementing commands with HTTP POST or PUT

The code needed in the Loyalty Program microservice to implement the handling of the two commands—the HTTP POST to register a new user and the HTTP PUT to update one—is similar to the code you saw in chapter 2. You'll start by implementing a handler for the command to register a user. A request to Loyalty Program to register a new user is shown in the following listing.

Listing 4.3 Request to register a user named Christian

```
POST /users HTTP/1.1
Host: localhost:5000
Content-Type: application/json
Accept: application/json

{
  "id":0,
  "name":"Christian",
  "loyaltyPoints":0,
  "settings":{ "interests" : ["whisky", "cycling"] }
}
```

JSON representation of the user being registered

To handle the command for registering a new user, you need to add a Nancy module to Loyalty Program by adding a file called UserModule.cs and putting the following code in it.

Listing 4.4   POST endpoint for registering users

```
using System.Collections.Generic;
using Nancy;
using Nancy.ModelBinding;


public class UsersModule : NancyModule
{
    public UsersModule() : base("/users")
    {
        Post("/", _ =>
        {
            var newUser = this.Bind<LoyaltyProgramUser>();
            this.AddRegisteredUser(newUser);
            return this.CreatedResponse(newUser);
        });
    }

    private dynamic CreatedResponse(LoyaltyProgramUser newUser)
    {
        return
          this.Negotiate
            .WithStatusCode(HttpStatusCode.Created)
            .WithHeader(
              "Location",
              this.Request.Url.SiteBase + "/users/" + newUser.Id)
            .WithModel(newUser);
    }

    private void AddRegisteredUser(LoyaltyProgramUser newUser)
    {
        // store the newUser to a data store
    }
}
```

The request must include a **LoyaltyProgramUser** in the body. If it doesn't, the request is malformed.

Negotiate is an entry point to Nancy's fluent API for creating responses.

Uses the 201 Created status code for the response

Returns the user in the response for convenience

Adds a location header to the response because this is expected by HTTP for 201 Created responses

The response to the preceding request looks like this:

The status code is 201 Created.

Nancy's content negotiation sets the Content-Type.

```
HTTP/1.1 201 Created
Content-Type: application/json; charset=utf-8
Location: http://localhost:5000/users/4

{
  "id": 4,
  "name": "Christian",
  "loyaltyPoints": 0,
  "settings": { "interests": ["whisky", "cycling"]
  }
}
```

The Location header points to the newly created resource.

The main new thing to notice in listing 4.4 is the use of Negotiate to create the response to the command. Negotiate is a property on the NancyModule class that you use as a base class for UserModule. Here, it mainly works as an entry point to Nancy's nice, fluent API for creating responses. In the handler, you use that API to set the status code, add a Location header, and add the user object to the response. The API will also allow you to do more things to the response, such as setting other headers and specifying a view that will be used when responding to requests that ask for HTML in the Accept header.

Negotiate also triggers Nancy's content-negotiation functionality. Content negotiation is how HTTP specifies that the format of data in responses should be decided. It essentially means reading the Accept header in the request and serializing to a format indicated there. In listing 4.3, the accept header is Accept: application/json, meaning the response should serialize data to JSON.

With the handler for the register-user command in place, let's turn our attention to implementing a handler for the update-user command. That handler is added to UserModule.

Listing 4.5   PUT endpoint for registering users

```
public class UsersModule : NancyModule
{
  public UsersModule() : base("/users")
  {
    Post("/", _ => ...);

    Put("/{userId:int}", parameters =>
    {
      int userId = parameters.userId;
      var updatedUser = this.Bind<LoyaltyProgramUser>();
      // store the updatedUser to a data store
      return updatedUser;              ◁──┐ Nancy turns the user object
    });                                    into a complete response.
  }
  ...
}
```

There's nothing in this code you haven't seen before.

The handlers for the commands are only one side of the collaboration. The other side is the code that sends the commands. Figure 4.2 shows that the API Gateway microservice sends commands to the Loyalty Program microservice. You won't build a complete API Gateway microservice here, but in the code download for this chapter, you'll find a console application that acts as API Gateway would with regard to collaborating with Loyalty Program. Here, we'll focus only on the code that sends the commands.

In the API Gateway microservice, you'll create a class called LoyaltyProgramClient that's responsible for dealing with communication with the Loyalty Program microservice. That class encapsulates everything involved in building HTTP requests, serializing data for requests, understanding HTTP responses, and deserializing response data.

The code for sending the registered-user command takes a `LoyaltyProgramUser` as input and creates an HTTP POST with the `LoyaltyProgramUser` object in the body, and it sends that to the Loyalty Program microservice. After it checks the response status code and confirms that it's 201 Created, it deserializes the body of the response to a `LoyaltyProgramUser` and returns it. If the status code is anything else, the method returns null. The following listing shows the implementation.

Listing 4.6   The API Gateway microservice registering new users

```
using System;
using System.Text;
using System.Threading.Tasks;
using System.Net;
using System.Net.Http;
using Newtonsoft.Json;

public class LoyaltyProgramClient
{
  public async Task<LoyaltyProgramUser>
  RegisterUser(LoyaltyProgramUser newUser)
  {
    using(var httpClient = new HttpClient())
    {
      httpClient.BaseAddress = new Uri($"http://{this.hostName}");
      var response = await
        httpClient.PostAsync(              ⟵── Sends the command to Loyalty Program
          "/users/",
          new StringContent(
            JsonConvert.SerializeObject(newUser),    ⟵── Serializes newUser as JSON
            Encoding.UTF8,
            "application/json"));          ⟵┐
      ThrowOnTransientFailure(response);         │ Sets the Content-Type header
      return JsonConvert.DeserializeObject<LoyaltyProgramUser>(   ⟵┐
          await response.Content.ReadAsStringAsync());           │
    }                                          Deserializes the response if the
  }                                            command was handled successfully
}
```

Similarly, `LoyaltyProgramClient` has a method for sending the update-user command. This method also encapsulates the HTTP communication involved in sending the command.

Listing 4.7   The API Gateway microservice updating users

```
public async Task<LoyaltyProgramUser> UpdateUser(LoyaltyProgramUser user)
{
  using(var httpClient = new HttpClient())
  {
    httpClient.BaseAddress = new Uri($"http://{this.hostName}");
    var response = await
```

```
      httpClient.PutAsync(
        $"/users/{user.Id}",
        new StringContent(
          JsonConvert.SerializeObject(user),
          Encoding.UTF8,
          "application/json"));
    ThrowOnTransientFailure(response);
    return JsonConvert.DeserializeObject<LoyaltyProgramUser>(
      await response.Content.ReadAsStringAsync());
  }
}
```

← **Sends the update-user command as a PUT request**

This code is similar to the code for the register-user command, except this HTTP request uses the PUT method. With the command handlers implemented in the Loyalty Program microservice and a LoyaltyProgramClient implemented in the API Gateway microservice, the command-based collaboration is implemented. API Gateway can register and update users, but it can't yet query users.

4.2.4   *Implementing queries with HTTP GET*

The Loyalty Program microservice can handle the commands it needs to handle, but it can't answers queries about registered users. Remember that Loyalty Program only needs one endpoint to handle queries. As mentioned previously, the endpoint handling queries is an HTTP GET endpoint at URLs of the form /users/{userId}, and it responds with a representation of the user. This endpoint implements both queries in figure 4.4.

Listing 4.8   GET endpoint to query a user by ID

```
public class UsersModule : NancyModule
{
  private static IDictionary<int, LoyaltyProgramUser> registeredUsers =
    new Dictionary<int, LoyaltyProgramUser>();

  public UsersModule() : base("/users")
  {
    Post("/", _ => ...);

    Put("/{userId:int}", parameters => ...);

    Get("/{userId:int}", parameters =>
    {
      int userId = parameters.userId;
      if (registerUsers.ContainsKey(userId))
        return registerUsers[userId];
      else
        return HttpStatusCode.NotFound;
    });
  }
  ...
}
```

There's nothing about this code that you haven't already seen several times. Likewise, the code needed in the API Gateway microservice to query this endpoint shouldn't come as a surprise:

```
public class LoyaltyProgramClient
{
  ...

  public async Task<LoyaltyProgramUser> QueryUser(int userId)
  {
    var userResource = $"/users/{userId}";
    using(var httpClient = new HttpClient())
    {
      httpClient.BaseAddress = new Uri($"http://{this.hostName}");
      var response = await httpClient.GetAsync(userResource);
      ThrowOnTransientFailure(response);
      return JsonConvert.DeserializeObject<LoyaltyProgramUser>(
        await response.Content.ReadAsStringAsync());
    }
  }
}
```

This is all that's needed for the query-based collaboration. You've now implemented the command- and query-based collaborations of the Loyalty Program microservice.

4.2.5   *Data formats*

Suppose you want the endpoints you just implemented to support YAML. You shouldn't implement support for a third data format in the endpoint handlers—it's not a concern of the application logic, it's a technical concern.

Nancy lets you support deserialization of another format by implementing the `IBodyDeserializer` interface. In typical Nancy style, any implementation of that interface is picked up at application startup and is hooked into Nancy's model binding. Likewise, to support serialization of response bodies in a third format, you can implement `IResponseProcessor`, which also is automatically discovered by Nancy and gets hooked into Nancy's content negotiation.

To implement YAML support in the Loyalty Program microservice, you'll first install the `YamlDotNet NuGet` package in the project. Then, you'll add a file called YamlSerializerDeserializer.cs. You'll use this file to implement both the deserialization and the serialization. The deserialization looks like this.

Listing 4.9   Deserializing from YAML

```
namespace LoyaltyProgram
{
  using System.IO;
  using Nancy.ModelBinding;
  using Nancy.Responses.Negotiation;
  using YamlDotNet.Serialization;
```

```
public class YamlBodyDeserializer : IBodyDeserializer
{
  public bool CanDeserialize(
    MediaRange mediaRange, BindingContext context)
      => mediaRange.Subtype.ToString().EndsWith("yaml");

  public object Deserialize(
    MediaRange mediaRange, Stream bodyStream, BindingContext context)
  {
    var yamlDeserializer = new Deserializer();
    var reader = new StreamReader(bodyStream);
    return yamlDeserializer.Deserialize(
      reader, context.DestinationType);
  }
}
}
```

Tells Nancy which content types this deserializer can handle

Tries to deserialize the request body to the type needed by the application code

This code mainly uses the YamlDotNet library to deserialize the data from the body of the request.

The implementation of the serialization support isn't as simple, but it's still only a matter of implementing two methods and a property.

Listing 4.10 Serializing to YAML

```
namespace LoyaltyProgram
{
  using System;
  using System.Collections.Generic;
  using System.IO;
  using Nancy;
  using Nancy.Responses.Negotiation;
  using YamlDotNet.Serialization;
  ...

  public class YamlBodySerializer : IResponseProcessor
  {
    public IEnumerable<Tuple<string, MediaRange>> ExtensionMappings
    {
      get
      {
        yield return new Tuple<string, MediaRange>(
          "yaml", new MediaRange("application/yaml"));
      }
    }
  public ProcessorMatch CanProcess(
    MediaRange requestedMediaRange, dynamic model, NancyContext context)
    =>
      requestedMediaRange.Subtype.ToString().EndsWith("yaml")
      ? new ProcessorMatch
        {
          ModelResult = MatchResult.DontCare,
```

Tells Nancy which file extensions can be handled by this response processor. You don't use this feature.

Tells Nancy that this processor can handle accept header values that end with "yaml"

```
              RequestedContentTypeResult = MatchResult.NonExactMatch
          }
        : ProcessorMatch.None;
```

Creates a new response object to use in the rest of Nancy's pipeline

```
  public Response Process(
    MediaRange requestedMediaRange, dynamic model, NancyContext context)
    =>
      new Response
      {
        Contents = stream =>
        {
          var yamlSerializer = new Serializer();
          var streamWriter = new StreamWriter(stream);
          yamlSerializer.Serialize(streamWriter, model);
          streamWriter.Flush();
        },
        ContentType = "application/yaml"
      };
  }
}
```

Sets up a function that writes the response body to a stream

Writes the YAML serialized object to the stream Nancy uses for the response body

The serialization is also handled by the YamlDotNet library. The code in `Extension-Mappings` and `CanProcess` in `YamlBodySerializer` tells Nancy which responses it applies to. The code in `Process` creates a response with a YAML-serialized body. This response may be processed more if the code in the handler customizes the response further. For instance, the response to the register-user command is created like this:

```
return
  this.Negotiate
    .WithStatusCode(HttpStatusCode.Created)
    .WithHeader(
      "Location",
      this.Request.Url.SiteBase + "/users/" + newUser.Id)
    .WithModel(newUser);
```

This code customizes the response through the `.With*` extension methods. After `YamlBodySerializer` has created the response, including the YAML-formatted body, the `WithStatusCode` and `WithHeader` methods further customize the response. As you've seen, all it takes to make your Nancy-based microservices support another data format is an implementation of `IBodyDeserializer` and an implementation of `IResponseProcessor`.

4.2.6   *Implementing an event-based collaboration*

Now that you know how to implement command- and query-based collaborations between microservices, it's time to turn our attention to the event-based collaboration. Figure 4.11 repeats the collaborations that the Loyalty Program microservice is involved in. Loyalty Program subscribes to events from Special Offers, and it uses the events to decide when to notify registered users about new special offers.

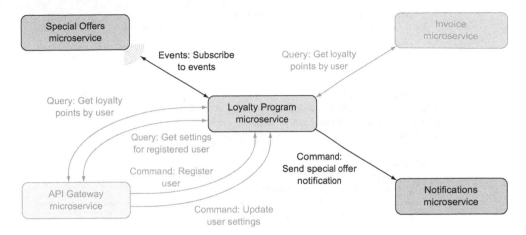

Figure 4.11 **The event-based collaboration in the Loyalty Program microservice is the subscription to the event feed in the Special Offers microservice.**

We'll first look at how Special Offers exposes its events in a feed. Then, you'll return to Loyalty Program and add a second process to that service, which will be responsible for subscribing to events and handling events.

IMPLEMENTING AN EVENT FEED

You saw a simple event feed in chapter 2. The Special Offers microservice implements its event feed the same way: it exposes an endpoint—/events—that returns a list of sequentially numbered events. The endpoint can take two query parameters—start and end—that specify a range of events. For example, a request to the event feed can look like this:

```
GET /events?start=10&end=110 HTTP/1.1

Host: specialoffers.mycompany.com
Accept: application/json
```

The response to this request might be the following, except that I've cut off the response after two events:

```
HTTP/1.1 200 OK
Content-Type: application/json; charset=utf-8

[
  {
    "sequenceNumber": 10,
    "occuredAt": "2015-10-02T18:37:00.7070659+00:00",
    "name": "NewSpecialOffer",
    "content": {
      "offerId": 123,
      "offer": {
        "productCatalogueId": 1,
```

```
            "productName": "Basic t-shirt",
            "description": "Get an awesome t-shirt at half price!",
          }
        }
      },
      {
        "sequenceNumber": 11,
        "occuredAt": "2015-10-02T20:01:00.3050629+00:00",
        "name": "UpdatedSpecialOffer",
        "content": {
          "offerId": 124,
          "offer": {
          "productCatalogueId": 10,
          "productName": "Hot teacup",
          "description": "Get a Cup<T>. Because you know you want to.",
          "update": "Now with 10% more inference"
        }
      }
    }
  }
}
```

Notice that the events have different names (`NewSpecialOffer` and `UpdatedSpecial-Offer`) and the two types of events don't have the same data fields. This is normal: different events carry different information. It's also something you need to be aware of when you implement the subscriber in the Loyalty Program microservice. You can't expect all events to have the exact same shape.

The implementation of the /events endpoint in the Special Offers microservice is a simple Nancy module, just like the one in chapter 2.

Listing 4.11   Endpoint that reads and returns events

```
namespace SpecialOffers.EventFeed
{
  using Nancy;

  public class EventsFeedModule : NancyModule
  {
    public EventsFeedModule(IEventStore eventStore) : base("/events")
    {
      Get("/", _ =>
      {
        long firstEventSequenceNumber, lastEventSequenceNumber;
        if (!long.TryParse(this.Request.Query.start.Value,
          out firstEventSequenceNumber))
          firstEventSequenceNumber = 0;
        if (!long.TryParse(this.Request.Query.end.Value,
          out lastEventSequenceNumber))
          lastEventSequenceNumber = long.MaxValue;

        return
          eventStore.GetEvents(
            firstEventSequenceNumber,
```

```
                        lastEventSequenceNumber);
        });
      }
    }
  }
}
```

This module only uses Nancy features that we've already discussed. You may notice, however, that it returns the result of eventStore.GetEvents directly, which is an IEnumerable<Event>; Nancy serializes it as an array. The Event is a struct that carries a little metadata and a Content field that's meant to hold the event data.

Listing 4.12   Event class that represents events

```
public struct Event
{
  public long SequenceNumber { get; }
  public DateTimeOffset OccuredAt { get; }
  public string Name { get; }
  public object Content { get; }

  public Event(
    long sequenceNumber,
    DateTimeOffset occuredAt,
    string name,
    object content)
  {
    this.SequenceNumber = sequenceNumber;
    this.OccuredAt = occuredAt;
    this.Name = name;
    this.Content = content;
  }
}
```

The Content property is used for event-specific data and is where the difference between a NewSpecialOffer event and an UpdatedSpecialOffer event appears. The former has one type of object in Content, and the latter has another.

This is all it takes to expose an event feed. This simplicity is the great advantage of using an HTTP-based event feed to publish events. Event-based collaboration can be implemented over a queue system, but that introduces another complex piece of technology that you have to learn to use and administer in production. That complexity is warranted in some situations, but certainly not always.

CREATING AND RUNNING AN EVENT-SUBSCRIBER PROCESS

The first step in implementing an event-subscriber process is to create a console application. You're using ASP.NET Core, which is based on .NET Core, for the web processes in the example microservices, so you'll create a console application that's .NET Core–based and call it LoyaltyProgramEventConsumer. You can create a .NET Core–based console application in Visual Studio 2015 by selecting the Console Application (Package) project type in the New Project dialog box. Alternatively, you can go to a PowerShell prompt, run the Yeoman ASP.NET generator,[1] and select the option to generate a Console Application.

> **Listing 4.13   Generating a console app with the Yeoman ASP.NET generator**

```
PS> yo aspnet
```

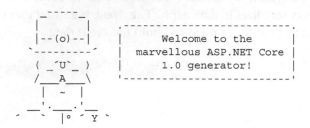

```
? What type of application do you want to create?
  Empty Web Application
> Console Application
  Web Application
  Web Application Basic [without Membership and Authorization]
  Web API Application
  Nancy ASP.NET Application
  Class Library
  Unit test project (xUnit.net)
```

Move the cursor here, and press Enter to generate a console app.

Whether you create the LoyaltyProgramEventConsumer with Visual Studio or Yeoman, you can run it by going to the project folder—the folder where the project.json file is—in PowerShell and using dotnet:

```
PS> dotnet run
```

The application is empty, so nothing interesting happens yet. Running LoyaltyProgramEventConsumer like that from PowerShell is something you'll only do for testing. In production, you might run LoyaltyProgramEventConsumer as a Windows service. If the production environment is based on Windows Servers that you (or your organization) run, a Windows service may well be the right choice; but if your production environment is in a cloud, in may not be.

> **WARNING** I'm implementing LoyaltyProgramEventConsumer as a Windows service, which only works on Windows. If you want to run on Linux, you can create a similar LoyaltyProgramEventConsumer as a Linux daemon.

Creating a Windows service is straightforward and is no different with a .NET Core–based console application than it was before .NET Core. The project already has a Program.cs file containing a Program class. The Program class has a Main method, which is

---

[1] See appendix A for instructions on installing Yeoman and the Yeoman ASP.NET generator.

the entry point to the application. To turn it into a Windows service, the `Program` class just has to inherit from `ServiceBase` and override the `OnStart` and `OnStop` methods, as in the following listing.

Listing 4.14 Making `Program` run as a Windows service

```
using System.ServiceProcess;

public class Program : ServiceBase
{
  private EventSubscriber subscriber;

  public void Main(string[] args)
  {
    // more to come
    Run(this);
  }

  protected override void OnStart(string[] args)
  {
    // more to come
  }

  protected override void OnStop()
  {
    // more to come
  }
}
```

Starts running as a Windows service ←

Called when the Windows service is started ←

Called when the Windows service is stopped ←

If you're coding along with this example, you'll get compile errors from the preceding code: the type `ServiceBase` isn't known. To load the assembly that contains the `ServiceBase` class, you have to add a line to the `dependencies` section of your project.json file and edit the `frameworks` section to indicate that this application uses the full .NET framework. The `frameworks` section should look like this:

```
"dependencies": {
  "Newtonsoft.Json": "8.0.3",
  "System.ServiceProcess.ServiceController": "4.1.0",
  "System.Net.Http": "4.1.0"
},

"frameworks": {
  "net461": { }
},
```

That should make the application compile again. To run it, you need to install it as a Windows service. And toward that end you need a binary version, so you need to explicitly compile the project. You do that with the `dotnet` command-line tool:

```
PS> dotnet build
```

This compiles the project into a bin folder under the project. You can run the compiled output by calling the compiled executable:

```
PS> .\bin\Debug\net452\LoyaltyProgramEventConsumer
```

Now you have a binary version, and you can install it as a Windows service using the sc.exe Windows utility. You must tell sc.exe the name of the Windows service and the command to execute as a Windows service. In this case, the command is the LoyaltyProgramEventConsumer executable. You end up with this command:

```
PS> sc.exe create loyalty-program-event-consumer binPath="<path-to-
    project>\bin\Debug\net452\LoyaltyProgramEventConsumer"
```

Once LoyaltyProgramEventConsumer is installed as a Windows service, you can start and stop it like any other Windows service.

SUBSCRIBING TO AN EVENT FEED

You now have a LoyaltyProgramEventConsumer console application that you can run as a Windows service. Its job is to subscribe to events from the Special Offers microservice and use the Notifications microservice to notify registered users of special offers. Figure 4.12 shows the collaboration of Loyalty Program, with the ones you've already implemented grayed out.

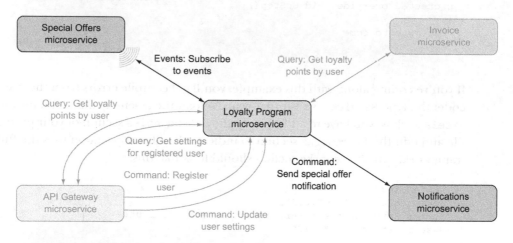

Figure 4.12   The event-based collaboration in the Loyalty Program microservice is the subscription to the event feed in the Special Offers microservice.

Subscribing to an event feed essentially means you'll poll the events endpoint of the microservice you subscribe to. At intervals, you'll send an HTTP GET request to the /events endpoint to check whether there are any events you haven't processed yet.

You'll start the implementation from the top down. The first thing to do is introduce a class called EventSubscriber and have it set up a timer that elapses after 10 seconds.

Listing 4.15 Starting a timer and setting up a callback function

```
public class EventSubscriber
{
  private readonly string loyaltyProgramHost;
  private long start = 0;
  private int chunkSize = 100;
  private readonly Timer timer;

  public EventSubscriber(string loyaltyProgramHost)
  {                                                              Sets up the timer
    this.loyaltyProgramHost = loyaltyProgramHost;                to elapse after 10
    this.timer = new Timer(10 * 1000);              ◁───┘        seconds
    this.timer.AutoReset = false;
    this.timer.Elapsed += (_, __) => SubscriptionCycleCallback().Wait();   ◁───┐
  }
}                                                     Called every time the timer elapses
```

After 10 seconds, you check for new events, handle any new events, and then sleep 10 seconds again before checking for new events. Every time the timer elapses, listing 4.15 calls SubscriptionCycleCallback, which tries to read new events from the event feed and then handles new events. Both these tasks are delegated to other methods that we'll get to in a moment. For now, here's the code for SubscriptionCycleCallback.

Listing 4.16 Reading and handling events

```
private async Task SubscriptionCycleCallback()
{
  var response = await ReadEvents().ConfigureAwait(false);      ◁───┐
  if (response.StatusCode == HttpStatusCode.OK)                Awaits the HTTP GET
    HandleEvents(response.Content);                            to the event feed
  this.timer.Start();
}
```

The ReadEvents method makes the HTTP GET request to the event feed. It uses Http-Client, which you've seen several times already.

Listing 4.17 Reading the next batch of events

```
private async Task<HttpResponseMessage> ReadEvents()
{
  using (var httpClient = new HttpClient())
  {
    httpClient.BaseAddress =                                   Awaits getting
      new Uri($"http://{this.loyaltyProgramHost}");            new events
    var response = await httpClient.GetAsync(          ◁───
      $"/events/?start={this.start}&end={this.start + this.chunkSize}")   ◁───┐
      .ConfigureAwait(false);                          Uses query parameters to limit
    return response;                                   the number of events read
  }
}
```

This method reads the events from the event feed and returns them to the Subscrip-tionCycleCallback method. If the request succeeded, the HandleEvents method is called. The events are first deserialized, and then each event is handled in turn.

> **Listing 4.18   Deserializing and then handling events**

```
private void HandleEvents(string content)                    Treats the content property ❶
{                                                               as a dynamic object
  var events = JsonConvert
    .DeserializeObject<IEnumerable<SpecialOfferEvent>>(content);
  foreach (var ev in events)
  {
    dynamic eventData = ev.Content;                          ◁──────┘
    // handle 'ev' using the eventData.
    this.start = Math.Max(this.start, ev.SequenceNumber + 1); ◁─────┐
  }
}                                                           Keeps track of the highest
                                                              event number handled ❷
```

There are a few things to notice here:

- This method keeps track of which events have been handled ❷. This makes sure you don't request events from the feed that you've already processed.
- You treat the Content property on the events as dynamic ❶. As you saw earlier, not all events carry the same data in the Content property, so treating it as dynamic allows you to access the properties you need on .Content and not care about the rest. This is a sound approach because you want to be liberal in accepting incoming data—it shouldn't cause problems if the Special Offers microservice decides to add an extra field to the event JSON. As long as the data you *need* is there, the rest can be ignored.
- The events are deserialized into the type SpecialOfferEvent. This is a different type than the Event type uses to serialize the events in Special Offers. This is intentional and is done because the two microservices don't need to have the exact same view of the events. As long as Loyalty Program doesn't depend on data that isn't there, all is well.

The SpecialOfferEvent type used here is simple and contains only the fields used in Loyalty Program:

```
public struct SpecialOfferEvent
{
  public long SequenceNumber { get; set; }
  public string Name { get; set; }
  public object Content { get; set; }
}
```

To tie the EventSubscriber code back into the Windows service you set up in listing 4.14 at the beginning of implementing the event-subscriber process, you'll add two more methods to the EventSubscriber: one that starts the timer and one that stops it. These two methods effectively start and stop the event subscription:

```
public void Start()
{
  this.timer.Start();
}

public void Stop()
{
  this.timer.Stop();
}
```

The Windows service can now create an EventSubscriber at startup and then call the Start and Stop methods when the Windows service is started or stopped. Filling in the missing pieces from listing 4.14, the Windows service becomes as follows.

Listing 4.19 Windows service to start and stop the subscription

```
public class Program : ServiceBase
{
    private EventSubscriber subscriber;

    public void Main(string[] args)
    {
      this.subscriber = new EventSubscriber("localhost:5000");
      Run(this);
    }

    protected override void OnStart(string[] args)
    {
      this.subscriber.Start();
    }

    protected override void OnStop()
    {
      this.subscriber.Stop();
    }
}
```

This concludes your implementation of event subscriptions. As you've seen, subscribing to an event feed means polling it for new events at intervals and then handling any new events.

4.3   Summary

- There are three types of microservice collaboration:
  - Command-based collaboration, where one microservice uses an HTTP POST or PUT to make another microservice perform an action

    – Query-based collaboration, where one microservice uses an HTTP GET to query the state of another microservice

    – Event-based collaboration, where one microservice exposes an event feed that other microservices can subscribe to by polling the feed for new events

- Event-based collaboration is more loosely coupled than command- and query-based collaboration.

- You can hook into Nancy's model binding and content negotiation to support data formats other than XML and JSON.

- The Nancy bootstrapper is used to configure Nancy itself and Nancy applications.

- You can use HttpClient to send commands to other microservices and to query other microservices.

- You can use Nancy to expose the endpoints for receiving and handling commands and queries.

- Nancy can expose a simple event feed.

- You can create a process that subscribes to events by

    – Creating a .NET Core console application

    – Implementing and installing a console application as a Windows service

    – Using a timer to make the console application poll an event feed

    – Using HttpClient to read events from an event feed

Data ownership
and data storage

5

This chapter covers

- Exploring microservices and their data stores
- Understanding how data ownership follows business capabilities
- Using data replication for speed and robustness
- Building read models from event feeds with event subscribers
- Understanding how microservices store data

Software systems create, use, and transform data. Without the data, most software systems wouldn't be worth much, and that's true for microservice systems. In this chapter, you'll learn where a piece of data should be stored and which microservice should be responsible for keeping it up to date. Furthermore, you'll learn how you can use data replication to make your microservice system both more robust and faster.

5.1   Each microservice has a data store

One of the characteristics of microservices identified in chapter 1 is that each microservice should own its data store. The data in that data store is solely under the control of the microservice, and it's exactly the data the microservice needs. It's primarily data belonging to the capability the microservice implements, but it also includes supporting data, like cached data and read models created from event feeds.

The fact that each microservice owns a data store means you don't need to use the same database technology for all microservices. You can choose a database technology that's suited to the data that each microservice needs to store.

A microservice typically needs to store three types of data:

- Data belonging to the capability the microservice implements. This is data that the microservice is responsible for and must keep safe and up to date.
- Events raised by the microservice. During command processing, the microservice may need to raise events to inform the rest of the system about updates to the data the microservice is responsible for.
- Read models based on queries to other microservices or on events from other microservices.

These three types of data may be stored in different databases and even in different types of databases.

5.2   Partitioning data between microservices

When you're deciding where to store data in a microservice system, competing forces are at play. The two main forces are data ownership and locality:

- *Ownership of data* means being responsible for keeping the data up to date.
- *Locality of data* refers to where the data a microservice needs is stored. Often, the data should be stored nearby—preferably in the microservice itself.

These two forces may be at odds, and in order to satisfy both, you'll often have to store data in several places. That's OK, but it's important that only one of those places be considered the authoritative source. Figure 5.1 illustrates that whereas one microservice stores the authoritative copy of a piece of data, other microservices can mirror that data in their own data stores.

5.2.1   Rule 1: Ownership of data follows business capabilities

The first rule when deciding where a piece of data belongs in a microservices system is that ownership of data follows business capabilities. As discussed in chapter 3, the primary driver in deciding on the responsibility of a microservice is that it should handle a business capability. The business capability defines the boundaries of the microservice—everything belonging to the capability should be implemented in the microservice. This includes storing the data that falls under the business capability.

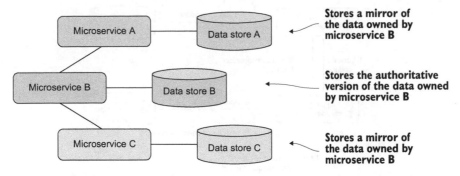

Figure 5.1 **Microservices A and C collaborate with microservice B. Microservices A and C can store mirrors of the data owned by microservice B, but the authoritative copy is stored in microservice B's own data store.**

Domain-driven design teaches that some concepts can appear in several business capabilities and that the meaning of the concepts may differ slightly. Several microservices may have the concept of a customer, and they will work on and store customer entities. There may be some overlap between the data stored in different microservices, but it's important to be clear about which microservice is in charge of what.

For instance, only one microservice should own the home address of a customer. Another microservice could own the customer's purchase history, and a third the customer's notification preferences. The way to decide which microservice is responsible for a given piece of data—the customer's home address, for instance—is to figure out which business process keeps that data up to date. The microservice responsible for the business capability is responsible for storing the data and keeping it up to date.

Let's consider again the e-commerce site from chapters 1 and 2. Figure 5.2 shows an overview of how that system handles user requests for adding an item to a shopping cart. Most of the microservices in figure 5.2 are dimmed, to put the focus on three microservices: Shopping Cart, Product Catalog, and Recommendations.

Each of the highlighted microservices in figure 5.2 handles a business capability: the Shopping Cart microservice is responsible for keeping track of users' shopping carts; the Product Catalog microservice is responsible for giving the rest of the system access to information from the product catalog; and the Recommendations microservice is responsible for calculating and giving product recommendations to users of the e-commerce site. Data is associated with each of these business capabilities, and each microservice owns and is responsible for the data associated with its capability. Figure 5.3 shows the data each of the three microservices owns. Saying that a microservice *owns* a piece of data means it must store that data and be the authoritative source for that piece of data.

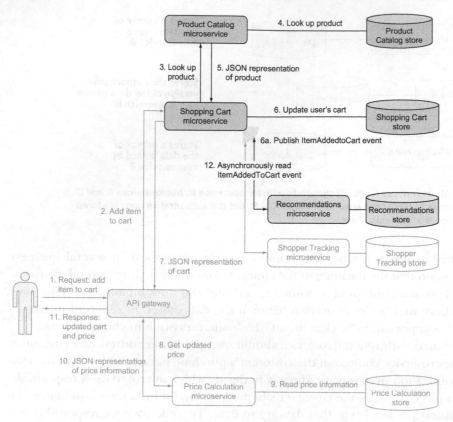

Figure 5.2   In this e-commerce example (from chapters 1 and 2), we'll focus on partitioning data between the Shopping Cart microservice, the Product Catalog microservice, and the Recommendations microservice.

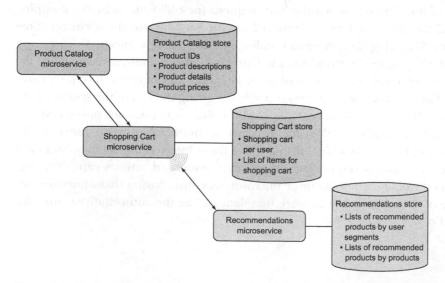

Figure 5.3   Each microservice owns the data belonging to the business capability it implements.

5.2.2   *Rule 2: Replicate for speed and robustness*

The second force at play when deciding where a piece of data should be stored in a microservices system is locality. There's a big difference between a microservice querying its own database for data and a microservice querying another microservice for that same data. Querying its own database is generally both faster and more reliable than querying another microservice.

Once you've decided on the ownership of data, you'll likely discover that your microservices need to ask each other for data. This type of collaboration creates a certain coupling: one microservice querying another means the first is *coupled* to the other. If the second microservice is down or slow, the first microservice will suffer.

To loosen this coupling, you can cache query responses. Sometimes you'll cache the responses as they are, but other times you can store a read model based on query responses. In both cases, you must decide when and how a cached piece of data becomes invalid. The microservice that owns the data is in the best position to decide when a piece of data is still valid and when it has become invalid. Therefore, endpoints responding to queries about data owned by the microservice should include cache headers in the response telling the caller how long it should cache the response data.

USING HTTP CACHE HEADERS TO CONTROL CACHING

HTTP defines a number of headers that can be used to control how HTTP responses can be cached. The purpose of the HTTP caching mechanisms is twofold:

- To eliminate the need, in many cases, to request information the caller already has
- To eliminate the need, in many other situations, to send full HTTP responses

To eliminate the need to make requests for information the caller already has, the server can add a `cache-control` header to responses. The HTTP specification defines a range of controls that can be set in the `cache-control` header. The most common are the `private|public` and the `max-age` directives. The first indicates whether only the caller—`private`—may cache the response or if intermediaries—proxy servers, for instance—may cache the response, too. The `max-age` directive indicates the number of seconds the response may be cached. For example, the following `cache-control` header indicates that the caller, and only the caller, can cache the response for 3,600 seconds:

```
cache-control: private, max-age:3600
```

That is, the caller, may reuse the response any time it wants to make an HTTP request to the same URL with the same method—GET, POST, PUT, DELETE—and the same body within 3,600 seconds. It's worth noting that the query string is part of the URL, so caching takes query strings into account.

To eliminate the need to send a full response in cases where the caller has a cached but stale response, the server can add an `etag` header to responses. This is an identifier for the response. When the caller makes a later request to the same URL using the same method and the same body, it can include the `etag` in a request header. The server can read the `etag` and, through it, know which response the caller already has cached. If the server decides the response is still valid, it can return a response with the 304 Not Modified status code to tell the client to use the already-cached response. Furthermore, the server can add a `cache-control` header to the 304 response to prolong the period the response may be cached. Note that the etag is set by the server and later read again by the same server.

Let's consider the microservices in figure 5.3 again. The Shopping Cart microservice uses product information that it gets by querying the Product Catalog microservice. How long the product catalog information for any given product is likely to be correct is best decided by Product Catalog, which owns the data. Therefore, Product Catalog should add cache headers to its responses, and Shopping Cart should use them to decide how long it can cache a response. Figure 5.4 shows a sequence of requests to Product Catalog that Shopping Cart wants to make.

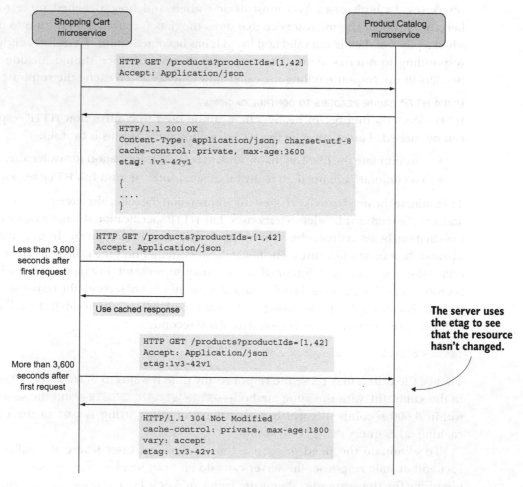

Figure 5.4   The Product Catalog microservice can allow its collaborators to cache responses by including cache headers in its HTTP responses. In this example, it sets `max-age` to indicate how long responses may be cached, and it also includes an `etag` built from the product IDs and versions.

In figure 5.4, the cache headers on the response to the first request tell the Shopping Cart microservice that it can cache the response for 3,600 seconds. The second time Shopping Cart wants to make the same request, the cached response is reused because fewer than 3,600 seconds have passed. The third time, the request to the Product Catalog microservice is made because more than 3,600 seconds have passed. That request includes the `etag` from the first response. Product Catalog uses the `etag` to decide that the response would still be the same, so it sends back the shorter 304 Not Modified response instead of a full response. The 304 response includes a new set of cache headers that allows Shopping Cart to cache the already-cached response for an additional 1,800 seconds.

In sections 5.3.3 and 5.3.4, we'll discuss how to include cache headers in responses from Nancy route handlers. We'll also look at reading them on the client side from the response.

USING READ MODELS TO MIRROR DATA OWNED BY OTHER MICROSERVICES

It's normal for a microservice to query its own database for data it owns, but querying its database for data it doesn't own may not seem as natural. The natural way to get data owned by another microservice is to query that microservice. But it's often possible to replace a query to another microservice with a query to the microservice's own database by creating a *read model*: a data model that can be queried easily and efficiently. This is in contrast to the model used to store the data owned by the microservice, where the purpose is to store an authoritative copy of the data and to be able to easily update it when necessary.

Data is, of course, also written to read models—otherwise they'd be empty—but the data is written as a consequence of changes somewhere else. You trade some additional complexity at write time for less complexity at read time.

Read models are often based on events from other microservices. One microservice subscribes to events from another microservice and updates its own model of the event data as events arrive.

Read models can also be built from responses to queries to other microservices. In this case, the lifetime of the data in the read model is decided by the cache headers on those responses, just as in a straight cache of the responses. The difference between a straight cache and a read model is that to build a read model, the data in the responses is transformed and possibly enriched to make later reads easy and efficient. This means the shape of the data is determined by the scenarios in which it will be read instead of the scenario in which it was written.

Let's consider an example. The Shopping Cart microservice publishes events every time an item is added to or removed from a shopping cart. Figure 5.5 shows a Shopper Tracking microservice that subscribes to those events and updates a read model based on the events. Shopper Tracking allows business users to query how many times specific items are added to or removed from shopping carts.

The events published from the Shopping Cart microservice aren't in themselves an efficient model to query when you want to find out how often a product has been

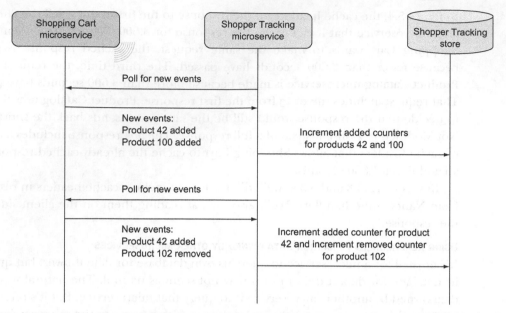

Figure 5.5   The Shopper Tracking microservice subscribes to events from the Shopping Cart microservice and keeps track of how many times products are added to or removed from shopping carts.

added to or removed from shopping carts. But the events are a good source from which to build such a model. The Shopper Tracking microservice keeps two counters for every product: one for how many times the product has been added to a shopping cart, and one for how many times it's been removed. Every time an event is received from Shopping Cart, one of the counters is updated; and every time a query is made about a product, the two counters for that product are read.

5.2.3 *Where does a microservice store its data?*

A microservice can use one, two, or more databases. Some of the data stored by the microservice may fit well into one type of database, and other data may fit better into another type. Many viable database technologies are available today, and I won't get into a comparison here. There are, however, some broad database categories that you can consider when you're making a choice, including relational databases, key/value stores, document databases, column stores, and graph databases.

The choice of database technology (or technologies) for a microservice can be influenced by many factors, including these:

- What shape is your data? Does it fit well into a relational model, a document model, or a key/value store, or is it a graph?
- What are the write scenarios? How much data is written? Do the writes come in bursts, or are they evenly distributed over time?
- What are the read scenarios? How much data is read at a time? How much is read altogether? Do the reads come in bursts?

- How much data is written compared to how much is read?
- Which databases do the team already know how to develop against *and* run in production?

Asking yourself these questions—and finding the answers—will not only help you decide on a suitable database but will also likely deepen your understanding of the nonfunctional qualities expected from the microservice. You'll learn how reliable the microservice must be, how much load it must handle, what the load looks like, how much latency is acceptable, and so on.

Gaining that deeper understanding is valuable, but note that I'm not recommending that you undertake a major analysis of the pros and cons of different databases each time you spin up a new microservice. You should be able to get a new microservice going and deployed to production quickly. The goal isn't to find a database technology that's perfect for the job—you just want to find one that's suitable given your answers to the previous questions. You may be faced with a situation in which a document base seems like a good choice and in which you're confident that both Couchbase and MongoDB would be well suited. In that case, choose one of them. It's better to get the microservice to production with one of them quickly and at a later stage possibly replace the microservice with an implementation that uses the other, than it is to delay getting the first version of the microservice to production because you're analyzing Couchbase and MongoDB in detail.

How many database technologies in the system?

The decision about which database you should use in a microservice isn't solely a matter of what fits well in that microservice. You need to take the broader landscape into consideration. In a microservice system, you'll have many microservices and many data stores. It's worth considering how many different database technologies you want to have in the system. There's a trade-off between standardizing on a few database technologies and having a free-for-all.

On the side of standardizing are goals like these:

- Running the databases reliably in production and continuing to do so in the long run.
- Developers being able to get into and work effectively in the codebase of a microservice they haven't touched before.

Favoring a free-for-all are these types of goals:

- Being able to choose the optimal database technology for each microservice in terms of maintainability, performance, security, reliability, and so on.
- Keeping microservices replaceable. If new developers take over a microservice and don't agree with the choice of database, they should be able to replace the database or even the microservice as a whole.

How these goals are weighed against each other changes from organization to organization, but it's important to be aware that there are trade-offs.

5.3   *Implementing data storage in a microservice*

We've discussed where data should go in a microservice system, including which data a microservice should own and which data it should mirror. It's time to switch gears and look at the code required to store the data.

I'll focus on how a microservice can store the data it owns, including how to store the events it raises. I'll first show you how to do this using SQL Server and the light-weight Dapper data access library. Then I'll show you how to store events in a database specifically designed for storing events—the aptly named Event Store database.

New technologies used in this chapter

In this chapter, you'll begin using a couple of technologies that you haven't used yet in this book:

- *SQL Server*—Microsoft's SQL database. You can find information about installing SQL Server in appendix A.
- *Dapper* (https://github.com/StackExchange/dapper-dot-net)—A lightweight object-relational mapper (ORM). I'll introduce Dapper next.
- *Event Store* (https://geteventstore.com)—A database product specifically designed to store events. I'll introduce Event Store in a moment.

Dapper: a lightweight O/RM

Dapper is a simple library for working with data in a SQL database from C#. It's part of a family of libraries sometimes referred to as *micro ORMs*, which also includes Simple.Data and Massive. These libraries focus on being simple to use and fast, and they embrace SQL.

Whereas a more traditional ORM writes all the SQL required to read data from and write it to the database, Dapper expects you to write your own SQL. I find this to be liberating when dealing with a database with a simple schema.

In the spirit of choosing lightweight technologies for microservices, I choose to use Dapper over a full-fledged ORM like Entity Framework or NHibernate. Often the database for a microservice is simple, and in such cases I find it easiest to add a thin layer—like Dapper—on top of it for a simpler solution overall. I could have chosen to use any of the other micro ORMs, but I like Dapper. In this chapter, you'll use Dapper to talk to SQL Server, but Dapper also works with other SQL databases like PostgreSQL and MySQL.

Event Store: a dedicated event database

Event Store is an open source database server designed specifically for storing events. Event Store stores events as JSON documents, but it differs from a document database by assuming that the JSON documents are part of a stream of events. Although Event Store is a niche product because it's so narrowly focused on storing events, it's in widespread use and has proven itself in heavy-load production scenarios.

In addition to storing events, Event Store has facilities for reading and subscribing to events. For instance, Event Store exposes its own event feeds—as ATOM feeds—that clients can subscribe to. If you don't mind depending on Event Store, using its ATOM event feed to expose events to other microservices can be a viable alternative to the way you'll implement event feeds in this book.

(continued)
Event Store works by exposing an HTTP API for storing, reading, and subscribing to events. There are a number of Event Store client libraries in various languages—including C#, F#, Java, Scala, Erlang, Haskell, and JavaScript—that make it easier to work with the database.

5.3.1 Storing data owned by a microservice

Once you've decided which data a microservice owns, storing that data is relatively straightforward. The details of how it's done depend on your choice of database. The only difference specific to microservices is that the data store is solely owned and accessed by the microservice itself.

As an example, let's go back to the Shopping Cart microservice. It owns the users' shopping carts and therefore stores them. You'll store the shopping carts in SQL Server using Dapper.

You implemented most of the Shopping Cart microservice in chapter 2. Here, you'll fill in the data store bits.

> **NOTE** To code along with this example, you'll need SQL Server. In appendix A, you'll find the information you need to install SQL Server. Alternatively, you can use PostgreSQL, but doing so will require various small changes to the code.

If you're familiar with storing data in SQL Server, the implementation should be no surprise, and that's the point. Storing the data owned by a microservice doesn't need to involve anything fancy. These are the steps for storing the shopping cart:

1 Create a database.
2 Use Dapper to implement the code to read, write, and update shopping carts.

First, you'll create a simple database for storing shopping carts. It will have two tables, as shown in figure 5.6.

Figure 5.6 `ShoppingCart` **has only two tables: one has a row for each shopping cart, and the other has a row per item in a shopping cart.**

In the code download, you'll find a SQL script for creating the ShoppingCart database called create-shopping-cart-db.sql in the folder \code\Chapter05\ShoppingCart\src\database-scripts\. You can execute the script in SQL Server Management Studio to create your own ShoppingCart database.

With the database in place, you can implement the code in the Shopping Cart microservice that reads, writes, and updates the database. You'll install the Dapper NuGet package into the microservice. Remember that you do this by adding Dapper to the project.json file and running the dotnet restore command from PowerShell. The dependencies section of the project.json file should look like this:

```
"dependencies": {
    "Microsoft.AspNetCore.Server.IISIntegration": "1.0.0",
    "Microsoft.AspNetCore.Server.Kestrel": "1.0.0",
    "Microsoft.AspNetCore.Owin": "1.0.0",
    "Nancy": "2.0.0-barneyrubble",
    "Polly": "4.2.1",
    "Dapper": "1.50.0-rc2a"          ⟵ Adds the Dapper
},                                      library
```

In chapter 2, the Shopping Cart microservice was expecting an implementation of an IShoppingCart interface. You'll change that interface slightly to allow the implementation of it to make asynchronous calls to the database. This is the modified interface:

```
public interface IShoppingCartStore
{
    Task<ShoppingCart> Get(int userId);
    Task Save(ShoppingCart shoppingCart);
}
```

Now it's time to look at the implementation of the IShoppingCartStore interface. First, let's consider the code for reading a shopping cart from the database.

Listing 5.1   Reading shopping carts with Dapper

```
namespace ShoppingCart.ShoppingCart
{
    using System.Threading.Tasks;
    using System.Data.SqlClient;
    using Dapper;
                                                      Connection
                                                      string to the
    public class ShoppingCartStore : IShoppingCartStore   ShoppingCart
    {                                                      database
        private string connectionString =          ⟵
@"Data Source=.\SQLEXPRESS;Initial Catalog=ShoppingCart;
Integrated Security=True";

        private const string readItemsSql =        ⟵   Dapper works with SQL, so you
@"select * from ShoppingCart, ShoppingCartItems         have SQL in the C# code.
where ShoppingCartItems.ShoppingCartId = ID
and ShoppingCart.UserId=@UserId";
```

```
public async Task<ShoppingCart> Get(int userId)
{
  using (var conn = new SqlConnection(connectionString))
  {
    var items = await
      conn.QueryAsync<ShoppingCartItem>(
        readItemsSql,
        new { UserId = userId });
    return new ShoppingCart(userId, items);
  }
}
```

Opens a connection to the ShoppingCart database

Uses a Dapper extension method to execute a SQL query and map the results back to an IEnumerable of ShoppingCartItem objects

Dapper is a simple tool that provides some convenient extension methods on IDbConnection to make working with SQL in C# easier. It also provides some basic mapping capabilities. For instance, in listing 5.1, Dapper maps the rows returned by the SQL query to an IEnumerable<ShoppingCartItem> because the column names in the database are equal to the property names in ShoppingCartItem.

Dapper doesn't try to hide the fact that you're working with SQL, so you see SQL strings in the code. This may feel like a throwback to the earliest days of .NET. I find that as long as I'm working with a simple database schema—as I usually am in microservices—the SQL strings in C# code aren't a problem.

Writing a shopping cart to the database is also done through Dapper. The implementation is the following method in ShoppingCartStore.

Listing 5.2 Writing shopping carts to the database

```
    private const string deleteAllForShoppingCartSql=
@"delete item from ShoppingCartItems item
inner join ShoppingCart cart on item.ShoppingCartId = cart.ID
and cart.UserId=@UserId";

    private const string addAllForShoppingCartSql=
@"insert into ShoppingCartItems
(ShoppingCartId, ProductCatalogId, ProductName,
ProductDescription, Amount, Currency)
values
(@ShoppingCartId, @ProductCatalogId, @ProductName,v
@ProductDescription, @Amount, @Currency)";

    public async Task Save(ShoppingCart shoppingCart)
    {
      using (var conn = new SqlConnection(connectionString))
      using (var tx = conn.BeginTransaction())
      {
        await conn.ExecuteAsync(
          deleteAllForShoppingCartSql,
          new { UserId = shoppingCart.UserId },
```

Deletes all preexisting shopping cart items

```
              tx).ConfigureAwait(false);
          await conn.ExecuteAsync(
              addAllForShoppingCartSql,
              shoppingCart.Items,
              tx).ConfigureAwait(false);
      }
  }
```

⟵ **Adds the current shopping cart items**

That concludes the implementation that stores shopping cart information in the Shopping Cart microservice. It's similar to storing data in a more traditional setting—like a monolith or traditional SOA service—except that the narrow scope of a microservice means the model is often so simple that little-to-no mapping between C# code and a database schema is needed.

5.3.2 *Storing events raised by a microservice*

This section looks at storing the events raised by a microservice. During command processing, a microservice can decide to raise events. Figure 5.7 shows the standard set of components in a microservice: the domain model raises the events. It typically does so when there's a change or a set of changes to the state of the data for which the microservice is responsible.

The events should reflect a change to the state of the data owned by the microservice. The events should also make sense in terms of the capability implemented by the microservice. For example, in a Shopping Cart microservice, when a user has added an item to their shopping cart, the event raised is `ItemAddedToShoppingCart`, not `RowAddedToShoppingCartTable`. The difference is that the first signifies an event of significance to the system—a user did something that's interesting in terms of the business—whereas the latter would report on a technical detail—a piece of software did something because a programmer decided to implement it that way. The events should be of

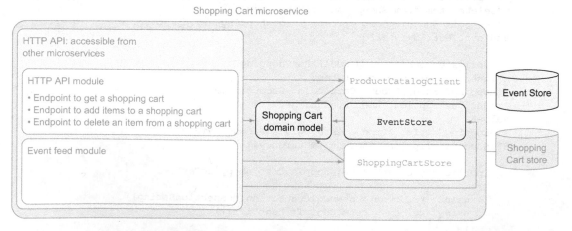

Figure 5.7   The components in the Shopping Cart microservice involved in raising and saving events are the Shopping Cart domain model, the `EventStore` component, and the Event Store database.

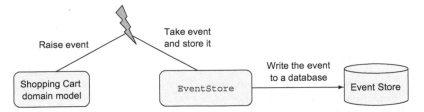

Figure 5.8 When the domain model raises an event, the `EventStore` component code must write it to the Event Store database.

significance at the level of abstraction of the capability implemented by the microservice, and they will often cover several updates to the underlying database. The events should correspond to business-level transactions, not to database transactions.

Whenever the domain logic in a microservice raises an event, it's stored to the event store in the microservice. In figure 5.8, this is done through the `EventStore` component, which is responsible for talking to the database where the events are stored.

The following two sections show two implementations of an `EventStore` component. The first stores the events by hand to a table in a SQL database, and the second uses the open source Event Store database.

STORING EVENTS BY HAND

Here, you'll build an implementation of the `EventStore` component in the Shopping Cart microservice that stores events to a table in SQL Server. The `EventStore` component is responsible for both writing events to and reading them from that database.

> **NOTE** This by-hand implementation demonstrates exactly what it means to store events. It demystifies the notion of an event store, but it isn't a production-ready implementation.

The following steps are involved in implementing the `EventStore` component:

1. Add an `EventStore` table to the `ShoppingCart` database. This table will contain a row for every event raised by the domain model.
2. Use Dapper to implement the writing part of the `EventStore` component.
3. Use Dapper to implement the reading part of the `EventStore` component.

Before we dive into implementing the `EventStore` component, here's a reminder of what the `Event` type in Shopping Cart looks like:

```
public struct Event
{
  public long SequenceNumber { get; }
  public DateTimeOffset OccurredAt { get; }
  public string Name { get; }
  public object Content { get; }
```

```
public Event(
  long sequenceNumber,
  DateTimeOffset occurredAt,
  string name,
  object content)
{
  this.SequenceNumber = sequenceNumber;
  this.OccurredAt = occurredAt;
  this.Name = name;
  this.Content = content;
}
}
```

It's events of this type that you'll store in the event store database. The first step is to go into the ShoppingCart database and add a table like the one shown in figure 5.9. The database script in Chapter05\ShoppingCart\src\database-scripts\create-shopping-cart-db.sql in the code download creates this table, along with the other two tables in the ShoppingCart database.

EventStore

Column Name	Data Type	Allow Nulls
🔑 ID	int	☐
Name	nvarchar(100)	☐
OccurredAt	datetimeoffset(7)	☐
[Content]	nvarchar(MAX)	☐
		☐

Figure 5.9 The EventStore table has four columns for these categories: event ID, event name, the time the event occurred, and the contents of the event.

Next, add a file named EventStore.cs to Shopping Cart, and add to it the following code for writing events.

Listing 5.3   Raising an event, which amounts to storing it

```
namespace ShoppingCart.EventFeed
{
  using System;
  using System.Threading.Tasks;
  using System.Collections.Generic;
  using System.Data.SqlClient;
  using System.Linq;
  using Dapper;
  using Newtonsoft.Json;
```

```
public interface IEventStore
{
  Task<IEnumerable<Event>> GetEvents(long firstEventSequenceNumber,
    long lastEventSequenceNumber);
  Task Raise(string eventName, object content);
}

public class EventStore : IEventStore
{
  private string connectionString =
    @"Data Source=.\SQLEXPRESS;Initial Catalog=ShoppingCart;Integrated
    ➥ Security=True";

  private const string writeEventSql =
    @"insert into EventStore(Name, OccurredAt, Content) values
    ➥ (@Name, @OccurredAt, @Content)";
  public Task Raise(string eventName, object content)
  {
    var jsonContent = JsonConvert.SerializeObject(content);
    using (var conn = new SqlConnection(connectionString))
    {
      return
        conn.ExecuteAsync(               ◁─── Uses Dapper to execute a
          writeEventSql,                      simple SQL insert statement
          new
          {
            Name = eventName,
            OccurredAt = DateTimeOffset.Now,
            Content = jsonContent
          });
    }
  }
}
}
```

This code doesn't compile yet, because the IEventStore interface has another method: one for reading events. That side is implemented as shown next.

NOTE Storing events essentially amounts to storing a JSON serialization of the content of the event in a row in EventTable along with the ID of the event, the name of the event, and the time at which the event was raised. The concept of storing events and publishing them through an event feed may be new, but the implementation is pretty simple.

Listing 5.4 EventStore method for reading events

```
private const string readEventsSql =
  @"select * from EventStore where ID >= @Start and ID <= @End";

public async Task<IEnumerable<Event>> GetEvents(
  long firstEventSequenceNumber,
```

```
    long lastEventSequenceNumber)
{
    using (var conn = new SqlConnection(connectionString))
    {
      return (await conn.QueryAsync<dynamic>(
        readEventsSql,
        new
        {
          Start = firstEventSequenceNumber,
          End = lastEventSequenceNumber
        }).ConfigureAwait(false))
        .Select(row =>
        {
          var content = JsonConvert.DeserializeObject(row.Content);
          return new Event(row.ID, row.OccurredAt, row.Name, content);
        });
    }
}
```

Reads EventStore table rows between start and end

Maps EventStore table rows to Event objects

That's all you need to implement a basic event store. The Shopping Cart microservice can now raise events in the domain model and rely on the EventStore component to write them to the EventStore table in the ShoppingCart database. Furthermore, Shopping Cart has an event feed that you implemented back in chapter 2, which now uses the EventStore component to read events from the database. It will send them to event subscribers when they poll the feed.

As noted earlier, this event store implementation isn't ready for production use. For instance, it will run into lock-contention problems as soon as the microservice starts raising events from several concurrent threads. These problems will only get worse when you begin scaling the microservice out to several servers that potentially have multiple threads raising events at the same time. This example does, however, show what it means to store events.

STORING EVENTS USING THE EVENT STORE DATABASE SYSTEM

You'll now implement another version of the EventStore component in the Shopping Cart microservice, this time using the open source Event Store database. The advantage of using Event Store over storing events in SQL Server is that its API is geared specifically toward storing events, reading events, and subscribing to new events. Event Store is an open source, mature, well-tested event store implementation that can scale and run stably under load. Furthermore, it comes with some nice added features out the box, such as a web interface for inspecting events and Atom event feeds. SQL Server is, of course, also mature, well-tested, scalable, and stable, but it isn't specifically geared toward storing events.

NOTE This implementation uses an existing, well-tested, scalable, reliable implementation of an event store. It's a production-ready implementation.

WARNING At the time of writing, the C# client library for communicating with Event Store hasn't been ported to .NET Core. Therefore, code in this section needs to run on the full .NET Framework and therefore on Windows.

You'll implement this version with the following steps. When you're finished, you'll have a fully working implementation of the `EventStore` component in the Shopping Cart microservice based on the Event Store database:

1 Install the Event Store database.
2 Write events to Event Store via the `EventStore` component.
3 Read events from Event Store via the `EventStore` component.

You can download Event Store for various platforms from http://getevent-store.com/downloads. The downloads are zip files containing the Event Store database. Download and unzip the download for your platform, and you'll have Event Store on your machine.

You can now open a shell and go to the folder where you unzipped the Event Store download. Run this command to start Event Store:

```
PS> ./EventStore.ClusterNode --db ./db --log ./logs
```

You can check whether the Event Store database is running by going to http://127.0.0.1:2113/. You should see a login prompt that lets you log in with the user name `admin` and the password `changeit`.

In order to use the Event Store database from the Shopping Cart microservice code, you first need to add the `EventStore.Client` NuGet package to the project. With that installed, you can implement the `EventStore` component against the Event Store database. The following listing shows the code for writing events.

Listing 5.5 Storing events to the Event Store database

```
namespace ShoppingCart.EventFeed
{
  using System;
  using System.Collections.Generic;
  using System.Linq;
  using System.Text;
  using System.Threading.Tasks;
  using global::EventStore.ClientAPI;
  using Newtonsoft.Json;

  public class EventStore : IEventStore
  {
    private const string connectionString =
      "discover://http://127.0.0.1:2113/";          Creates a connection
    private IEventStoreConnection connection =    ◁─┘ to EventStore
      EventStoreConnection.Create(connectionString);

    public async Task Raise(string eventName, object content)
```

```
    {
      await connection.ConnectAsync().ConfigureAwait(false);        ◄──┐ Opens the
      var contentJson = JsonConvert.SerializeObject(content);            connection to
      var metaDataJson =                                                 EventStore
        JsonConvert.SerializeObject(new EventMetadata        ◄───┐
        {                                                       Maps OccurredAt and
          OccurredAt = DateTimeOffset.Now,                      EventName to metadata to be
          EventName = eventName                                 stored along with the event
        });

      var eventData = new EventData(              ◄───┐ EventData is EventStore's
        Guid.NewGuid(),                                representation of an event.
        "ShoppingCartEvent",
        isJson: true,
        data: Encoding.UTF8.GetBytes(contentJson),
        metadata: Encoding.UTF8.GetBytes(metaDataJson)
      );

      await
        connection.AppendToStreamAsync(
          "ShoppingCart",                         ◄──┐ Writes the event
          ExpectedVersion.Any,                         to EventStore
           eventData);
    }

    private class EventMetadata
    {
      public DateTimeOffset OccurredAt { get; set; }
      public string EventName { get; set; }
    }
  }
}
```

This code maps the Shopping Cart microservice's own `Event` type to the Event Store database's `EventData` type, and then stores that to the Event Store database. The implementation for reading events back from the Event Store database is shown next.

Listing 5.6   Reading events from the Event Store database

```
public async Task<IEnumerable<Event>>
  GetEvents(long firstEventSequenceNumber, long lastEventSequenceNumber)
{
  await connection.ConnectAsync().ConfigureAwait(false);

  var result = await connection.ReadStreamEventsForwardAsync(        ◄───┐
    "ShoppingCart",
    start:(int) firstEventSequenceNumber,
    count: (int) (lastEventSequenceNumber - firstEventSequenceNumber),
    resolveLinkTos: false).ConfigureAwait(false);
                                                      Reads events from
  return                                              the Event Store
```

```
        result.Events
          .Select(ev =>
            new
            {
              Content = JsonConvert.DeserializeObject(
                Encoding.UTF8.GetString(ev.Event.Data)),
              Metadata = JsonConvert.DeserializeObject<EventMetadata>(
                Encoding.UTF8.GetString(ev.Event.Data))
            })
          .Select((ev, i) =>
            new Event(
              i + firstEventSequenceNumber,
              ev.Metadata.OccurredAt,
              ev.Metadata.EventName,
              ev.Content));
    }
```

> **Accesses the events on the result from the Event Store**

> **Deserializes the content part of each event**

> **Deserializes the metadata part of each event**

> **Maps to events from Event Store Event objects**

This code reads the events from Event Store, deserializes the content and metadata parts of the events, and then maps them back to the Shopping Cart Microservice's own Event type.

This completes the implementation of the `EventStore` component based on the Event Store database. Let's now look at using caching.

5.3.3 *Setting cache headers in Nancy responses*

Let's consider the microservices in figure 5.2 again. The Shopping Cart microservice uses product information that it gets by querying the Product Catalog microservice; you implemented the Shopping Catalog microservice part of that collaboration in chapter 2. Here, you'll first set cache headers in the code implementing the endpoint in Product Catalog. Then, you'll rewrite the code in Shopping Cart that calls Product Catalog to read and use the cache header.

Assume that the /products endpoint in the Product Catalog microservice is implemented in a Nancy module called `ProductsModule`. You'll take a comma-separated list of product IDs as a query parameter. The endpoint returns the product information for each of the products identified by that list of product IDs. The implementation is similar to the Nancy modules you've already seen in this book. The new part is that you'll add a `cache-control` header to the response that allows clients to cache the response for 24 hours.

Listing 5.7   Adding cache headers to the product list

```
namespace ProductCatalog
{
  using System;
  using System.Collections.Generic;
  using System.Linq;
  using Nancy;

  public class ProductsModule : NancyModule
```

```
  {
    public ProductsModule(ProductStore productStore) : base("/products")
    {
      Get("", _ =>
      {
        string productIdsString = this.Request.Query.productIds;
        var productIds = ParseProductIdsFromQueryString(productIdsString);
        var products = productStore.GetProductsByIds(productIds);

        return
          this
          .Negotiate
          .WithModel(products)
          .WithHeader("cache-control", "max-age:86400");
      });
    }

    private IEnumerable<int>
      ParseProductIdsFromQueryString(string productIdsString)
    {
      ...
    }
  }
}
```

> Adds a cache-control header, with max-age in seconds

This implementation adds a cache-control header to the response that looks like this:

```
cache-control: max-age:86400
```

The header tells callers that the response may be cached for as long as indicated by max-value, which is given in seconds. In this case, callers may cache the response for 86,400 seconds (24 hours).

5.3.4 Reading and using cache headers

In chapter 2, you saw code make calls to the /products endpoint from the Shopping Cart microservice. That code is as follows; it's part of the ProductCatalogClient class.

> Listing 5.8 Calling the Product Catalog microservice

```
private static async Task<HttpResponseMessage>
  RequestProductFromProductCatalogue(int[] productCatalogueIds)
{
  var productsResource = string.Format(
    getProductPathTemplate, string.Join(",", productCatalogueIds));
  using (var httpClient = new HttpClient())
  {
    httpClient.BaseAddress = new Uri(productCatalogueBaseUrl);
    return await
      httpClient.GetAsync(productsResource).ConfigureAwait(false);
  }
}
```

With this code, an HTTP request is made every time Shopping Cart needs product information, regardless of any cache headers. This is inefficient in cases where Shopping Cart needs information about the same products several times within 24 hours, because that's the `max-age` value set in the responses from the Product Catalog microservice. Such cases will occur every time a user adds to their shopping cart an item that another user has added to their shopping cart within the preceding 24 hours. That's likely to happen often.

Let's extend the code making the call to the /products endpoint in Product Catalog to take cache headers into account. Add a dependency to `ProductCatalogClient` on a cache that implements an `ICache` interface:

```
private ICache cache;

public ProductCatalogClient(ICache cache)
{
  this.cache = cache;
}
```

As you'll recall, Nancy handles dependency injection for you, so as long as there's an implementation of the `ICache` interface in the solution, Nancy will inject it. Here, I'll only show the interface, but in the code download, you can find a simple static cache implementing the interface. The interface is straightforward and has two methods:

```
public interface ICache
{
  void Add(string key, object value, TimeSpan ttl);
  object Get(string key);
}
```

"ttl" means time to live.

You'll use the `cache` variable on `ProductCatalogClient` to check whether there's a valid object in the cache before making an HTTP request.

Listing 5.9 Making requests when there's no valid response in the cache

Tries to retrieve a valid response from the cache

```
private async Task<HttpResponseMessage>
   RequestProductFromProductCatalogue(int[] productCatalogueIds)
{
  var productsResource = string.Format(
    getProductPathTemplate, string.Join(",", productCatalogueIds));
  var response = this.cache.Get(productsResource) as HttpResponseMessage;
  if (response == null)
  {
    using (var httpClient = new HttpClient())
    {
      httpClient.BaseAddress = new Uri(productCatalogueBaseUrl);
      response = await
        httpClient.GetAsync(productsResource).ConfigureAwait(false);
```

Only makes the HTTP request if there's no response in the cache

```
        AddToCache(productsResource, response);
    }
}
return response;                                              Reads the cache-control
}                                                             header from the response

private void AddToCache(string resource, HttpResponseMessage response)
{
  var cacheHeader = response
    .Headers
    .FirstOrDefault(h => h.Key == "cache-control");           Parses the cache-control
  if (string.IsNullOrEmpty(cacheHeader.Key))                  value and extracts max-
    return;                                                   age from it
  var maxAge =
    CacheControlHeaderValue.Parse(cacheHeader.Value.ToString())
      .MaxAge;
  if (maxAge.HasValue)
    this.cache.Add(key: resource, value: response, ttl: maxAge.Value);
}
```

Adds the response to the cache if
it has a max-age value

With this code in place in the Shopping Cart microservice, the responses from the
Product Catalog microservice will be used for as long as the max-age value in the
cache-control header allows (24 hours, in this example).

5.4   Summary

- A microservice stores and owns all the data that belongs to the capability the
  microservice implements.
- A microservice is the authoritative source for the data it owns.
- A microservice stores its data in its own dedicated database.
- A microservice will often also cache data owned by other microservices for sev-
  eral reasons:
  - To reduce coupling to other microservices. This makes the overall system
    more stable.
  - To speed up processing by avoiding making remote calls.
  - To build up its own custom representations—known as read models—of data
    owned by another microservice to make its code simpler.
  - To build read models based on events from other microservices to avoid que-
    rying the other microservices, thus using an event-based collaboration style
    instead of a query-based one. Remember from chapter 4 that event-based
    collaboration is preferable because of the reduced coupling.
- Which database or databases a microservice uses is a design decision particular
  to that microservice. Different microservices can use different databases.
- Storing the data owned by a microservice is similar to storing data in other
  kinds of systems.

- You can use Dapper to read data from and write data to a SQL database.
- Storing events is essentially a matter of storing a serialized event to a database.
- A simple version of an event store involves storing events to a table in a SQL database.
- You can also implement an event store by storing events to the open source Event Store database, which is specifically designed to store events.

Designing for robustness

This chapter introduces strategies for making a system of microservices robust in the face of failures. In general, whenever one microservice communicates with another microservice, the communication may fail. In this chapter, you'll learn about and implement some patterns for dealing with such failures. The strategies are fairly simple, yet they'll make the overall system much more robust.

Failures and errors

I'll distinguish between the terms *failure* and *error*. A *failure* happens when something goes wrong in the system and the issue is caused by something outside the system. Some typical sources of failures are as follows:

- Lost network packets cause communication to fail.
- Lost connections cause communication to fail.
- Hardware failures cause microservices to fail.

> **(continued)**
> An *error* happens when the system can't serve its users properly. Some typical examples of errors are these:
>
> - A user sees an error page.
> - The system hangs and never responds to a user action.
> - The system gives back the wrong response to a user action.
>
> Errors often stem from failures. On the other hand, failures only become errors if the software can't cope properly with failures. It follows that a perfect system would see failures, but no errors. Unfortunately, our systems aren't perfect, and we may as well accept that errors will occur.

6.1 Expect failures

When working with any nontrivial software system, you must expect failures to occur. Hardware can fail. Software may fail due to, for instance, unforeseen usage or corrupt data. A distinguishing factor of a microservice system is that there's a lot of communication between microservices. Figure 6.1 repeats the diagram from chapter 1 that shows the communication resulting from a user adding an item to a shopping cart. You see that just one user action results in quite a bit of communication—and a real system will likely have many concurrent users all performing many actions, and thus lots of communication going on. You must expect communication to fail from time to time. Communication between two microservices may not fail often, but looking at a microservice system as a whole, communication failures are likely to occur often due to the amount of communication.

Because you have to expect that some of the communication in your microservice system will fail, you should design your microservices to be able to cope with those failures. As discussed in chapter 4, you can divide the collaborations between microservices into three categories: query-, command-, and event-based collaborations. When a communication fails, the impact depends on the type of collaboration and the way the microservices cope with it:

- *Query-based collaboration*—When a query fails, the caller doesn't get the information it needs. If the caller copes well with that, the system keeps working, but with degraded functionality. If the caller doesn't cope well, the result could be an error.
- *Command-based collaboration*—When sending a command fails, the sender can't know whether the receiver got the command. Again, depending on how the sender copes, this could result in an error, or it could result in degraded functionality.
- *Event-based collaboration*—When a subscriber polls an event feed, but the call fails, the impact is limited. The subscriber will poll the event feed again later and, assuming the event feed is up again, receive the events at that time. In other words, the subscriber will still get all events, but some of them will be delayed. This shouldn't be a problem for an event-based collaboration, because it's asynchronous anyway.

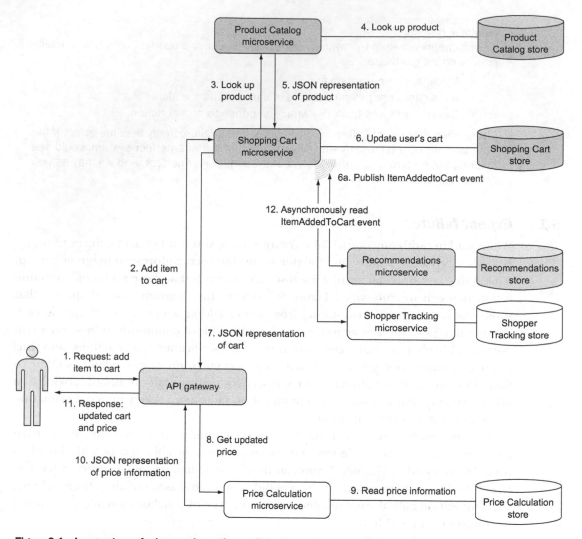

Figure 6.1 In a system of microservices, there will be many communication paths.

The following subsection discusses some important ways to prepare for handling failure well.

6.1.1 *Keeping good logs*

Once you accept that failures are bound to happen and that some of them may result not just in a degraded end user experience but also in errors, you must make sure you're able to understand what went wrong when an error occurs. That means you need good logs that allow you to trace what happened in the system and led to an error situation. "What happened" will often span several microservices, which is why you should consider introducing a central Log microservice, as shown in figure 6.2; all

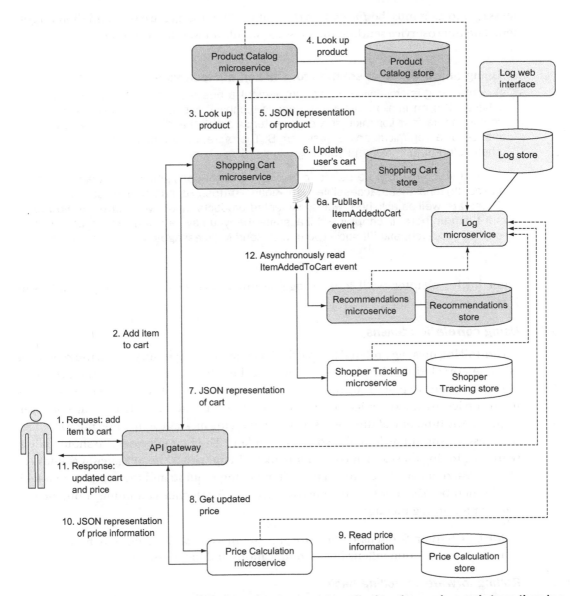

Figure 6.2 A central Log microservice receives log messages from all other microservices and stores them in a database or a search engine. The log data is accessible through a web interface. The dotted arrows shows microservices sending log messages to the central Log microservice.

the other microservices send log messages to it, and you can inspect and search the logs when you need to.

The Log microservice is a central component that all other microservices use. You need to make certain that a failure in Log doesn't bring down the whole system by causing all other microservice to fail if they can't log messages. Therefore, sending log messages to Log must be *fire and forget*—that is, the messages are sent and then forgotten. The microservice sending the message shouldn't wait for a response.

Using an off-the-shelf solution for the Log microservice

A central Log microservice doesn't implement a business capability of a particular system. It's an implementation of generic technical capability. In other words, the requirements for a Log microservice in system A aren't that different from the requirements for a Log microservice in system B. Therefore, I recommend using an off-the-shelf solution to implement your Log microservice.

For instance, logs can be stored in Elasticsearch (https://github.com/elastic/elasticsearch) and made accessible with Kibana (https://github.com/elastic/kibana). These are well-established, well-documented products, and I won't dive into how to set them up here. In chapter 9, I'll assume that you have a Log microservice based on Elasticsearch, and I'll show you how to send log messages to it.

Later in this chapter, we'll look at logging unhandled errors by adding handlers to Nancy's error pipeline.

6.1.2 Using correlation tokens

To find all log messages related to a particular action in the system, you can use *correlation tokens*. A correlation token is an identifier attached, for example, to a request from an end user when it comes into the system. The correlation token is passed along from microservice to microservice in any communication that stems from that end user request. Any time one of the microservices sends a log message to the Log microservice, the message should include the correlation token. The Log microservice should allow searching for log messages by correlation token. In figure 6.2, the API gateway would create and assign a correlation token to each incoming request; and the correlation token would then be passed with every microservice-to-microservice communication, including events and log messages.

> **NOTE** Chapter 9 discusses how to implement request logging and how to include correlation tokens in communications and log messages.

6.1.3 Rolling forward vs. rolling back

When errors happen in production, you're faced with the question of how to fix them. In many traditional systems, if errors begin to occur shortly after deployment, the default response is to roll back to the previous version of the system. In a microservice system, the default can be different. As discussed in chapter 1, microservices lend themselves to continuous delivery. With continuous delivery, microservices are deployed frequently, and each deployment should be both fast and easy to perform. Furthermore, microservices are sufficiently small and simple that many bug fixes are also easy. This opens the possibility of *rolling forward* rather than rolling backward.

Why would you want to default to rolling forward? In some situations, rolling backward is complicated—in particular, when database changes are involved. When a new version that changes the database is deployed, the microservice begins to produce data that fits in the updated database. Once that data is in the database, it has to stay there, which may not be compatible with rolling back to an earlier version. In such a case, rolling forward may be easier.

6.1.4 Don't propagate failures

Sometimes, things happen around a microservice that may disturb its normal operation. We say that the microservice is *under stress* in such situations. There are many sources of stress, including the following:

- One of the machines in the cluster on which the microservice's data store runs has crashed.
- The microservice has lost network connectivity to one of its collaborators.
- The microservice is receiving unusually high amounts of traffic.
- One of its collaborators is down.

In all these situations, the microservice under stress can't continue to operate the way it normally does. That doesn't mean it's down, but it must cope with the situation.

When one microservice fails, its collaborators are put under stress. That means the collaborators are also at risk of failing. While the microservice is failing, its collaborators can't query, send commands, or poll events from the failing microservice. As illustrated in figure 6.3, if the collaborators fail, even more microservices become at risk of failing: the failure begins to propagate through the system of microservices. Such a situation can quickly escalate from one microservice failing to many microservices failing.

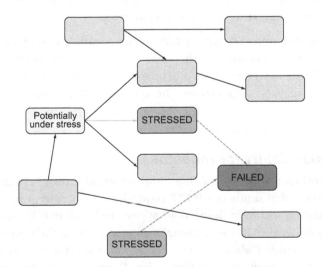

Figure 6.3 If the microservice marked FAILED is failing, so is communication with it. That means the microservices at the other end of those communications are under stress. If the stressed microservices fail due to the stress, the microservices communicating with them are put under stress. In that situation, the failure in one failed microservice can propagate to several other microservices.

Here are some examples of how you can stop failures from propagating:

- When one microservice tries to send a command to another microservice that happens to be failing at the time, that request will fail. If the sender fails too, you get the situation illustrated in figure 6.3, with failures propagating throughout the system. To stop the propagation, the sender can act as if the command succeeded, but actually store the command in a list of failed commands. The sending microservice can periodically go through the list of failed commands and try to send them again. This isn't possible in all situations, because the command may need to be handled immediately; but when this approach is feasible, it stops the failure in one microservice from propagating. This approach can be combined with a circuit, which we'll talk about later in the chapter.

- When one microservice queries another that's failing, the caller can use a cached response. In chapter 5, you saw how to cache query responses and how to respect the cache header set by the microservice being queried. If the caller has a stale response in the cache, but a query for a fresh response fails, it may decide to use the stale response anyway. Again, this isn't possible in all situations, but when it is, the failure won't propagate.

- An API gateway that's stressed because of high amounts of traffic from a certain client can throttle that client by not responding to more than a certain number of requests per second from the client. Note that the client may be sending an unusually high number of requests because it's failing internally. When throttled, the client will get a degraded experience but will still receive some responses. Without the throttling, the API gateway may become slow for all clients or fail completely. Moreover, because the API gateway collaborates with other microservices, handling all the incoming requests would push the stress of those requests onto other microservices, too. Again, throttling stops the failure in the client from propagating to other microservices.

As you can see from these examples, stopping failure propagation comes in many shapes and sizes. The important takeaway is the idea of building into your systems safeguards that are specifically designed to stop propagation of the kinds of failures you anticipate. How that's realized depends on the specifics of the systems you're building. Building in safeguards may take some effort, but it's often well worth the effort because of the robustness they give the system as a whole.

6.2   *The client side's responsibility for robustness*

When two microservices collaborate, there's a client and server, as shown in figure 6.4. The client is the microservice that sends out HTTP requests, and the server microservice handles them. The request shown in figure 6.4 happens to fail; it may fail because the server fails, or it may fail because it doesn't reach the server. Once the request has failed, the server can't do anything about it. The server can't send a response to a failed request—the request is already gone at that point. Responsibility for handling

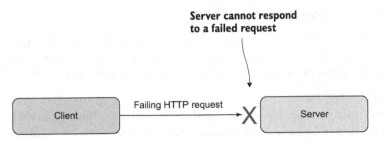

Figure 6.4   All collaborations between microservices have a client and a server. The client sends HTTP requests to the server. The client is responsible for handling failed requests.

requests therefore must fall on the client. In other words, the client is responsible making the collaboration robust in the face of failing requests.

When you look at an event-based collaboration, you see a degree of robustness in the face of failing requests built into the collaboration itself. Figure 6.5 shows an event subscriber in one microservice and an event feed in another microservice. As you saw in chapter 3, an event subscriber polls the event feed at intervals for new events. That way of collaborating means that if a request for new events fails, the event subscriber will ask for the same events the next time it polls for events. The subscriber can catch up to events in the event feed even though some requests fail, and thus the subscriber is robust with regard to failing requests for events.

You can see that with regard to command- and query-based collaboration, robustness doesn't come easily. The next two sections talk about patterns for building robustness into command- and query-based collaborations.

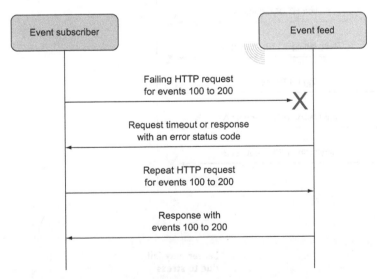

Figure 6.5   If a request for events from an event feed fails, the subscriber will request the same events the next time it polls for events.

6.2.1   *Robustness pattern: retry*

The client in a command- or query-based collaboration may choose to try again when a request fails. If the reason for the failed request is transient, the next attempt may be successful. Transient failures are common, and the reasons for them include the following:

- Network congestion.
- The server microservice being deployed. Depending on how the microservice is deployed, there may be a short window when the microservice is unavailable or slow—for example, while a load balancer is switched over to a new version. Even if the server is slow only during deployment, requests may fail due to timeouts.

Retrying is a double-edged sword. If the reason for the failures isn't transient, retrying requests won't help. On the contrary, retrying indiscriminately puts stress on the server, because it's getting not only its usual number of requests but also the retries (see figure 6.6). This may not seem like a big deal, but imagine a system that's already under high load. During normal operation, the client sends many requests to the server. If requests start failing and the client retries all of them, the client ends up sending more and more requests to the server. If the reason for the failing requests is that the server is already having trouble keeping up with the number of requests it receives, sending even more requests certainly isn't going to help.

Does this mean retrying is a bad pattern? No; it means you shouldn't continue retrying or retry too aggressively. The first thing to consider is how many times it

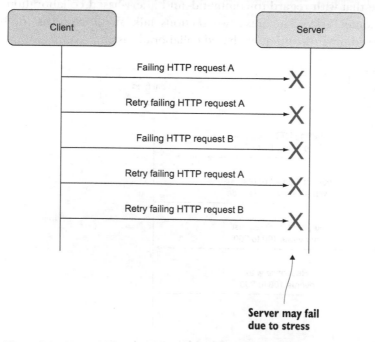

Figure 6.6   If a client keeps retrying a request that continues to fail at the server, the stress on the server will grow, and it may eventually fail completely.

makes sense to retry. If the request fails three times, is there any reason to believe it will succeed the fourth time? Second, you can use an exponential *backoff* between each retry. That is, instead of retrying after a constant amount of time (say, 100 ms), wait two or three times longer between each retry: maybe 100 ms before the first retry, 200 ms between the first and the second, and 400 ms between the second and third. These two simple additions mean the stress on the server builds up more slowly; you should always use them when you retry command or query requests. Later in this chapter, I'll show how the Polly library makes it easy to set up such retry strategies.

You may even want to consider making the interval between retries much longer. Instead of waiting a fraction of a second before retrying, you could wait a few minutes or even hours. Figure 6.7 shows a retry strategy in which the intervals are long and become exponentially longer. This type of retry doesn't place nearly as much stress on the server as the fast retries used in many software systems.

This approach clearly doesn't work for all situations. If a user is waiting for a response, it makes no sense to retry an hour later, because the user will have given up long before, so the software should also give up and give a degraded response sooner.

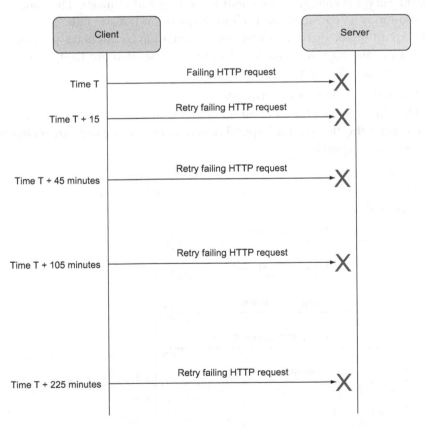

Figure 6.7 To avoid putting unnecessary stress on the server, the client can wait exponentially longer and longer between retries.

On the other hand, if the request is initiated based on something the system does on its own—for example, as part of handling an event—you can often wait a long time.

Next, we'll discuss another useful pattern for making collaborations robust: the circuit breaker pattern. Then we'll move on to code and implement both the fast-paced and slow-paced styles of retries.

6.2.2 *Robustness pattern: circuit breaker*

The circuit breaker pattern is a different take on dealing with failing requests. As you saw in the previous section, retrying failing requests can add to the problem by putting the server under stress; therefore, you must limit the number of retries. The circuit breaker pattern takes this line of thinking a step further: it assumes that if a number of different requests in a row fail, then the next request is also likely to fail.

Figure 6.8 illustrates this situation. The client has already made HTTP requests A, B, C, and D. Is it then likely that E will succeed? In many cases, no. The fact that a number of requests failed indicates that the problem isn't with the individual requests. Rather, it has to do with the communication—the client can't reach the server, the server is failing, or the client is sending bad requests. The issue with communication may be transient, but even so, request E often also fails.

The circuit breaker pattern addresses this situation by not making request E at all, but instead assuming it will fail. Not making requests that are likely to fail alleviates stress on both the client and the server:

- The server receives fewer requests.
- The client doesn't have to wait for requests to fail, but rather assumes they will, meaning the client doesn't spend resources on waiting and can get its own work done more quickly.

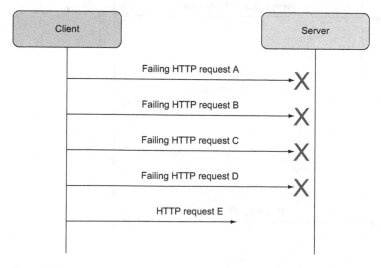

Figure 6.8 **If several requests in a row have failed, is the next one likely to fail? In many cases, yes.**

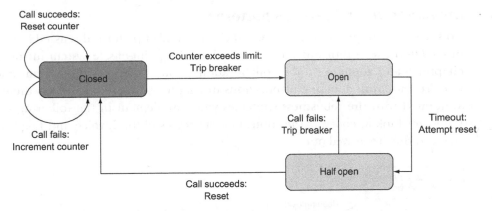

Figure 6.9 A circuit breaker is a state machine with three states. When the circuit breaker is closed, real HTTP requests are made. When the circuit breaker is open, no requests are made. A circuit breaker helps avoid making HTTP requests that are likely to fail.

A circuit breaker wraps HTTP requests in a state machine like the one shown in figure 6.9. When the microservice needs to make an HTTP request, it does so through the circuit breaker.

The circuit breaker state machine starts in the closed state and works as follows:

- While the circuit breaker is in the *closed state*, it makes a real HTTP request when asked to. If the HTTP request fails, the circuit breaker increments a counter. If the request succeeds, the circuit breaker resets the counter to zero. When and if that counter exceeds a preset limit—say, five failed requests in a row—the circuit breaker goes to the open state.

- While the circuit breaker is in the *open state*, it doesn't make any HTTP requests. Instead, it errors immediately. The circuit breaker stays in the open state for a preset period—say, 30 seconds—and then goes to the half-open state.

- While the circuit breaker is in the *half-open state*, it makes an HTTP request the first time it's asked to. After that one HTTP request, it goes to the closed state if the request succeeded, or the open state if it failed.

The result of these simple rules is a state machine that stops making HTTP requests when they're likely to fail anyway. Later in this chapter, I'll show you how to use Polly to create circuit breakers around HTTP requests.

> **TIP** Circuit breakers not only are useful for HTTP requests, but also can be used to add robustness around any operation that can fail.

For the remainder of the chapter, we'll get down to the code level and see how to implement retry strategies and circuit breakers using Polly and general error handling using Nancy's error pipelines.

6.3   *Implementing robustness patterns*

To see how to implement the retry and circuit breaker patterns discussed in the previous sections, let's turn our attention back to the point-of-sale system introduced in chapter 3 and zoom in on the collaborations around the Loyalty Program microservice. You identified these collaborations in chapter 4; figure 6.10 shows them again, annotated with the robustness strategies you'll implement in the following sections. We won't look at code for the robustness strategies of the Invoice and Log microservices, so they're grayed out.

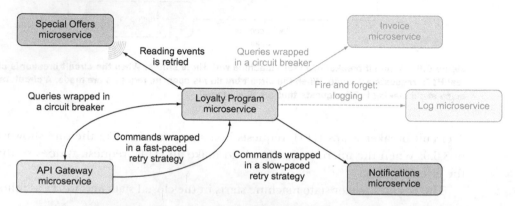

Figure 6.10   The Loyalty Program microservice collaborates with several other microservices. Each collaboration is annotated with a robustness strategy.

In the following sections, you'll do the following:

- Implement a fast-paced retry strategy in the API Gateway microservice for the commands it sends to the Loyalty Program microservice. The implementation is based on the Polly library.
- Implement a circuit breaker in the API Gateway microservice for the queries it makes to the Loyalty Program microservice. This implementation is also based on the Polly library.
- Implement a slow-paced retry strategy in the Loyalty Program microservice for the commands it sends to the Notifications microservice, based on the way the event subscription already works.
- Implement general exception handlers in the HTTP API in the Loyalty Program microservice using the error pipeline built into Nancy.

> ### Polly
> Polly is a convenient library for creating and using error-handling strategies. Creating a strategy with Polly is done in a declarative way via a fluent API. Once created, a strategy can be applied to any `Func` or `Action`—which essentially means you can apply the strategy to any code you want.

(continued)

Polly is a convenient library for creating and using error-handling strategies. Creating a strategy with Polly is done in a declarative way via a fluent API. Once created, a strategy can be applied to any `Func` or `Action`—which essentially means you can apply the strategy to any code you want.

The three steps to using Polly are as follows:

1 Decide which exceptions to handle, such as HttpException.
2 Decide which policy to use, such as a retry policy.
3 Apply the policy to a function.

The entry point to working with Polly is the `Policy` class:

```
var retryStrategy =
  Policy
    .Handle<HttpException>()        Step I: Decide which
    .Retry();                       exceptions to handle.

                                    Step 2: Decide
                                    which policy to use.

retryStrategy.Execute(() => DoHttpRequest());    Step 3: Use the strategy
                                                 to wrap a function call.
```

Polly comes with a number of built-in policies, including variations of retry strategies and various circuit breaker strategies.

The API Gateway microservice consists of the components shown in figure 6.11. In the next two sections, we'll zoom in on `LoyaltyProgramClient`.

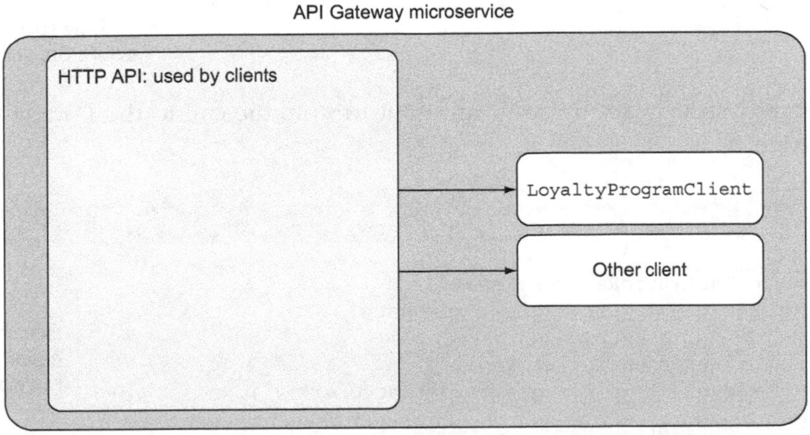

API Gateway microservice

Figure 6.11 The API Gateway microservice consists of the same standard set of components you've seen several times already.

6.3.1 Implementing a fast-paced retry strategy with Polly

As shown in figure 6.10, the API Gateway microservice sends commands to the Loyalty Program microservice. We'll only look at adding a retry strategy to the register-user command here, because the code for adding a retry strategy to the update-user command is essentially the same.

First, you need to add the Polly NuGet package to the API Gateway microservice. The code that sends the commands to the Loyalty Program microservice is in `Loyal-tyProgramClient`. You use Polly to set up a retry policy that uses an exponential back-off. Polly splits the setup of a policy from the execution of the policy: that is, Polly allows you to set up different policies—a retry policy, for instance—and then later execute a piece of code under the policy. In the case of a retry strategy, that means retrying the piece of code if it fails. The retry policy for the register-user command is set up as shown next.

Listing 6.1   Polly retry policy

```
using System;
using Polly;

public class LoyaltyProgramClient
{
  private static Policy exponentialRetryPolicy =
    Policy
      .Handle<Exception>()            ◁─── Handles all exceptions
      .WaitAndRetryAsync(
        3,
        attempt =>
          TimeSpan.FromMilliseconds(100 * Math.Pow(2, attempt)),
      );
}
```

Number of retries → (points to `3`)

Chooses an async policy because you'll use it with async code later (points to `.WaitAndRetryAsync(`)

Time span to wait before the next retry (points to `TimeSpan.FromMilliseconds(100 * Math.Pow(2, attempt)),`)

With the retry strategy set up, you can use it to wrap the call to the Loyalty Program microservice.

Listing 6.2   Using a Polly policy around an HTTP request

```
public async Task<HttpResponseMessage>
  RegisterUser(LoyaltyProgramUser newUser)
{
  return await exponentialRetryPolicy
    .ExecuteAsync(() => DoRegisterUser(newUser));
}

private async Task<HttpResponseMessage>
  DoRegisterUser(LoyaltyProgramUser newUser)
{
  using (var httpClient = new HttpClient())
```

Executes an Action with the retry policy (points to `.ExecuteAsync(() => DoRegisterUser(newUser));`)

```
  {
    httpClient.BaseAddress = new Uri($"http://{this.hostName}");
    var response = await
      httpClient.PostAsync("/users/",
        new StringContent(JsonConvert.SerializeObject(newUser),
        Encoding.UTF8,
        "application/json"));
    ThrowOnTransientFailure(response);
    return response;
  }
}
```

Makes the HTTP request → `httpClient.PostAsync("/users/",`

`ThrowOnTransientFailure(response);` ← **Throwing an exception tells the policy to retry.**

```
private static void ThrowOnTransientFailure(HttpResponseMessage response)
{
  if (((int) response.StatusCode) < 200 || ((int) response.StatusCode) > 499)
    throw new Exception(response.StatusCode.ToString());
}
```

That is how easy it is to set up retrying with Polly. Next, you'll use Polly to create a circuit breaker.

6.3.2 *Implementing a circuit breaker with Polly*

Now you'll add a circuit breaker to the API Gateway microservice's queries to the Loyalty Program microservice. This time, you'll use Polly's built-in support for circuit breaker policies.

Listing 6.3 Polly circuit breaker policy

```
private static Policy circuitBreaker =
  Policy
    .Handle<Exception>()
    .CircuitBreaker(5, TimeSpan.FromMinutes(3));
```

Sets the failure limit to 5 and the time-in-open-state limit to 3 minutes

Even though the circuit breaker pattern may seem more complicated than retrying, Polly makes it just as easy to set up a circuit breaker policy as a retry policy. Using a policy is the same no matter what the policy is, so wrapping queries to the Loyalty Program microservice in the circuit breaker policy is just like the code for wrapping register-user commands in the retry policy.

Listing 6.4 Wrapping a query in a circuit breaker

```
public async Task<HttpResponseMessage> QueryUser(int userId)
{
  return await circuitBreaker
    .ExecuteAsync(() => DoUserQuery(userId));
}

private async Task<HttpResponseMessage> DoUserQuery(int userId)
```

Uses the circuit breaker policy

```
{
  var userResource = $"/users/{userId}";
  using (var httpClient = new HttpClient())
  {
    httpClient.BaseAddress = new Uri($"http://{this.hostName}");
    var response = await httpClient.GetAsync(userResource);
    ThrowOnTransientFailure(response);          <---
    return response;
  }
}
```

> **Signals a failure to the circuit breaker by throwing an exception**

With these two policies in place, API Gateway takes responsibility for adding robustness to the collaboration with Loyalty Program. Next, we'll move on to the Loyalty Program microservice.

6.3.3   *Implementing a slow-paced retry strategy*

The Loyalty Program microservice subscribes to events from the Special Offers microservice. Based on the events, Loyalty Program sends commands to the Notifications microservice, asking it to notify users about new special offers. If sending a command to Notifications fails, you want to retry. Because sending out notifications isn't particularly time critical, you'll choose not to retry immediately; instead, you'll retry the next time the event subscriber would otherwise poll for new events. To do this, all you have to do is keep track of what the last successful event was.

Remember from chapter 4 that an event subscriber works by periodically waking up and polling the event feed for new events. On each such cycle, the next batch of events is read and handled. The next batch of events will begin one event after the last successfully handled event. This means all failed events are retried. It also means you may as well abort the rest of a batch as soon as one event fails—the rest will be retried later anyway. The method from chapter 4 that handled each cycle looked like this.

Listing 6.5   Single-event subscription cycle

```
private async Task SubscriptionCycleCallback()
{
  var response = await ReadEvents().ConfigureAwait(false);
  if (response.StatusCode == HttpStatusCode.OK)
    HandleEvents(
      await response.Content.ReadAsStringAsync().ConfigureAwait(false));
  this.timer.Start();
}
```

This method relies on other methods to read and handle events. Event reading in chapter 4 was as shown next.

Listing 6.6 Reading events from an event feed

```
private async Task<HttpResponseMessage> ReadEvents()
{
  using (var httpClient = new HttpClient())
  {
    httpClient.BaseAddress =
      new Uri($"http://{this.loyaltyProgramHost}");
    var resource =
      $"/events/?start={this.start}&end={this.start + this.chunkSize}";     <─┐
    var response = await
      httpClient
        .GetAsync(resource)
        .ConfigureAwait(false);
    PrettyPrintResponse(response);
    return response;
  }
}
```

**Holds the starting point
of a batch in memory**

And finally, the handling of events looked like this.

Listing 6.7 Handling a batch of events

**All events were assumed to be
successfully handled, and "start"
was updated for each one.**

```
private async Task HandleEvents(string content)
{
  var events = JsonConvert.DeserializeObject<IEnumerable<Event>>(content);
  foreach (var ev in events)
  {
    dynamic eventData = ev.Content;
    if (ShouldSendNotification(eventData))
      await SendNoitifcation(eventData).ConfigureAwait(false);
    this.start = ev.SequenceNumber + 1;                                    <─┐
  }
}

private bool ShouldSendNotification(dynamic eventData)
{
  // decide if notification should be sent based on business rules
}

private Task SendNotification(dynamic eventData)
{
  // use HttpClient to send command to notification microservice
}
```

To begin implementing the retry strategy, modify the reading of events to use a start
number read from the database.

Listing 6.8   Reading events starting from the stored start number

Reads the start number
from the database

```
private async Task<HttpResponseMessage> ReadEvents()
{
  var startNumber = await ReadStartNumber().ConfigureAwait(false);     ⟵
  using (var httpClient = new HttpClient())
  {
    httpClient.BaseAddress = new Uri($"http://{this.loyaltyProgramHost}");
    var resource =
      $"/events/?start={startNumber}&end={this.start + this.chunkSize}";     ⟵

    var response = await httpClient.GetAsync(resource).ConfigureAwait(false);
    PrettyPrintResponse(response);
    return response;                                   Uses startNumber when
  }                                           requesting an event from the feed
}


private async Task<long> ReadStartNumber()
{
  // Read start number from database
}
```

Next, modify the handling of events to abort when an event fails and to write the number of the last successfully handled event to the database.

Listing 6.9   Keeping track of which events have been handled

```
private async Task HandleEvents(string content)          Keeps track of events
{                                                        successfully handled
  var lastSucceededEvent = 0L;                    ⟵
  var events = JsonConvert.DeserializeObject<IEnumerable<Event>>(content);
  foreach (var ev in events)
  {
    dynamic eventData = ev.Content;                       Not all events
    if (ShouldSendNotification(eventData))               are assumed to be
    {                                                  handled successfully.
      var notificationSucceeded = await
        SendNoitifcation(eventData).ConfigureAwait(false);     ⟵
      if (!notificationSucceeded)
        return;                                        Updates to the last
    }                                             successfully handled event
    lastSucceededEvent = ev.SequenceNumber + 1;     ⟵
  }
  await WriteStartNumber(lastSucceededEvent).ConfigureAwait(false);     ⟵
}
                                                        Updates where the
                                                        next batch starts
private bool ShouldSendNotification(dynamic eventData)
{
  // decide if notification should be sent based on business rules
}
```

Aborts when
handling one
event fails

```
private Task<bool> SendNotification(dynamic eventData)
{
  // use HttpClient to send command to notification microservice
  // return true if the command succeeded, false otherwise
}

private async Task WriteStartNumber()
{
    // Write start number to database
}
```

As you can see, the changes necessary to introduce the slow-paced retry strategy aren't significant.

6.3.4 *Logging all unhandled exceptions*

Finally, we'll turn our attention to the HTTP API of the Loyalty Program microservice. As stated earlier, you want to keep good logs of everything that goes wrong in the system. That means you should log any unhandled exceptions thrown in the handlers for the endpoints in the microservices. You can uses Nancy's application-level error pipeline for this. The error pipeline allows you to add handlers that will be called every time a route handler in the microservice throws an unhandled exception. You add the handler to the error pipeline in the Nancy bootstrapper by overriding the `ApplicationStartup` method and accessing the error pipeline through the `IPipelines` interface.

You already wrote a Nancy bootstrapper for Loyalty Program in chapter 4. Now you'll extend it with the following code, which adds a handler to the error pipeline.

> **Listing 6.10 Registering a global error handler with Nancy**

```
namespace LoyaltyProgram
{
  using Nancy;
  using Nancy.Bootstrapper;
  using Nancy.TinyIoc;

  public class Bootstrapper : DefaultNancyBootstrapper
  {
    ...

    protected override void ApplicationStartup(
      TinyIoCContainer container,
      IPipelines pipelines)
    {
      pipelines.OnError += (ctx, ex) =>        ◁─┐ Adds a handler to
      {                                             the error pipeline
        Log("Unhandled", ex);
        return null;                           ◁─┐ Doesn't override the
      };                                            default response
    }
```

```
    private void Log(string message, Exception ex)
    {
        // send message and ex to central log store
        // in chapter 9 we will see how to do this
    }
  }
}
```

The handler added to the error pipeline returns null. It could also have returned a Nancy.Response object; Nancy would then have used that as the response to the client. When you return null, as shown here, you choose not to override the response. Therefore, the client gets a default 500 status code response.

The IPipelines interface also provides access to the Before pipeline and the After pipeline. You could add handlers to these pipelines in a similar fashion, and they would be called before and after any route handler is invoked, respectively.

Nancy also has Before, After, and OnError pipelines on NancyModule. These pipelines work the same way, except that they only apply to handlers in the module where they're set up.

This concludes the implementation of robustness measures in collaborations around the Loyalty Program microservice. With these fairly simple measures in place, the collaborations are likely to be a good deal more robust under production load.

6.4   *Summary*

- Due to the amount of communication between microservices, you must expect some communication to fail. It's vital for the robustness of the system that your microservices handle such failures gracefully.
- You should design robustness into your microservices such that failures don't propagate through the system and eventually become errors.
- The client side of a collaboration is responsible for making communication robust in the face of failures.
- You should have good logs that are easy to access and search through when you need to investigate production problems. A central Log microservice should receive all log messages and provide access to them.
- The most important strategies for making communications robust are the retry and circuit breaker patterns.
- Polly makes it easy to set up and use retry policies as well as circuit breakers.
- Nancy has application- and module-level error pipelines that allow you to react to unhandled exceptions. At minimum, you should write them to the central log.

Writing
tests for microservices

This chapter covers
- Writing good automated tests
- Understanding the test pyramid and how it applies to microservices
- Testing microservices from the outside
- Writing fast, in-process tests for endpoints
- Using Nancy.Testing for integration and unit tests

Up to this point, you've written a few microservices and set up collaborations between some of them. The implementations are fine, but you haven't written any tests for them. As you write more and more microservices, developing systems without good automated tests becomes unmanageable. In the first half of this chapter, I'll discuss what you need to test for each individual microservice. Then we'll dive into code, looking first at testing endpoints using the Nancy.Testing library, and then at testing a complete microservice as if you were sending it requests from another microservice.

155

7.1   What and how to test

In chapter 1, you saw three characteristics of a microservice that make it good for continuous delivery:

- *Individually deployable*—As soon as any small, safe change has been made to a microservice, the microservice can be deployed to production. But how do you know a change is safe? This is where testing and, particularly, test automation come into the picture. Several other activities, like code reviews, static code analysis, and designing public APIs for backward compatibility, also play into determining that a change is safe, but testing is where much of your confidence will come from.
- *Replaceable*—You should strive to be able to replace the implementation of a microservice with another functionally equivalent implementation within the normal pace of work. Again, tests play an important role, because a good set of tests lets you assess whether the new implementation really is equivalent to the old one.
- *Maintainable by a small team*—Microservices are sufficiently small and focused that a team can maintain several of them. This has the advantage that you can write tests that cover all parts of your microservices.

If you want to become confident about changes quickly and be able to replace a badly implemented microservice, testing has to be fast and repeatable. To make testing fast and repeatable, you must automate a significant part of it—and that's the focus of this chapter.

7.1.1   The test pyramid: what to test in a microservices system

The *test pyramid* shown in figure 7.1 is a tool you can use to guide which kinds of tests you should write and how many you should have of each kind. You can find variations of the test pyramid in different writings; all of them put tests on different levels, where the levels at the top of the pyramid are broad in scope and the tests at the bottom are narrow. The test pyramid illustrates that you should aim for having many narrowly focused tests (the ones at the wide bottom of the pyramid) and only a few broadly scoped tests (the ones at the narrow top).

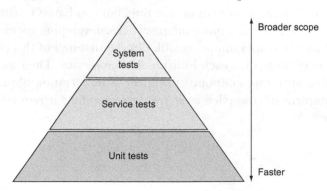

Figure 7.1   The test pyramid illustrates that you should have a few system-level tests, many service-level tests, and even more unit-level tests.

The version of the test pyramid that I use here has three levels:

- *System tests (top level)*—Tests that span the complete system of microservices and are usually implemented through the GUI.
- *Service tests (middle level)*—Tests that work against one, but only one, complete microservice.
- *Unit tests (bottom level)*—Tests that test one small piece of functionality in a microservice. Unit tests call code in the microservice under test in-process and usually involve only part of a microservice.

Note that when I use the term *unit test*, the word *unit* refers to a small piece of functionality. I define the scope of a unit test not in terms of any particular code construct, like a class or a method, but rather in terms of functionality. When we look at implementations of unit tests later, you'll see that unit tests can easily span all layers of a microservice: for example, from a Nancy module, through a domain object, down to a data access class.

Although the test pyramid tells you to have more tests as you move down the levels, exactly how many tests you should have on each level is situational. It depends on such factors as the size of the system, the complexity of the system, and the cost of failure.

7.1.2 *System-level tests: testing a complete microservice system end-to-end*

The tests at the top of the pyramid have a very broad scope and therefore cover a lot of code with just a few tests. Because they have such a broad scope, they're also imprecise. When a system-level test breaks, it isn't immediately clear where the problem lies. The test can potentially use the entire system, so the issue could be anywhere.

An example of a system-level test is one that uses the web UI of the point-of-sale system we talked about in earlier chapters to add a number of items to an invoice, apply a discount code, and pay using a test credit card. If that test passes, it gives you confidence that invoices are created, that discounts can be applied, and that you can receive credit card payments. During such a system test, you might assert that the amount due on the invoice is as expected. If that assertion fails, any number of things could have caused the problem: you might be using the wrong price for one or more items, you might have applied the discount incorrectly, or you might have misinterpreted the invoice data. In other words, such a failure could be caused by at least a handful of different microservices. To figure out which one is the culprit, you need to investigate.

The specific way a system-level test fails can give some hints as to where the problem lies, but there's usually a lot of code that could be at fault. From the system test alone, it won't even be clear which microservice caused the failure. On the other hand, when system-level tests pass, they give you a good deal of confidence.

The second downside to system-level tests is that they tend to be slow. This again is the flip side of them involving the complete system: real HTTP requests are made, things are written to real data stores, and real event feeds are polled.

Considering that system-level tests, when successful, can give you good confidence, but that they're both slow and imprecise, my advice is to *write system-level tests for the success path of the most important use cases.* This should give you coverage for the success paths of all the most important parts of the system. You can, optionally, supplement this with some tests for the most common and important failure scenarios. Exactly how many system tests this amounts to is, as mentioned earlier, entirely situational. This advice applies equally to microservices, traditional SOA, and monoliths. There's nothing microservice-specific about system-level tests. For this reason, I won't show implementations of any system-level tests in this chapter.

7.1.3 *Service-level tests: testing a microservice from outside its process*

The tests in the middle level of the test pyramid interact with one microservice as a whole and in isolation—the collaborators of the microservice under test are replaced with *microservice mocks.* Like system tests, these tests interact with the microservice under test from the outside. But unlike system-level tests, they interact directly with the public API of the microservice and make assertions about responses to the microservice as well as the interactions the microservice has with other microservices: for instance, about the commands the microservice under test sends to other microservices.

> **A microservice mock simulates a real microservice and records interactions**
>
> A *microservice mock* can be used in place of a real microservice in service-level tests. It implements the same endpoints as the real microservice, but instead of using real business logic to implement the endpoints, the mock has dumbed-down endpoint implementations; usually endpoints in a mock return hardcoded responses. Furthermore, a mock often records the requests made to the endpoints, so the test code can inspect the requests made during the test.
>
> This is similar to the mock objects widely used in tests for object-oriented code. But where mock objects replace a real object, a microservice mock replaces a real microservice.

Like system-level tests, service-level tests test scenarios rather than single requests. That is, they make a sequence of requests that together form a meaningful scenario. The requests made from the microservice under test to its mocked collaborators are real HTTP requests, and the responses are real HTTP responses.

For examples, recall the Loyalty Program microservice from the example point-of-sale system. In chapter 4, you saw that it collaborated with a number of other microservices, as shown in figure 7.2, using all three collaboration styles: events, queries, and commands.

To test Loyalty Program in isolation, you can create mock versions of its collaborators. As shown in figure 7.3, when Loyalty Program interacts with a mocked collaborator, it gets back a hardcoded response.

Figure 7.2   The Loyalty Program microservice collaborates with a number of other microservices through all three types of collaboration: events, queries, and commands.

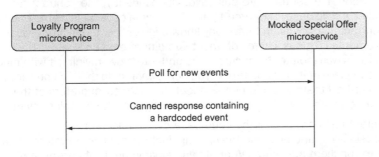

Figure 7.3   For service-level testing, the Loyalty Program microservice interacts with mocked versions of its collaborators. The mocked microservices respond to requests with hardcoded responses.

A service-level test for the Loyalty Program microservice could do the following:

- Send a command to create a user
- Wait for the Loyalty Program microservice to query a mock Special Offer microservice for events, and get back a hardcoded event about a new special offer
- Record any commands sent to the Notifications microservice, and assert that a command for a notification to the new user about the new special offer was sent

When a test like this passes, you can have confidence that important aspects of the Loyalty Program microservice work. When it fails, you know that the problem is within Loyalty Program itself.

Service-level tests are much more precise than system-level tests, because they cover only a single microservice: if such a test fails, the problem should lie within the microservice under test, assuming the test setup itself isn't buggy. Because microservices are small—they're replaceable, after all—knowing that a problem lies within a certain microservice is a lot more precise than what you get from system-level tests.

On the other hand, service-level tests are still slow, because they interact with the microservice under test over HTTP, because the microservice uses a real database, and because it interacts with its mocked collaborators over HTTP.

Contract tests

As you know by now, there's a lot of collaboration between microservices in a micro-services system. You implement the collaborations as requests from one microservice to another. If you aren't careful, changes in an endpoint can break the microservices that call that endpoint. This is where contract tests come into the picture.

When any two microservices in the system collaborate, the one making requests to the other has some expectations about how the other microservice will behave. That is, given a collaboration, the calling microservice expects the called microservice to implement a certain contract. A *contract test* is a test with the purpose of determining whether the called microservice implements the contract expected by the calling microservice.

Contract tests are written from the point of view of the caller and are there for the sake of the calling microservice: as long as the contract test passes, the assumptions the caller makes about the contract are still valid. Consequently, the contract tests are part of the caller's code base. They aren't part of the same code base as the endpoints they test. Contract tests shouldn't have any knowledge of how the microservices they test are implemented. This is where contract tests differ from service-level tests. With service-level tests, you isolate the microservice under test by providing it with mocked microservices in place of its collaborators. You don't want to do that for contract tests, because the contract tests shouldn't know about the other collaborators of the micro-service they test. In other words, contract tests run against the complete system.

Because contact tests are part of the code base of one microservice but test things in other microservices, and because they run against the complete system, it can be a good idea to run them against a QA or staging environment. Moreover, it's a good idea to have them run automatically every time the microservice under test is deployed. When a contract breaks, it's a strong indication that the collaboration between the microservice the contract test belongs to and the microservice under test is broken, too.

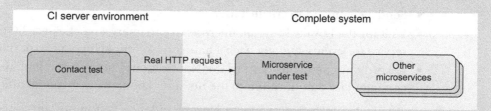

A contract test runs against the complete system. It may, for instance, run against a staging or QA environment, where the complete microservices system is deployed.

In terms of implementation, contract tests look a bit like the service-level tests you'll write later in this chapter. The difference is that contract tests are a slightly higher level in the test pyramid, between system-level tests and service-level tests. Contract tests don't set up mocked collaborators, whereas service-level tests do; but just like service-level tests, they work by making real HTTP requests to the microservice under test.

My recommendation regarding service-level tests is that you should write such tests for the success versions of all functionality the microservice under test offers. Such tests will naturally use all endpoints of the microservice as well as rely on any event subscriptions in the microservice. In other words, they will cover all success paths in the microservice. In general, I recommend writing service-level tests only for the most important failure scenarios. Again, the number of service-level tests needed and how many failure scenarios they should cover depends on the system and the cost of failure in that particular system.

7.1.4   *Unit-level tests: testing endpoints from within the process*

The tests at the bottom of the test pyramid also deal with a single microservice, but these tests don't work over HTTP and don't deal with the entire microservice. These unit tests interact with the parts of the microservice under test directly and in memory. To call the endpoints implemented in your Nancy modules, you'll use the Nancy.Testing library that comes as a companion library alongside Nancy. Nancy.Testing lets you write tests that make calls to Nancy endpoints in memory. The calls go through Nancy in exactly the same way HTTP requests would, but without going through the network stack. To the code in your Nancy modules, calls made with Nancy.Testing look exactly like real HTTP requests.

At the unit-test level, I'll show you two kinds of tests (see figure 7.4): one that uses a database and one that uses a mock in place of the database. I consider both to be unit tests, even though the first type uses a database. Two things make a test a unit test: its scope is a small piece of functionality, and the test

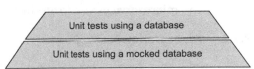

Figure 7.4   At the unit-test level, there are two kinds of tests: those that use a database and those that don't.

code and the production code in the microservice run in the same process.

The narrow scope of a unit test makes it precise: when it fails, the problem lies in a small amount of code. A narrow scope also enables you to write tests that cover failure scenarios properly. Both types of unit tests are faster than service-level tests, but of course the tests that mock out databases are faster than those that use a database. Therefore, you can have both and will probably have more tests that mock the database than tests that don't.

Sometimes you may also have even narrower unit tests that test the business logic in the microservices directly by instantiating domain objects and testing them directly. I take a pragmatic approach to deciding how narrow the narrowest unit tests should be: I use a test-first workflow that starts from the outside, with tests that use Nancy.Testing making calls to endpoint handlers in Nancy modules. I start with tests that cover the broad strokes of what the endpoint should do, an then I progressively add tests for more details. Only when it becomes awkward to test a particular detail through the endpoint handler do I begin to write narrower unit tests. For instance, covering a particular case in the business logic with tests that call through the endpoint handler might require a lot of setup code. That's a signal to switch down to a test that has a narrower scope: just those cases in the business logic. I'll write tests for those cases that work directly on the classes that should implement that particular part of the business logic.

For the Loyalty Program microservice, you need unit tests that test the endpoint that lets you create users with a number of different inputs covering both possible valid inputs and invalid inputs. Likewise, you need tests that try to read both existing and nonexistent users from the query endpoint that lets you read users. You need similar tests for the other endpoints in the microservice. Loyalty Program is sufficiently simple that you don't need to switch down to tests that are narrower than the microservice's endpoints. So, the units tests I'll show you later all work by calling endpoint handlers through Nancy.Testing.

7.2   Testing libraries: Nancy.Testing and xUnit

In this chapter, you'll use two new libraries:

- Nancy.Testing (https://github.com/NancyFx/Nancy/wiki/Testing-your-application)
- xUnit (https://xunit.github.io/)

I'll give you a brief introduction to each, and then you'll implement tests for some of the microservices you wrote in earlier chapters.

7.2.1   Meet Nancy.Testing

The Nancy.Testing library is a companion to Nancy that makes it easy to test endpoints implemented in Nancy modules. The main entry point into Nancy.Testing is the `Browser` type, which accepts method calls like `Get("/")`, `Post("/user")`, `Put("/user/42")`, and `Delete("/user/42")` that let tests call GET, POST, PUT, and DELETE endpoints in Nancy modules, respectively. When a test calls an endpoint through the `Browser` type, the call goes through the real Nancy pipeline. This means routes are resolved the same way as for real HTTP requests, the dependency injection container is set up and used as usual, and serialization and deserialization run as they normally do. In short, to the endpoint, the call looks exactly like a real HTTP request. The cool thing is that it's all done in process, so it's much faster than a real HTTP request would be. The return value of each method is a `NancyResponse` object and contains everything a real HTTP response would, including headers, status codes, and a body.

In addition to the `Browser` type, the Nancy.Testing library provides `Configurable-Bootstrapper`, which offers a nice API for creating ad hoc bootstrappers used in tests. Among other things, `ConfigurableBootstrapper` allows you to do the following:

- Create `Browser` objects that see only one Nancy module instead of all modules in the application
- Override registrations in the dependency injection container: for instance, to provide mock objects in place of real ones
- Add hooks to the Nancy pipeline, such as an error handler

Finally, Nancy.Testing comes with a bunch of convenience methods that make writing assertions against `NancyResponse` objects easy.

Nancy.Testing offers a wealth of functionality that makes it easier to write tests. Going through all of it is beyond the scope of this chapter, but you'll see some of its power. I find the APIs in the library to be quite discoverable, so I'm sure once you get going, you'll discover more of what Nancy.Testing has to offer.

You can find further information on Nancy.Testing in the Nancy documentation (https://github.com/NancyFx/Nancy/wiki/Testing-your-application), or you can jump right in and start using it. I think you'll find that the APIs are quite discoverable through IntelliSense.

7.2.2 Meet xUnit

xUnit (http://xunit.github.io) is a unit-test tool for .NET. It has a library part that allows you to write automated tests and a runner part that can run those tests. To write a test with xUnit, you create a method with a `Fact` attribute over it and put the code to perform the test there. The xUnit runner scans for methods with a `Fact` attribute and executes all of them. In addition, xUnit has an API for making assertions in tests. If an assertion fails, the xUnit runner picks up the failure and reports it back when it's finished running tests. The xUnit test runner can be run by `dotnet` and is therefore well suited for the projects you're building in this book.

Other .NET test tools similar to xUnit—NUnit, for instance—are available that you can also use. This book sticks with xUnit because it's used for the test projects that Yeoman and Visual Studio create. If you prefer another tool, feel free to use it, as long as it works with `dotnet`.

7.2.3 xUnit and Nancy.Testing working together

Putting Nancy.Testing and xUnit together, you can write succinct tests for endpoints implemented in Nancy modules. In section 7.3.1, you'll set up a project for these unit tests and run them with `dotnet`; but for now, I just want to give you a quick peek at how the tests will look. The following test calls the `Get` endpoint in `TestModule` and makes the assertion that the response status code is 200 OK.

Listing 7.1 Simple test using xUnit and Nancy.Testing

```
namespace LoyaltyProgramUnitTests
{
  using Nancy;
  using Nancy.Testing;
  using Xunit;

  public class TestModule_should
  {
    public class TestModule : NancyModule
    {
```

```
                    public TestModule()
                    {
                        Get("/", _ => 200;)        ◁──── Endpoint used in the test
                    }
                }
```

Configures a Nancy bootstrapper with TestModule ⟶

```
                [Fact]
                public async Task respond_ok_to_request_to_root()
                {
                    var sut = new Browser(with => with.Module<TestModule>());
                    var actual = await sut.Get("/");
                    Assert.Equal(HttpStatusCode.OK, actual.StatusCode);
                }
            }
        }
```

Asserts that the endpoint returns a 200 OK response ⟶

Calls the Get endpoint in TestModule ⟵

Naming conventions

My tests follow these naming conventions:

- My tests work on an object called sut for *system under test*. In the previous test, sut is a Browser object that I use to make a call to an endpoint.
- I name my test classes after the thing they test—TestModule in this example test—followed by _should.
- I name the Fact method after the scenario being tested and the expected result. I separate the words in Fact method names with underscores and try to make sure they form a sentence when combined with the name of the surrounding class. For instance, in this test, concatenating the class name and the Fact method name and replacing underscores with spaces, you get "TestModule should respond ok to requests to root."

Whether you like these conventions is a matter of taste. I happen to like them, but they're in no way essential to writing good tests.

You can run the previous test with dotnet; it will execute in-memory and give you good coverage because the call to sut.Get("/") executes the real Nancy pipeline, including the implementation of the endpoint in TestModule. The string argument "/" is the relative URL to which the fake request is made. In section 7.3.1, we'll look at setting up a project for these unit tests and how to run them with dotnet.

For the rest of this chapter, we'll work at the code level and implement unit tests and service-level tests for the Loyalty Program microservice. When you implemented Loyalty Program in chapter 4, it didn't have an event feed; but for these examples you'll add an event feed that other microservices can subscribe to.

7.3   *Writing unit tests using Nancy.Testing*

In this section, you'll implement some unit tests for the endpoints in the Loyalty Program microservice. In chapter 4, you saw that Loyalty Program has three command and query endpoints:

- An HTTP GET endpoint at URLs of the form /users/{userId} that responds with a representation of the user
- An HTTP POST endpoint to /users/ that expects a representation of a user in the body of the request and then registers that user in the loyalty program
- An HTTP PUT endpoint at URLs of the form /users/{userId} that expects a representation of a user in the body of the request and then updates an already-registered user

Let's write tests for these endpoints. The Loyalty Program microservice has an event feed for which you'll also write a test. You won't write comprehensive tests for the endpoints and event feed in Loyalty Program—only enough to see how tests against Nancy endpoints are written.

In the following subsections, you'll do the following:

- Set up a test project to house unit tests for the Loyalty Program microservice.
- Write tests that use Browser from Nancy.Testing to test endpoints in Loyalty Program and that let the code in the microservice use the real database. You'll write three such tests, one for each of these pieces of functionality:
  - A test that tries to read a user that doesn't exist
  - A test that creates a user and reads it back out
  - A test that modifies a user and reads it back out
- Write tests that also use Browser to test an endpoint but are limited in scope by a mocked database injected in the endpoint under test. These tests test the event feed in the microservice.

When you're finished, you'll have learned to write unit tests for Nancy endpoints both with and without a real database.

7.3.1 Setting up a unit-test project

Before you can start writing tests, you need a project to house them. For that, create a new project next to the LoyaltyProgram project, and call it LoyaltyProgramUnit-Tests. If you create the project with Visual Studio, choose the Class Library (.NET Core) template from the dialog; and if you use you Yeoman, choose Unit Test Project (xUnit.net) from the menu.

Your solution should look similar to this:

```
C:.
├──LoyaltyProgram
│      Bootstrapper.cs
│      project.json
│      README.md
│      Startup.cs
│      UsersModule.cs
│      YamlSerializerDeserializer.cs
│
├──LoyaltyProgram
```

```
    |    └──────EventFeed
    |               Event.cs
    |               EventsFeedModule.cs
    |               EventStore.cs
    |               IEventStore.cs
    |
    ├──LoyaltyProgramEventConsumer
    |       Program.cs
    |       project.json
    |
    └──LoyaltyProgramUnitTests
            project.json
            Class1.cs
```

If you used Yeoman to create the new LoyaltyProgramUnitTests project, you're
ready to run your first tests. But if you used the Visual Studio template, you need to
edit the Class1.cs and project.json files a bit. The following listing shows how Class1.cs
should look.

Listing 7.2   Class1.cs file

```csharp
using Xunit;

namespace UnitTest
{
    // see example explanation on xUnit.net website:
    // https://xunit.github.io/docs/getting-started-dotnet-core.html
    public class Class1
    {
        [Fact]
        public void PassingTest()
        {
            Assert.Equal(4, Add(2, 2));
        }

        [Fact]
        public void FailingTest()
        {
            Assert.Equal(5, Add(2, 2));
        }

        int Add(int x, int y)
        {
            return x + y;
        }
    }
}
```

In the project.json file, add the following to set up a test command that refers to the
xunit test runner:

```
"testRunner": "xunit",
```

The xunit test runner is added to the project via the NuGet package dotnet-test-xunit, and the xUnit package is installed. Here are all the dependencies:

```
"dependencies": {
    "dotnet-test-xunit": "2.2.0-preview2-build1029",
    "Microsoft.NETCore.App": {
      "version": "1.0.0",
      "type": "platform"
    },
    "xunit": "2.1.0"
  },
```

You can now go to the LoyaltyProgramUnitTests folder in PowerShell and restore the NuGet packages as usual, using dotnet:

```
PS> dotnet restore
```

The Class1.cs file now contains two small xUnit tests: one that passes and one that fails. You run them with dotnet like this:

```
PS> dotnet test
```

Once you have the initial tests running, add a dependency on Nancy.Testing so you can use Browser and later ConfigurableBootstrapper. Also add a dependency on LoyaltyProgram so you can begin testing it. The dependencies now look like this:

```
"dependencies": {
    "dotnet-test-xunit": "2.2.0-preview2-build1029",
    "Microsoft.NETCore.App": {
      "version": "1.0.0",
      "type": "platform"
    },
    "xunit": "2.1.0",
    "Nancy.Testing": "2.0.0--barneyrubble",
    "LoyaltyProgram": {"target": "project"}       ◁——— Project reference
  },
```

The last line is the reference to the LoyaltyProgram project. As you can see, the project references in project.json look almost like NuGet references. You don't specify a version for LoyaltyProgram because you want the test to run against the version of the LoyaltyProgram code that you have next to the LoyaltyProgramUnitTests project.

7.3.2 Using the Browser object to unit-test endpoints

Now that you have a test project set up, you can begin adding tests to it. The first test you'll add is very simple: given that there are no registered users in the Loyalty Program microservice, the test queries for a user and expects to get back a response with a 404 Not Found status code. Add a file called userModule_should.cs to the LoyaltyProgramUnitTests project, and put the following code in it.

Listing 7.3   First test for the users endpoint

```
namespace LoyaltyProgramUnitTests
{
  using LoyaltyProgram;
  using Nancy;
  using Nancy.Testing;
  using Xunit;

  public class UserModule_should
  {
    private Browser sut;

    public UserModule_should()
    {
      this.sut = new Browser(
        new Bootstrapper(),
        defaultsTo => defaultsTo.Accept("application/json"));
    }

    [Fact]
    public void respond_not_found_when_queried_for_unregistered_user()
    {
      var actual = await sut.Get("/users/1000");
      Assert.Equal(HttpStatusCode.NotFound, actual.StatusCode);
    }
  }
}
```

Remember that sut stands for "system under test."

Real LoyaltyProgram bootstrapper

All "requests" accept JSON

Requests a user that doesn't exist

The most interesting part of this test class is in the constructor, where you create a Browser object. When xUnit runs, it creates an instance of UserModule_should and then calls a method with the Fact attribute on that instance. Unlike most other .NET test frameworks, xUnit create a new, clean instance for each Fact method.

The Browser object in listing 7.3 is initialized with the real bootstrapper from LoyaltyProgram. This means the LoyaltyProgram application that the Browser calls into is wired up exactly the same way it is when it runs on top of a real web server and receives real HTTP requests. Furthermore, for convenience, you set a default Accept header on Browser. This header will be added to all requests made through the Browser object unless explicitly overridden. For instance, sut.Get("/users/1000") has the Accept header set.

Let's move on to a test that registers a new user and then queries it to check that it was registered as it should be. Add the following test to the UserModule_should class.

Listing 7.4   Test for registering a user through the users endpoint

```
[Fact]
public void allow_to_register_new_user()
{
  var expected =
    new LoyaltyProgramUser() { Name = "Chr" };
```

Reads the new user from the body of the response from the POST

Registers a new user through the POST endpoint

Reads the new user through the GET endpoint

```
var registrationResponse = await
    sut.Post("/users", with => with.JsonBody(expected));
var newUser =
    registrationResponse.Body.DeserializeJson<LoyaltyProgramUser>();

var actual = await sut.Get($"/users/{newUser.Id}");

Assert.Equal(HttpStatusCode.OK, actual.StatusCode);
Assert.Equal(
    expected.Name,
    actual.Body.DeserializeJson<LoyaltyProgramUser>().Name);
// more assertions on the response from the GET
}
```

Checks that the response from the GET is correct

Here, you see another use of the Browser object. For instance, you add a body to the Post via the lambda in the second argument. In that lambda, you can do a variety of things to the request, such as adding headers, cookies, form values, a host name, or an identity, or choosing between HTTP and HTTPS. Here, you add a body to the request.

The last test you'll add registers a user and then modifies it via the PUT endpoint in the Loyalty Program microservice. Add it to UserModule_should.cs.

Listing 7.5 Test for modifying users through the users endpoint

```
[Fact]
public void allow_modifying_users()
{
  var expected = "jane";
  var user = new LoyaltyProgramUser() { Name = "Chr" };
  var registrationResponse = await
    sut.Post("/users", with => with.JsonBody(user));          <—— Registers a user
  var newUser =
    registrationResponse.Body.DeserializeJson<LoyaltyProgramUser>();

  newUser.Name = expected;                                    Updates the user
  var actual = await
    sut.Put($"/users/{newUser.Id}", with => with.JsonBody(newUser));   <—

  Assert.Equal(                          <—— Asserts that the update was done
    expected,
    actual.Body.DeserializeJson<LoyaltyProgramUser>().Name);
}
```

There's nothing new in this code compared to what you've seen in the two previous tests. But I wanted to include it because it's a good illustration of the kind of unit tests I think you should write for the endpoints in your microservices: unit tests that focus on the behavior the endpoints provide rather than on testing just one endpoint in isolation.

7.3.3   *Using a configurable bootstrapper to inject mocks into endpoints*

Now that you've tested the endpoints in `UserModule`, let's turn to testing the `Loyal-tyProgram` event feed. The event feed is a Nancy module that depends on an `IEvent-Store` to store and read events. Here's the `IEventStore` interface.

Listing 7.6   `IEventStore` interface

```
using System.Collections.Generic;

namespace LoyaltyProgram.EventFeed
{
  public interface IEventStore
  {
    IEnumerable<Event> GetEvents(          ◄─┐ Reads events from
      long firstEventSequenceNumber,           the event store
      long lastEventSequenceNumber);
    void Raise(string eventName, object content);  ◄─┐ Stores events to
  }                                                     the event store
}
```

You saw an event feed in chapter 4, but I'll repeat it here, to remind you how it works.

Listing 7.7   Event feed

```
namespace LoyaltyProgram.EventFeed
{
  using Nancy;

  public class EventsFeedModule : NancyModule
  {
    public EventsFeedModule(IEventStore eventStore) : base("/events")
    {
      Get("/", _ =>
      {
        long firstEventSequenceNumber, lastEventSequenceNumber;
        if (!long.TryParse(this.Request.Query.start.Value,        ◄─┐ Gets the
          out firstEventSequenceNumber))                              start value
          firstEventSequenceNumber = 0;                               from the
                                                                      query string
        if (!long.TryParse(this.Request.Query.end.Value,   ◄─┐ Gets the end value
          out lastEventSequenceNumber))                          from the query string
          lastEventSequenceNumber = 50;

        return
          eventStore.GetEvents(              ◄─┐ Reads events "start"
            firstEventSequenceNumber,            through "end" from
            lastEventSequenceNumber);            the event store
      });
    }
  }
}
```

As you can see, the event feed is a Nancy module that responds to requests to /events with the events it reads from IEventStore. You want to write a test to check whether the event feed returns exactly the event from the IEventFeed. Toward that end, you want to control which events IEventStore returns. So, you'll create a fake implementation of IEventStore and use that in the test.

Listing 7.8   Fake IEventStore to use in tests

```
public class FakeEventStore : IEventStore
{
  public IEnumerable<Event> GetEvents(
    long firstEventSequenceNumber,
    long lastEventSequenceNumber)
  {
    if (firstEventSequenceNumber > 100)
      return Enumerable.Empty<Event>();
    else
      return
        Enumerable
        .Range((int) firstEventSequenceNumber,
               (int) (lastEventSequenceNumber - firstEventSequenceNumber))
        .Select(i =>
          new Event(
            i,
            DateTimeOffset.Now,
            "some event",
            new Object()));
  }

  public void Raise(string eventName, object content) {}
}
```

> **Returns a list of fake events when firstEventSequenceNumber is less than 100**

With this fake implementation of an event store, you know the event store will return a list of events only if the firstEventSequenceNumber argument is less than 100. Otherwise, FakeEventStore will return an empty list of events. If you inject this IEventStore implementation into EventsFeedModule, you'll know which events EventsFeedModule will get from the event store and therefore which events it should return.

You can use another feature of Nancy.Testing to inject the fake IEventStore implementation into EventsFeedModule: ConfigurableBootstrapper, which allows you to modify how the Nancy application under test is configured. Here, you'll use ConfigurableBootstrapper to set up FakeEventStore as the implementation of IEventStore when creating the Browser object. That is done with the following piece of code.

Listing 7.9   Using the fake event store while testing

```
this.sut = new Browser(
  with => with
    .Module<EventsFeedModule>()
    .Dependency<IEventStore>(typeof(FakeEventStore)),
  withDefault => withDefault.Accept("application/json"));
```

with has the type ConfigurableBootstrapper

Limits Browser to using EventsFeedModule only

Registers FakeEventStore as the implementation of IEventStore

Adds a JSON Accept header to all requests

With this code in the tests, constructor instances of `EventsFeedModule` will have `FakeEventStore` injected. You can use that to write two tests:

- A test that asserts that events are returned from the feed when the start number in the request is less than 100
- A test that asserts that no events are returned when the start number is greater than 100

Listing 7.10   Tests for the event feed, using the fake event store

```
using System;
using System.Collections.Generic;
using System.Linq;
using LoyaltyProgram.EventFeed;
using Nancy;
using Nancy.Testing;
using Xunit;

public class EventFeed_should
{
  private Browser sut;

  public EventFeed_should()
  {
    this.sut = new Browser(
      with => with
        .Module<EventsFeedModule>()
        .Dependency<IEventStore>(typeof(FakeEventStore)),
      withDefault => withDefault.Accept("application/json"));
  }

  [Fact]
  public void return_events_when_from_event_store()
  {
    var actual = await sut.Get("/events/", with =>
    {
      with.Query("start", "0");
      with.Query("end", "100");
    });
```

Creates Browser configured to use FakeEventStore

Makes a request to /events with the query string "start=0&end=100"

```
      Assert.Equal(HttpStatusCode.OK, actual.StatusCode);
      Assert.StartsWith("application/json", actual.ContentType);
      Assert.Equal(100,
         actual.Body.DeserializeJson<IEnumerable<Event>>().Count());
   }

   [Fact]
   public void return_empty_response_when_there_are_no_more_events()
   {
      var actual = wait sut.Get("/events/", with =>        ◁─┐  Makes a request to /events
      {                                                       │  with the query string
         with.Query("start", "200");                         │  "start=200&end=300"
         with.Query("end", "300");
      });

      Assert.Empty(actual.Body.DeserializeJson<IEnumerable<Event>>());
   }
}
```

Now that you have some unit tests in place, you can run them with dotnet, as you saw earlier. When you do, xUnit will scan for classes with Fact methods and then execute each Fact method. The output from the tests shows a summary of how many tests ran, how many errors there were, how many tests failed, and how many were skipped:

```
PS > dotnet test
xUnit.net .NET CLI test runner (64-bit .NET Core win10-x64)
   Discovering: LoyaltyProgramUnitTests
   Discovered:  LoyaltyProgramUnitTests
   Starting:    LoyaltyProgramUnitTests
   Finished:    LoyaltyProgramUnitTests
=== TEST EXECUTION SUMMARY ===
   LoyaltyProgramUnitTests  Total: 6, Errors: 0, Failed: 0, Skipped: 0, Time:
      2.375s
SUMMARY: Total: 1 targets, Passed: 1, Failed: 0.
```

As you can see, six tests were run, and none of them failed. In other words, all tests passed.

Now that you have tests for EventsFeedModule and UsersModule, you're off to a good start writing unit tests for endpoints in your microservices. In real life, these tests aren't sufficient; I'd write more tests for edge cases and error scenarios. But now you know how to write those tests using Nancy.Testing.

7.4 *Writing service-level tests*

Let's move on to writing service-level tests for the entire Loyalty Program microservice. Service-level tests interact with a microservice from the outside and provide the microservice with mocked versions of its collaborators.

Loyalty Program makes requests to two collaborators: the event feed in the Special Offers microservice and the API of the Notifications microservice. The service-level tests for Loyalty Program go through these steps:

1 Set up two endpoints in the same process as the test:
   - One that works as a mocked special-offer event feed
   - One that works as a mocked notification endpoint
2 Start the Loyalty Program microservice in separate processes, and configure it to use the mocked endpoints in place of the real collaborators. This means whenever Loyalty Program needs to call one of its collaborators, it will call one of the mocked endpoints.
3 Execute a scenario against Loyalty Program as a sequence of HTTP requests.
4 Record any calls to the mocked endpoints.
5 Make assertions on the responses from Loyalty Program and on the requests made to the mocked endpoints.

Figure 7.5 shows the runtime setup for the service-level tests for the Loyalty Program microservice.

You'll follow these steps to create the test setup from figure 7.5:

1 Create a test project for the service-level tests.
2 Create the mocked endpoints for the special-offers event feed and the notification endpoint.
3 Start both processes of the Loyalty Program microservice: the Nancy application containing the HTTP API and the event consumer.
4 Write test code that executes a test scenario against Loyalty Program.

When that setup is in place, you'll write a test that uses it.

Service-level test process

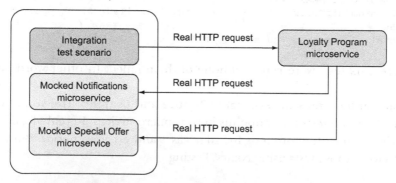

Figure 7.5 A service-level test executes a scenario against the API of the microservice under test but configures the microservice to use mocked endpoints running in the same process as the test, in place of real collaborators. When a service-level test runs, it makes real HTTP requests to the microservice under test, which makes real HTTP requests back to mocked endpoints as needed. The test can inspect the responses from the microservice under test as well as the calls it makes to the mocked endpoints.

7.4.1 Creating a service-level test project

For the service-level tests, you'll create a new test project exactly like the unit-test project you create earlier. That is, create a project based on either the ASP.NET Test Project Template in Visual Studio or the Unit Test project template in Yeoman, and call it `LoyaltyProgramIntegrationTest`. Just like the unit-test project, place this new project side by side with `LoyaltyProgram`. You now have four projects:

```
Mode                LastWriteTime         Length Name
----                -------------         ------ ----
d-----       4/6/2016    8:53 PM                 LoyaltyProgram
d-----       4/6/2016    8:53 PM                 LoyaltyProgramEventConsumer
d-----       4/6/2016    8:53 PM                 LoyaltyProgramIntegrationTest
d-----       8/6/2016   10:59 PM                 LoyaltyProgramUnitTests
```

These are the two projects that make up the Loyalty Program microservice—the Nancy application and the event consumer—and the test projects that go along with the microservice.

7.4.2 Creating mocked endpoints

As shown in figure 7.5, you need to create mocked versions of the endpoints in the Special Offers microservice and the Notifications microservice that the Loyalty Program microservice uses. You'll do so by writing two simple Nancy modules, each of which implements an endpoint that returns a hardcoded response. Listing 7.11 shows the mocked special-offers event feed endpoint, and listing 7.12 shows the mocked notifications endpoint.

Listing 7.11 Mock event feed returning hardcoded events

```
public class MockEventFeed : NancyModule
{
  public static AutoResetEvent polled =          ◁─── Signals to the test that
    new AutoResetEvent(initialState: false);            Loyalty Program has
                                                         been polled for events
  public MockEventFeed()
  {
    this.Get("/events", _ =>
    {
      polled.Set();
      return new []                              ◁─── Returns a hardcoded
      {                                                response
        new
        {
          SequenceNumber = 1,
          Name= "baz",
          Content = new
          {
```

```
                        OfferName = "foo",
                        Description = "bar",
                        item = new { ProductName = "name" }
                    }
                }
            };
        });
    }
}
```

Listing 7.12 Mock endpoint that records when it was called

```
public class MockNotifications : NancyModule
{
  public static AutoResetEvent notificationWasSent =
    new AutoResetEvent(initialState: false);          ◁─── Used later in
                                                           the test to make
                                                           assertions on
  public MockNotifications()
  {
    this.Get("/notify", _ =>
    {
      notificationWasSent.Set();
      return 200;                                     ◁─── Returns a hardcoded
    });                                                    response
  }
}
```

The plan is to run these two modules in the test process. To do that, you'll use Nancy
on top of ASP.NET Core like you usually do. You need to add the Microsoft.AspNet-
Core.Owin NuGet packages and add Nancy and LoyaltyProgram as dependencies.
The dependencies section in the project.json file now looks like this.

Listing 7.13 Integration project dependencies, including Nancy

```
"dependencies": {
    "dotnet-test-xunit": "2.2.0-preview2-build1029",
    "Microsoft.NETCore.App": {
      "version": "1.0.0",
      "type": "platform"
    },
    "xunit": "2.1.0",
    "Microsoft.AspNetCore.Owin": "1.0.0",
    "Nancy": "2.0.0-barneyrubble",
    "LoyaltyProgram": { "target": "project" }
  },
```

Next, add a file called RegisterUserAndGetNotification.cs containing the following
code, which uses Nancy.Hosting.Self to start a Nancy application in the test process.

Listing 7.14 Starting up Nancy inside the test process

```
public class RegisterUserAndGetNotification : IDisposable
{
  private readonly NancyHost hostForMockEndpoints;

  public RegisterUserAndGetNotification()
  {
    StartFakeEndpoints();
  }

  private void StartFakeEndpoints()
  {
    this.hostForFakeEndpoints = new WebHostBuilder()
      .UseKestrel()
      .UseContentRoot(Directory.GetCurrentDirectory())
      .UseStartup<FakeStartup>()
      .UseUrls("http://localhost:5001")
      .Build();

    new Thread(() => this.hostForFakeEndpoints.Run()).Start();
  }
}

public class FakeStartup
{
  public void Configure(IApplicationBuilder app)
  {
    app.UseOwin(buildFunc => buildFunc.UseNancy());
  }
}
```

Creates an ASP.NET Core application

Uses FakeStartup to bootstrap the ASP.NET Core application

Lets the ASP.NET Core application listen on port 5001

Adds Nancy to the ASP.NET Core application

Later, you'll add a Fact method to this class: then, when you run xUnit, it will find this class and instantiate it to execute Fact. The constructor starts up Nancy, which will automatically discover the MockEventsFeed and MockUsersModule modules and expose the endpoints defined in them. This is all you need to create mocked endpoints in the service-level test process.

7.4.3 Starting all the processes of the microservice under test

With the mocked endpoints running, you're ready to start up Loyalty Program. The microservice consists of two processes: a Nancy application and the event consumer. You add the code to start those to the setup in RegisterUserAndGetNotification. The following listing shows only new code—leave the existing code to start and stop Nancy.

Listing 7.15 Starting the microservice in a separate process

```
public class RegisterUserAndGetNotification : IDisposable
{
  ...
  private Process eventConsumer;
```

```
private Process web;

public RegisterUserAndGetNotification()
{
  StartLoyaltyProgram();
  ...
}

private void StartLoyaltyProgram()
{
  StartEventConsumer();
  StartLoyaltyProgramApi();
}

private void StartLoyaltyProgramApi()
{
  var apiInfo = new ProcessStartInfo("dotnet.exe")      ◄─┐  Setup for running the
  {                                                         command "dotnet run"
    Arguments = "run",                                      in the LoyaltyProgram
    WorkingDirectory = "../LoyaltyProgram"                  folder
  };
  this.api = Process.Start(apiInfo);                    ◄─┐  Starts the
}                                                          LoyaltyProgram process

private void StartEventConsumer()                      ◄─┐  Setup for running
{                                                          the event consumer
  var eventConsumerInfo = new ProcessStartInfo("dotnet.exe")
  {
    Arguments = "run localhost:5001",
    WorkingDirectory = "../LoyaltyProgramEventConsumer"
  };                                                     ◄─┐  Starts the event-
  this.eventConsumer = Process.Start(eventConsumerInfo);    consumer process
}

public void Dispose()                                  ◄─┐  Closes the processes,
{                                                          and releases resources
  this.eventConsumer.Dispose();
  this.api.Dispose();
}
}
```

This code spawns two dotnet processes, one for each process in the Loyalty Program microservice. This is like running dotnet from the command line, so running the Nancy application is the same as usual. Running the event consumer is different, and you need to solve these two problems:

- The event consumer expects to run as a Windows service. Now it also needs to be able to run like a simple process.
- In the following line from listing 7.15, the event consumer doesn't understand the command-line argument localhost:5001, which is the host name for the mocked endpoints you want the event consumer to use in place of the real collaborators:

```
Arguments = "run localhost:5001",
```

Both of these issues are easy to solve. You just change the Main method in the event consumer to the following.

Reads the host name from the command-line argument

```
public static void Main(string[] args) => new Program().Entry(args);

public void Entry(string[] args)
{
  this.subscriber = new EventSubscriber(args[0]);
  if (args.Length >= 2 && args[1].Equals("--service"))
    Run(this);
  else
  {
    OnStart(null);
    Console.ReadLine();
  }
}
```

Runs as a service if there's a --service in the command-line arguments

Runs the start method by hand

Now both processes of the Loyalty Program microservice are started from the test startup code. A nice side effect of the changes to the event consumer is that it's also easier to run by hand for testing reasons.

7.4.4   *Executing the test scenario against the microservice under test*

Finally, you're ready to write the test. It has three steps:

1 Make an HTTP request to register a user.
2 Wait for the Loyalty Program microservice to poll for events.
3 Assert that a request to the notifications endpoint was made.

In code, the test goes in the RegisterUserAndGetNotification file and is as follows.

```
[Fact]
public void Scenario()
{
  RegisterNewUser();
  WaitForConsumerToReadSpecialOffersEvents();
  AssertNotificationWassent();
}

private async Task RegisterNewUser()
{
  using (var httpClient = new HttpClient())
  {
    httpClient.BaseAddress = new Uri("http://localhost:5000");
    var response = await
```

Sends a request to register a user

Puts a user into the request

```
httpClient.PostAsync(
    "/users/",
    new StringContent(
        JsonConvert.SerializeObject(new LoyaltyProgramUser()),
        Encoding.UTF8,
        "application/json")).ConfigureAwait(false);
    Assert.Equal(HttpStatusCode.Created, response.StatusCode);
    Console.WriteLine("registered users");
    }
}

private static void WaitForConsumerToReadSpecialOffersEvents()
{
    Assert.True(MockEventFeed.polled.WaitOne(30000));
    Thread.Sleep(100);
}

private static void AssertNotificationWassent()
{
    Assert.True(MockNotifications.NotificationWasSent);
}
```

Waits for the microservice to poll the event feed, and fails if it doesn't poll

Waits to give the microservice time to handle the event from the feed

You can run the test in PowerShell with dotnet:

```
PS> dotnet test
```

This will open two command windows: one with each of the processes in the Loyalty Program microservice. The test runs, and, when it finishes, the two windows are closed. The output from xUnit is as follows:

```
Discovering: LoyaltyProgramIntegrationTest
  Discovered:  LoyaltyProgramIntegrationTest
  Starting:    LoyaltyProgramIntegrationTest
    LoyaltyProgramIntegrationTests.RegisterUserAndGetNotification.Scenario
  Finished:    LoyaltyProgramIntegrationTest
=== TEST EXECUTION SUMMARY ===
  LoyaltyProgramIntegrationTest  Total: 1, Errors: 0, Failed: 0, Skipped:
  ➥ 0, Time: 12.563s
```

This test is slow, and you had to do some setup before you were ready to write it. This is why such tests are higher on the test pyramid than the unit tests you wrote earlier. You should have only a few of this kind of test, whereas you can have many unit tests.

7.5   Summary

- The test pyramid tells you to have few system-level tests that test the complete system, several service-level tests for each microservice, and many unit tests for each microservice.
- System-level tests are likely to be slow and are very imprecise.

- You should write system-level tests for important success scenarios, to provide some test coverage for most of the system.

- Service-level tests are likely to be slow, but they're faster and more precise than system-level tests.

- You should write service-level tests for success scenarios and important failure scenarios for each microservice. This adds more test coverage to each microservice than just the system-level tests.

- You can use the process for writing service-level tests as the basis for writing contract tests that verify the assumption one microservice makes about the API and behavior of another microservice. In terms of the test pyramid, contract tests are between system-level tests and service-level tests.

- Unit tests are fast and should be kept fast. They're also precise, because they target a specific, narrow piece of functionality.

- You should write unit tests for success and failure scenarios alike. Use them to cover edge cases that are harder to cover with higher-level tests.

- I recommend working in an outside-in fashion with each microservice: write service-level tests first, and then begin writing unit tests when the service-level tests become awkward to work with.

- The Nancy.Testing library is a powerful companion to Nancy that makes it easy to test endpoints in Nancy modules.

- You use the `Browser` type in Nancy.Testing to test endpoints through a nice API that lets you simulate HTTP requests. Calls through the `Browser` object look exactly like real HTTP requests to the endpoint handlers in Nancy modules.

- You test endpoints through `Browser` both with real data stores and with mocked data stores.

- You can write service-level tests where you do the following:
  - Write mocked endpoints for the collaborators of the microservice under test, and use Nancy to host these in the test process.
  - Start up all the processes of the microservice under test, passing in the configuration through command-line arguments.
  - Write scenarios that interact with the microservice under test via HTTP requests.
  - Make assertions both on the response from the microservice under test and on the requests it makes to its collaborators.

- You can use the xUnit test framework to write and run your automated tests.

- xUnit can be run with `dotnet`.

Part 3

Handling cross-cutting concerns: building a reusable microservice platform

In this part, you'll build a platform that handles some important cross-cutting concerns and that's ready to be used across many microservices. The cross-cutting concerns you'll implement include monitoring, logging, passing correlation tokens along with requests between microservices, and security concerns around microservice-to-microservice requests. All these concerns make microservices behave well in production. With them in place, you can gain insight into the health of each microservice and trace business transactions across microservices.

You can implement such concerns in each microservice or create reusable implementations to use in many microservices. Implementing concerns in each microservice obviously incurs some duplication of effort, but reusing an implementation creates coupling between microservices. How much you want to reuse is, in other words, a tradeoff between keeping microservices independent of each other and avoiding repeated effort. Where you land on this tradeoff is a decision you'll have to make in the context of your system. In this book I demonstrate reusable handling of request logging, performance logging, passing around correlation tokens, and securing microservice-to-microservice calls. (Note that you should be cautious about reuse and only build reusable implementations for concerns that cut across many microservices with little or no variation among microservices.)

Chapter 1 touched briefly on OWIN middleware; chapter 8 will dive deeper into how OWIN works and what middleware is. In chapters 9 and 10, you'll implement cross-cutting concerns as OWIN middleware. In chapter 11, you'll build a reusable microservice platform from the middleware you've built. You can easily add this platform to new microservices, enabling you to quickly create microservices that behave well with regard to cross-cutting concerns.

Introducing OWIN: writing and testing OWIN middleware

This chapter covers

- Handling concerns that cut across several microservices
- Understanding OWIN, OWIN middleware, and OWIN pipelines
- Writing OWIN middleware
- Testing OWIN middleware and an OWIN pipeline

When you're implementing a system of microservices, some concerns cut across the entire system. These are the things you need every microservice to do, and they're often related to keeping the system healthy in production:

- Monitoring
- Logging errors, requests, performance, and so on
- Security
- Policies related to technologies you use in many microservices—for example, handling database connections

All of these lend themselves well to being implemented as OWIN middleware. This chapter explores how to use OWIN middleware to handle cross-cutting concerns.

8.1 Handling cross-cutting concerns

When you look at a single microservice, you see number of components. For instance, chapter 2 broke the Shopping Cart microservice down into the components shown in figure 8.1.

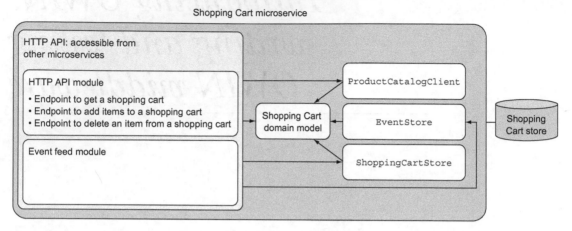

Figure 8.1   **The view of the Shopping Cart microservice you've seen in earlier chapters shows a small number of components that together implement the Shopping microservice behavior.**

None of these components address the cross-cutting concerns mentioned in the introduction to this chapter: monitoring, request logging, and so on. Furthermore, none of these components are good candidates for places to implement those cross-cutting concerns. Why? Because all the components in figure 8.1 implement things specific to the Shopping Cart microservice. In contrast, cross-cutting concerns aren't specific to any one microservice. Therefore, you need to implement them in components separate from those in figure 8.1. Looking at Shopping Cart from a different angle, in figure 8.2, you see that it gets HTTP requests through a web server, handles them using its various components, and returns responses to the web server, which then sends them back to the caller.

As I just mentioned, you want to keep the code for cross-cutting concerns separated from the components in figure 8.1. Furthermore, cross-cutting concerns apply to the microservice as a whole. This means a good place for the code that handles cross-cutting concerns is between the web server and the endpoint handlers in your Nancy modules (see figure 8.3).

The pieces of code between the web server and the endpoint handlers form a pipeline: every request flows through each piece in turn before reaching the endpoint handler in the Nancy module. Likewise, the response from the endpoint handler flows back through the same pipeline before reaching the web server, which sends the response back to the caller. In this chapter, you'll use OWIN to implement such a pipeline; each piece of the pipeline is called *OWIN middleware*.

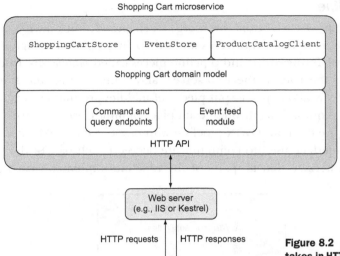

Figure 8.2 The Shopping Cart microservice takes in HTTP requests through a web server.

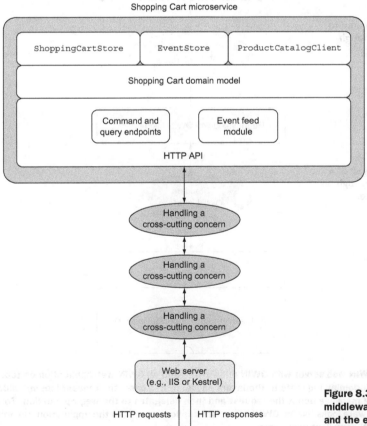

Figure 8.3 You can use a pipeline of middleware between the web server and the endpoint handler to handle cross-cutting concerns.

8.2   *The OWIN pipeline*

We touched briefly on OWIN (http://owin.org) in chapter 1, but now it's time for a closer look. OWIN is a community-driven standard for interoperability between .NET web servers, .NET web frameworks, and pipeline pieces called *middleware*. In this case, ASP.NET Core plays the role of the web server, and Nancy is the web framework. Between the two, OWIN allows you to put pieces of middleware that are executed for every request. Each request flows through each piece of middleware in turn.

The setup in figure 8.4 is an OWIN pipeline with one piece of OWIN middleware. OWIN defines the interface used to communicate between each part of the pipeline. This is a uniform interface that all parts of the pipeline implement: each piece of

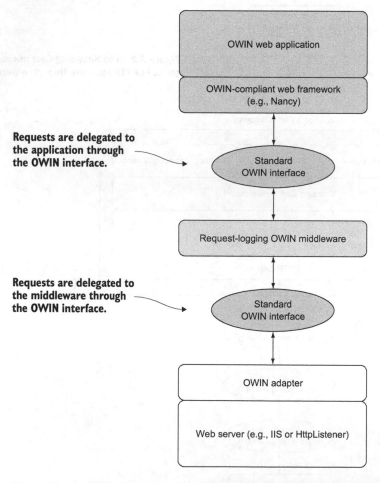

Figure 8.4   An OWIN web server with OWIN middleware and an OWIN web application on top. The web server delegates incoming requests to the layers above: in this case, the request-logging middleware, which writes a log message about the request and then delegates to the web application. To the web server, the middleware looks like an OWIN-compliant application; and to the application, the middleware looks like an OWIN-compliant web server.

middleware implements the interface, and so does the web framework. The web server doesn't implement the interface but communicates with the rest of the pipeline through the interface. By having one uniform interface, you can compose a pipeline as you like. You can put more middleware into it, you can take pieces out, or you can swap them around. Because they all use the same interface, they can be rearranged as needed.

When the request and the response pass through the middleware, the middleware can read them and even change them. The interface used between the pieces of an OWIN pipeline isn't a C# interface, but a function signature. Each piece of middleware, and even the web framework at the end of the pipeline, is a function with a signature compatible with this definition of the `AppFunc` type:

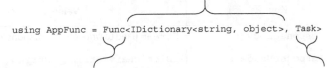

The OWIN environment is a dictionary that contains all information about the request and response. This data is in the environment under a set of standardized keys.

```
using AppFunc = Func<IDictionary<string, object>, Task>
```

The AppFunc takes an OWIN environment and returns a task. The web server initializes the environment with all request data under the standardized keys. The web server also adds the standardized response keys but adds only empty or placeholder values for response data.

The task captures the work done in the AppFunc. Because an AppFunc can be an OWIN pipeline or part of a pipeline, the task can capture the work of a complete pipeline or part of one.

The name `AppFunc` is commonly used to refer to this function signature, and I'll follow that convention, too. The idea is that you chain `AppFunc`s together, and that the OWIN environment is passed from one piece of middleware to the next when a request is being handled.

The OWIN environment contains all request and response data under keys specified by the OWIN standard. Table 8.1 gives an overview of the request keys specified by OWIN. You can find more details about each key in the OWIN standard, but for all you'll do here, this will suffice. Table 8.2 gives the same overview for the response keys.

Table 8.1 OWIN request environment keys

Required	Key	Value
Yes	`owin.RequestBody`	`Stream` with the request body, if any
Yes	`owin.RequestHeaders`	`IDictionary<string, string[]>` of request headers
Yes	`owin.RequestMethod`	HTTP request method as a string (for example, `"GET"`, `"POST"`)

Table 8.1 OWIN request environment keys (continued)

Required	Key	Value
Yes	owin.RequestPath	`string` containing the request path relative to a root
Yes	owin.RequestPathBase	`string` containing the root portion request path
Yes	owin.RequestProtocol	Request protocol name and version as a `string` (for example, "HTTP/1.1")
Yes	owin.RequestQueryString	`string` containing the query string of the HTTP request
Yes	owin.RequestScheme	URI scheme of the request as a `string` (for example, "http", "https")

Table 8.2 OWIN response environment keys

Required	Key	Value
Yes	owin.ResponseBody	`Stream` used to write out the response body, if any.
Yes	owin.ResponseHeaders	`IDictionary<string, string[]>` of response headers.
No	owin.ResponseStatusCode	HTTP response status code as an `int`. The default is 200.
No	owin.ResponseReasonPhrase	`string` containing the reason phrase associated with the given status code.
No	owin.ResponseProtocol	`string` containing the protocol name and version (such as "HTTP/1.1"). If none is provided, then the owin.RequestProtocol key's value is the default.

Because the OWIN environment is passed through the pipeline, any piece of middleware along the way can modify any key. For instance, to set the response status, a piece middleware just needs to set the value of the owin.ResponseStatusCode key.

Notice that an AppFunc can be not only a single piece of OWIN middleware, but also a pipeline. For instance, the web server calls into an AppFunc not knowing or caring whether it's a single piece of middleware or a long pipeline ending at a web framework.

When you build up a pipeline of OWIN middleware pieces, you essentially chain AppFuncs together: the first piece of middleware is given a reference to the next piece, and so on. The middleware in front of the web framework holds on to a reference to an AppFunc implementation in the web framework. When the pipeline is built and a request comes in, the server builds an OWIN environment and passes it into the pipeline.

To facilitate the chaining of OWIN middleware, you use functions of another type, MidFunc:

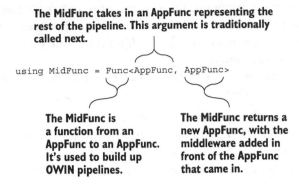

The MidFunc takes in an AppFunc representing the rest of the pipeline. This argument is traditionally called next.

```
using MidFunc = Func<AppFunc, AppFunc>
```

The MidFunc is a function from an AppFunc to an AppFunc. It's used to build up OWIN pipelines.

The MidFunc returns a new AppFunc, with the middleware added in front of the AppFunc that came in.

A function that takes in an `AppFunc` returns another `AppFunc`. A `MidFunc` is a function that takes in an `AppFunc` implementing an OWIN pipeline consisting of zero or more pieces of OWIN middleware, adds a piece of middleware in front of that, and returns an `AppFunc` for the new pipeline.

This may sound difficult, but it turns out that implementing a `MidFunc` is easy. As an example, let's turn to this short example of a piece of OWIN middleware that you saw in chapter 1:

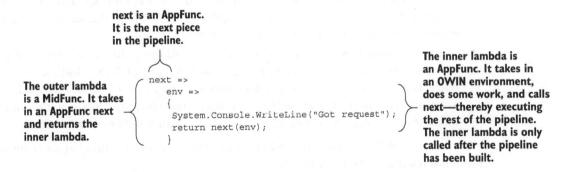

next is an AppFunc. It is the next piece in the pipeline.

The outer lambda is a MidFunc. It takes in an AppFunc next and returns the inner lambda.

```
next =>
    env =>
    {
        System.Console.WriteLine("Got request");
        return next(env);
    }
```

The inner lambda is an AppFunc. It takes in an OWIN environment, does some work, and calls next—thereby executing the rest of the pipeline. The inner lambda is only called after the pipeline has been built.

You're now well equipped to understand this code: the lambda function implements the `MidFunc`. It takes an argument (next) that implements the `AppFunc` and returns another `AppFunc` that calls the original `AppFunc` passed in (next) but does a little work first: writing to the console. Once the pipeline is set up, the value of next doesn't change; but at each request, a new environment is built and passed into the env argument.

The idea of OWIN middleware takes a little getting used to, but once you grasp it, you'll appreciate it's powerful simplicity, as shown in the following chapters.

8.2.1 What belongs in OWIN, and what belongs in Nancy?

OWIN gives you a way to build a pipeline that each request flows through. The different parts of the pipeline can react to the request and write to the response. Likewise, Nancy lets you handle requests and write responses. With Nancy, you primarily handle requests in route handlers in Nancy modules, but you can also add code that's executed before and after the route handler. You do that by adding to the Nancy `Before` or `After` pipelines, as mentioned briefly in chapter 6. Effectively, Nancy also lets you build up a pipeline. But what belongs where?

To decide what to implement in OWIN middleware and what to implement in Nancy, you can follow a few simple rules:

- Code addressing a cross-cutting concern and meant to be used across many microservices belongs in OWIN middleware. These reusable pieces of code should have few dependencies so they don't enforce too many technology choices on the microservices in which they're used. Therefore, you want to keep them independent of Nancy.

- Code that addresses a domain or business rule of a single microservice belongs in application code behind a Nancy module. This type of code doesn't depend on HTTP and therefore doesn't need to depend on OWIN or Nancy. Putting it in a separate component—for example, a domain model—enables you to keep the implementation of business and domain rules clean and readable.

- Code that handles HTTP requests and responses in a way that's specific to a particular endpoint belongs in a Nancy module. This code interprets the incoming HTTP requests and then hands off control to the domain model. That interpretation is at the same time tightly coupled to HTTP and to the specifics of the endpoint, making the Nancy module the right place for it.

- Code that addresses a concern that cuts across all endpoints in a microservice, but not across several microservices, usually belongs in OWIN middleware, but not always. The more technical the concern is, the more I lean toward middleware; and the more domain or business logic there is in the concern, the more I lean toward Nancy modules or, in rare cases, a Nancy `Before` or `After` handler.

I've introduced OWIN and discussed what it's used for. The rest of this chapter is about writing and testing OWIN middleware.

8.3   Writing middleware

We'll look at two ways to write OWIN middleware:

- *As a lambda*—You've seen middleware as a lambda in chapter 1 as well as earlier in this chapter. In the next section, I'll reiterate this style.
- *As a class that has a method that implements* `AppFunc`—You'll see this style in section 8.3.2.

In both cases, you can use the convenient *LibOwin* library, which allows you to work with the OWIN environment through types rather than working directly with the `IDictionary<string, object>` environment.

LibOwin

LibOwin is a small library that will help you work with OWIN. It's a little different from other libraries you use: it's a *source code library*, which means it consists of source code rather than .NET assemblies. LibOwin consists of a single file, LibOwin.cs, that contains a number of types that make working with OWIN easier. Primarily you'll use the `OwinContext` type, which wraps the OWIN environment dictionary and lets you access the keys in the environment dictionary through strongly typed properties. This, for instance, gets the HTTP method of the HTTP request from the environment:

```
// env is an OWIN environment dictionary
var context = new OwinContext(env);
var method = context.Request.Method
// do something with the method
```

In addition to using LibOwin in middleware implementations, you'll use it when writing tests for middleware, to create and work with OWIN environments that you'll send into middleware to test it.

At the time of writing, `dotnet restore` doesn't support distributing source code through NuGet packages; so instead of using the LibOwin NuGet package, you need to download the LibOwin.cs file. LibOwin can be found on GitHub at https://github.com/damianh/LibOwin, and LibOwin.cs is at http://mng.bz/8pRq. From PowerShell, you can use the `wget` command to download the file like this:

```
PS> wget https://raw.githubusercontent.com/<lineArrow />damianh/LibOwin/
➥ master/src/LibOwin

/LibOwin.cs -OutFile LibOwin.cs
```

Having run this, you'll have your own copy of LibOwin.cs to add to your projects like any other source file. The code in LibOwin.cs requires two NuGet packages, System.Security.Claims and System.Globalization, which you add like any other NuGet package.

8.3.1 Middleware as lambdas

You've already seen middleware implemented with a lambda function. In this section, I'll show you how to use LibOwin in a middleware lambda and then reiterate how to add lambda middleware to the OWIN pipeline in a startup.cs file.

This is the lambda middleware you've seen a few times before:

```
next =>                                    next is an AppFunc. The
  env =>                                   entire lambda is a MidFunc.
  {
    System.Console.WriteLine("Got request");     The inner lambda is an
    return next(env);                            AppFunc and takes in an
  }                                              OWIN environment in env.
```

If you want to write not just a static string to the console but, say, the path and method of the request, you can use the `OwinContext` type from LibOwin.

Listing 8.1   Using `OwinContext` to get request details

```
next =>
  env =>
  {                                    env is the OWIN
                                       environment dictionary.
    var context = new OwinContext(env);      Creates the strongly typed
    var method = context.Request.Method;     OwinContext from the
    var path = context.Request.Path;         OWIN environment
    System.Console.WriteLine($"Got request: {method} {path}");
    return next(env);
  }                            Picks out request data conveniently
                                via properties on OwinContext
```

You instantiate an `OwinContext` from the environment and dot into the properties. To add this kind of middleware to the OWIN pipeline, you use the `UseOwin` extension method on `IAppBuilder`, which is provided by ASP.NET Core in the `Startup` class.

Listing 8.2   Using `UseOwin` to build up the OWIN pipeline

```
public class Startup
{                                                        ASP.NET Core calls
  public void Configure(IApplicationBuilder app)         this during startup.
  {
    app.UseOwin(
      buildFunc => buildFunc(next => env =>              buildFunc builds an
    {                                                    OWIN pipeline from
      var context = new OwinContext(env);                MidFunc.
      var method = context.Request.Method;
      var path = context.Request.Path;
      System.Console.WriteLine($"Got request: {method} {path}");
      return next(env);
    }));
  }
}
```

Lets you use OWIN with ASP.NET Core

You've used the `UseOwin` extension method in previous chapters in every HTTP API project to add Nancy to the OWIN pipeline.

8.3.2   *Middleware classes*

Writing middleware as lambda functions works, but it becomes somewhat difficult when the middleware is more complex. In such cases, it's nicer to use a class to implement the middleware.

To use a class to implement middleware, you can create a class that has a method whose signature is the `AppFunc`.

Listing 8.3 Middleware implemented in a class

```
public class ConsoleMiddleware
{
  private AppFunc next;

  public ConsoleMiddleware(AppFunc next)
  {
    this.next = next;
  }

  public Task Invoke(IDictionary<string, object> env)
  {
    var context = new OwinContext(env);
    var method = context.Request.Method;
    var path = context.Request.Path;
    System.Console.WriteLine($"Got request: {method} {path}");
    return next(env);
  }
}
```

Holds on to next when instantiated

Has the AppFunc signature

Middleware in this style takes in the next AppFunc in the constructor and stores it in a private variable, such that it can be called as needed in the Invoke method, which implements the middleware's behavior. To add this kind of middleware to the OWIN pipeline, you instantiate it and then use the Invoke method as a delegate:

```
app.UseOwin(buildFunc =>
    buildFunc(next => new ConsoleMiddleware(next).Invoke));
```

Now you know how to implement middleware as lambdas as well as classes. Next, let's look at testing middleware.

8.4 *Testing middleware and pipelines*

Testing OWIN middleware is straightforward: you use LibOwin to create an OWIN environment for the cases you want to test, and then you call the middleware, passing in that OWIN environment.

> **NOTE** As detailed in the previous chapter, you can create test projects from Visual Studio or using Yeoman. These projects use xUnit, and that's also the test framework used here.

There's one small issue to overcome: in order to call middleware, you first need to provide it with a value for next. You get around that by passing in an AppFunc that does nothing, like this:

```
AppFunc noOp = env => Task.FromResult(0);     <--- "noOp" is short for "no operation."
```

You'll use no-operation middleware in tests as a stub to provide to middleware under test.

With this in place, you can write tests for your middleware. Suppose you have the following lambda-based middleware that you want to test.

Listing 8.4   An example of a piece of middleware

```
namespace Middleware
{
  using System;
  using System.Collections.Generic;
  using System.Threading.Tasks;
  using LibOwin;

  using AppFunc = Func<IDictionary<string, object>, Task>;

  public class Middleware
  {
    public Func<AppFunc, AppFunc> Impl =        <──── Middleware lambda
      next => async env =>
      {
        var ctx = new OwinContext(env);
        if (ctx.Request.Path.Value == "/test/path")     <──┐  If the request path is
          ctx.Response.StatusCode = 404;                   │  /test/path, respond
        else                                               │  with 404 Not Found.
          await next(env);                                 │  Otherwise, call the
      };                                                   │  rest of the pipeline.
  }
}
```

You can write a test for this middleware as shown next.

Listing 8.5   Test that invokes middleware directly

```
namespace OwinMiddlewareTests
{
  using System;
  using System.Collections.Generic;
  using System.Threading.Tasks;
  using Xunit;
  using LibOwin;

  using AppFunc = Func<IDictionary<string, object>, Task>;

  public class Middleware_should
  {                                                              No-operation
    private AppFunc noOp = env => Task.FromResult(0);      <──┘  AppFunc

    [Fact]
    public void Return404_for_test_path()
    {                                                         Sets up the OWIN
      var ctx = new OwinContext();                       <──┘ environment for this test
      ctx.Request.Scheme =
        LibOwin.Infrastructure.Constants.Https;
```

Constructs a pipeline of the
middleware under test and the
no-operation AppFunc

```
ctx.Request.Path = new PathString("/test/path");
ctx.Request.Method = "GET";

var pipeline = Middleware.Middleware.Impl(noOp));

var env = ctx.Environment;
pipeline(env);

Assert.Equal(404, ctx.Response.StatusCode);
    }
  }
}
```

Invokes the pipeline
with the middleware
under test

Asserts on the contents
of the OWIN environment

The pattern of this test is to do the following:

1 Set up an OWIN environment that mimics the scenario you want to test. This is done using the helper types in LibOwin.

2 Create a small OWIN pipeline consisting of the middleware under test followed by the no-operation middleware. The result is an `AppFunc` that's ready to be called with an OWIN environment.

3 Call the pipeline with the OWIN environment set up at the beginning of the test.

4 Make assertions on the contents of the OWIN environment or other things that the middleware under test is expected to work on. If, for instance, the middleware under test creates a response, that should be part of the environment and therefore accessible through the `OwinContext` object.

You can use the same pattern when testing class-based middleware. The only difference is in the line that constructs the pipeline. In listing 8.5, it looks like this:

```
var pipeline = Middleware.Middleware.Impl(noOp));
```

In a test for the class-based middleware in listing 8.4, it looks like this:

```
var pipeline = new ConsoleMiddleware(noOp).Invoke)
```

Notice that, once again, you pass in the no-operation `AppFunc`—the noOp—to the middleware under test.

To test a longer pipeline of several pieces of middleware, you build the pipeline by passing one into the other as next, just as you passed noOp into your middleware. Once the pipeline is built, the rest is just like the middleware test in listing 8.5. If, for instance, you want to test the lambda-based middleware and the class-based middleware together, the line setting up the pipeline changes to this:

```
var pipeline =
  new ConsoleMiddleware(Middleware.Middleware.Impl(noOp)))
    .Invoke)
```

You compose the two pieces of middleware to form a short pipeline, resulting in an `AppFunc` that you can test by calling it with an OWIN environment.

Now that you've learned how write and test OWIN middleware, you're ready to build middleware to address some important cross-cutting concerns in the coming chapters.

8.5   Summary

- Some concerns cut across all or many microservices in a system. Reusing code that addresses these concerns can save you a significant amount of duplicated effort.

- Reusing code that addresses cross-cutting concerns ensures consistency across microservices. For the cross-cutting concerns that make your microservices well-behaved citizens in the production environment—like request logging and monitoring—consistency is important.

- OWIN gives you a clean, flexible way to compose middleware into pipelines.

- OWIN middleware is nicely separated from the business logic of any microservice.

- OWIN middleware lends itself to reuse across many microservices.

- Many cross-cutting concerns can be implemented as OWIN middleware.

- OWIN middleware can be a lambda function. The lambda implements the `MidFunc`.

- OWIN middleware can be implemented with a class. The class takes in an `App-Func` in the constructor and has an `Invoke` method that implements another `AppFunc`. When you use class-based middleware, you form a `MidFunc` from the constructor and the `Invoke` method.

- LibOwin is a library that provides some convenient types that make it easier to work with OWIN. For instance, LibOwin gives you the `OwinContext` type, which is a strongly typed wrapper around the OWIN environment dictionary.

- OWIN middleware is straightforward to test: you call it with an OWIN environment, wait for the task to be returned, and then assert on the contents of the OWIN environment.

- OWIN pipelines are straightforward to test. Just like individual pieces of middleware, you call them with an OWIN dictionary and assert on the environment after the pipeline has executed.

Cross-cutting concerns: monitoring and logging

9

In this chapter, you'll start using the knowledge about OWIN you gained in chapter 8 to create reusable pieces of OWIN middleware that address some important cross-cutting concerns: monitoring and logging. Both are needed across all microservices, and they play an important role in making a microservice system operation-friendly. Once your system is in production, you need to know whether all your microservices are up, which is why you need to monitor them. In addition, as discussed in chapter 6, you need good logging to be able to diagnose the system.

Here, you'll build middleware in the context of one microservice. Then, in chapter 11, you'll take that middleware and put it into NuGet packages, ready to be reused easily across all your microservices.

9.1   *Monitoring needs in microservices*

When you deploy any server-side system into production, you need to be able to check the health of the system. You want to know whether the system is up, whether it's experiencing failures or errors, and whether it's performing as well as it usually does. This is true of any system. With a traditional monolithic system, you'd most likely set up some monitoring and add logging to the system, as shown in figure 9.1. Logging is often done many places in the code base—where there's something important to log—and the messages are often stored in a database.

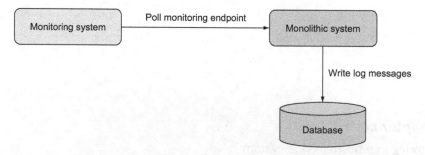

Figure 9.1   Traditionally, you set up monitoring around a system and add logging to the system code that logs messages to a database.

The situation for a system of microservices is similar. You have the same overarching need to monitor the health of the system, in terms of availability, performance, throughput, and error rates. The difference is that a microservice system consists of many small pieces that run independently and are deployed independently, and you need to monitor all of those small parts. In figure 9.2, that seems complicated; but it doesn't have to be, if you build an infrastructure that lets you easily make your microservices monitoring friendly. We'll get to that in a bit.

In order to monitor a microservice, you add to it two endpoints that the monitoring system will poll. As long as a microservice responds successfully to the polling to both endpoints, it's considered to be up. Figure 9.3 shows a microservice where two monitoring endpoints have been added: one at /_monitor/shallow and one at /_monitor/deep.

The first endpoint—at /_monitor/shallow—does nothing but respond to every request with a 204 No Content status code, when successful:

```
HTTP/1.1 204 No Content
```

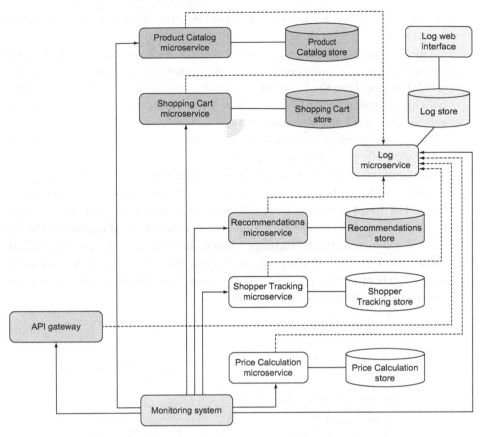

Figure 9.2 Each microservice is monitored by polling an endpoint.

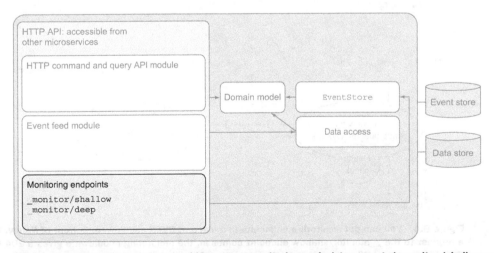

Figure 9.3 Every microservice should have two monitoring endpoints: one at /_monitor/shallow and one at /_monitor/deep. The monitoring system polls both endpoints. As long as both respond with a success response, the monitor considers the microservice to be up.

If this endpoint doesn't respond as expected, the microservice is most likely completely down.

The second endpoint—at /_monitor/deep—checks the internal health of the microservice and, if everything is OK, also responds with a 204 No Content status code. What checking the internal health of a microservice entails differs from microservice to microservice, but it's typical to run a simple query toward the microservice's database and check that the result makes sense.

You can implement both monitoring endpoints in OWIN middleware, resulting in an OWIN pipeline like the one shown in figure 9.4

You implement the monitoring endpoints in OWIN middleware because doing so lets you keep the monitoring concerns separated from the business logic of the microservice. Furthermore, because you'll put the middleware in a NuGet package and reuse it in many microservices, it's nice that it has minimal dependencies and therefore doesn't dictate the technology choices made in the microservices that use the middleware. Later in this chapter, you'll implement the monitoring middleware and see how each microservice can provide its own implementation of the health check done in the /_monitor/deep endpoint.

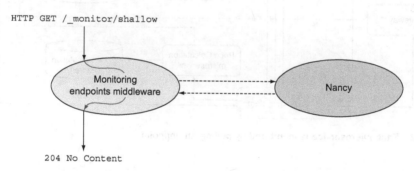

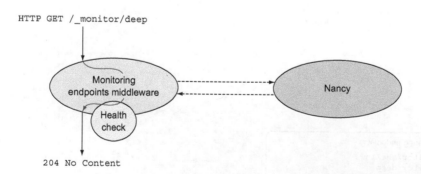

Figure 9.4   You can put monitoring endpoints in a piece of OWIN middleware in front of Nancy. When a request to the /_monitor/shallow endpoint comes in, the monitoring middleware gives a 204 No Content response. When a request to the /_monitor/deep endpoint comes in, the monitoring middleware calls a function that performs a health check and then responds with 204 No Content if the health check succeeded. Other requests pass through the monitoring middleware and on to Nancy.

9.2 Logging needs in microservices

In addition to monitoring each individual microservice, you also need to send out log messages regarding failures, errors, performance, and whatever else you need insight into. As discussed in chapter 6, you can introduce a centralized Logging microservice that receives log messages from all the other microservices, saves them (for example, in a search engine), and provides easy access to them through dashboards and search UIs (see figure 9.5). Again, you want to be able to easily set up each microservice to send log messages to the Logging microservice.

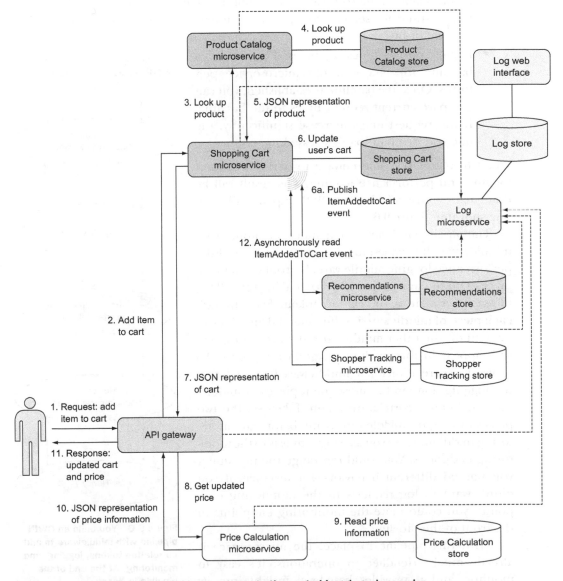

Figure 9.5   All microservices send log messages to the central Logging microservice.

You also want each microservice to perform a base level of logging. All microservices should log HTTP requests, HTTP responses, and the processing time for each request. These logs provide insight into the microservice's health:

- The HTTP request log provides invaluable insight into what's going on in production when you need to debug problems. Request logs aren't enough for debugging, though. The microservice's business logic should also send log messages to the Logging microservice about all unusual occurrences.
- The logged HTTP responses reveal whether requests to a microservice are failing. In particular, a microservice that responds often with status codes in the 500 range—used for server errors, such as unhandled exceptions—is most likely stressed or buggy.
- Logged request times can be used to establish a baseline for how well the microservice performs. Once the baseline is established, you can compare current request times to the baseline. If the request times increase significantly, the microservice is probably stressed.

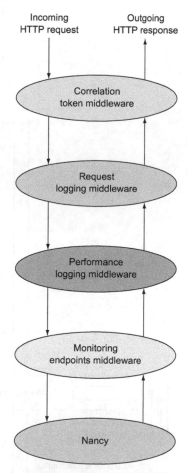

You'll turn to OWIN middleware to perform request logging and performance logging. The result will be that each microservice has an OWIN pipeline like the one shown in figure 9.6.

The pipeline in figure 9.6 includes the monitoring middleware, the request-logging middleware, and the performance-logging middleware. In front of them is a piece of middleware responsible for making sure all log messages contain a correlation token. Even though each piece of middleware is self-contained and doesn't depend on the other middleware, the order in which they appear in the pipeline is significant. Figure 9.6 shows the correlation token middleware first, such that the logging done in the subsequent pieces of middleware includes a correlation token. Likewise, the two pieces of logging middleware come before the monitoring middleware, so you also log requests to the monitoring endpoints. You could rearrange the pipeline if you wanted different behavior—for instance, if you didn't want to log requests to the monitoring endpoints, you could move the monitoring endpoints to the front of the pipeline.

With this pipeline in place, the microservice is already much friendlier to operations: it's easy to monitor, and it provides base-level insight into its

Figure 9.6 You build an OWIN pipeline with middleware to add correlation tokens, logging, and monitoring. At the end of the pipeline is Nancy.

health through the logs. In chapter 11, you'll create NuGet packages containing the OWIN middleware pieces, to make it easy to set up new microservices with the standard monitoring endpoints and good basic logging behavior.

9.2.1 *Structured logging with Serilog*

Traditional logging libraries treat log messages as simple strings, possibly with an exception attached, but we'll use something better: a *structured logging* library named Serilog. The idea of structured logging is to allow log messages to contain structured data: a log message contains not only a flat message—like "something went wrong"—but also objects.

Serilog introduces a bit of syntax to log messages on top of .NET format strings. The extra syntax lets you give names to parameters and control whether a parameter's value should be converted to a string with a .ToString() call, or whether the object should be included as a whole in the log message. Named parameters are enclosed in braces: for example, "{RequestTime}". You tell Serilog to include the entire value in the message by putting an @ in front of the name: "{@Request}". As with .NET format strings, you add formatting directives to parameters without a leading @.

For instance, you can use Serilog to send a log message like this, assuming that log is an object of the Serilog type Ilogger:

```
var simplyfiedRequest = new
{
  Path = "/foo",
  Method = "GET",
  Protocol = "HTTP",
};

var requestTime = 200;

log.Information(
    "Processed request: {@Request} in {RequestTime:000} ms.",
    simplyfiedRequest,
    requestTime);
```

simplyfiedRequest and requestTime are objects that are part of the message. Like other logging frameworks, Serilog lets you configure different *sinks* to which log messages are written. The sink you'll use here is the console. When the previous log message is written to the console, simplyfiedRequest and requestTime are JSON serialized and inserted into the log message string. Serilog also adds some metadata, so the message written to the console looks like this:

```
09:14:22 [Information] Processed request { Path: "/foo", Method: "GET",
⇒ Protocol: "HTTP" } in 200 ms.
```

As you can see, this preserves all the data from the original log message, because the complete simplyfiedRequest object and requestTime are included in the message written to the console. This is nice, but it becomes even better when the sink is a search engine like Elasticsearch. When you use the Elasticsearch sink, the objects included in the log messages—like `simplyfiedRequest`—are stored and indexed in the search engine. This means you can search for log messages based on values of particular properties of the objects included in the messages. For instance, you might search for log messages with a `Request` object that has a `Path` property with the value `/foo`. The previous message would be included, but a log message about a request to `/bar` wouldn't.

Preserving the structure of the data included in log messages means the web frontend of the Logging microservice can present the log message in a structured way. The end results are logs that are easier to search, easier to get an overview from, and include more data, and that you can drill into as needed. One such frontend is Kibana, which works well with logs stored in Elasticsearch and provides powerful search and visualization tools.

As you'll see when you implement the logging middleware later, you can configure Serilog to include extra data with every log message. You'll use this ability to add a correlation token to every log message.

For the remainder of this chapter, you'll be implementing monitoring and logging. You want to do this in all microservices, so you can work in the context of any one of the microservices you've already implemented. You'll use the Shopping Cart microservice as an example and build on top of the code from chapter 5, but the code fits just the same in the other microservices.

9.3   *Implementing the monitoring middleware*

In this section, you'll create a piece of middleware that implements the two monitoring endpoints we discussed earlier. The endpoints will behave as follows:

- /_monitor/shallow responds to every request with a 204 No Content status.
- /_monitor/deep performs a basic health check and then responds with 204 No Content if the health check succeeds. If the health check fails, it responds with 503 Service Unavailable. The health check will query the Shopping Cart microservice database to see how many shopping carts there are. As long as that number is above a certain threshold, the health check is successful; but if the count drops below the threshold, the health check fails. A health check like this must be built based on knowledge of the system: this particular check makes sense only if you have enough traffic on the e-commerce site that there should always be more active shopping carts than the threshold. Over time, you gain more insight into how the system runs and how it looks when it's healthy. You can and should exploit this knowledge to make health checks better over time.

The plan to implement the monitoring endpoint is as follows:

1 Add LibOwin to the Shopping Cart microservice.
2 Add a new MonitoringMiddleware.cs file to the microservice.
3 Create a piece of OWIN middleware that implements the /_monitor/shallow endpoint.

4 Add the implementation of the /_monitor/deep endpoint to the monitoring middleware.
5 Create the health check for Shopping Cart.
6 Add the monitoring middleware to the Shopping Cart OWIN pipeline.

Let's get started.

9.3.1 *Implementing the shallow monitoring endpoint*

The first thing to do is to add LibOwin to the Shopping Cart microservice as described in chapter 8.

Next, add a file called MonitoringMiddleware.cs to Shopping Cart. Put the following code in it, to implements the /_monitor/shallow endpoint as a piece of OWIN middleware.

Listing 9.1 OWIN middleware that implements a shallow monitoring endpoint

```
namespace ShoppingCart.Infrastructure
{
  using System.Collections.Generic;
  using System.Threading.Tasks;              OWIN AppFunc
  using LibOwin;                             signature, discussed
                                             in depth in chapter 8
  using AppFunc =
    System.Func<System.Collections.Generic.IDictionary<string, object>,
                System.Threading.Tasks.Task>;

  public class MonitoringMiddleware
  {
    private AppFunc next;

    public MonitoringMiddleware(AppFunc next)
    {                                          Stores a reference to
      this.next = next;                        the rest of the pipeline
    }

    public Task Invoke(IDictionary<string, object> env)
    {
      var context = new OwinContext(env);
      if (context.Request.Path.Equals("/_monitor/shallow"))
        return ShallowEndpoint(context);
      else
        return this.next(env);                 Sets the response status code
    }                                          to 204, and short-circuits the
                                                                    pipeline
    private Task ShallowEndpoint(OwinContext context)
    {
      context.Response.StatusCode = 204;
      return Task.FromResult(0);
    }
  }
}
```

Checks whether the incoming request is for the /_monitor/shallow endpoint

Invokes the rest of the pipeline if the request isn't for a monitoring endpoint

This code implements a piece of OWIN middleware that responds to the shallow endpoint. The middleware uses the class style you learned about in chapter 8. You use the OwinContext type from LibOwin to make it easier to work with the OWIN environment.

9.3.2 *Implementing the deep monitoring endpoint*

You'll enhance the piece of middleware that responds to the shallow monitoring endpoint to also implement the other monitoring endpoint: /_monitor/deep. To do so, assume that a function that performs a health check is injected into MonitoringMiddleware when it's created. The health check is expected to be a function that takes no arguments and returns a bool indicating whether the health check was successful. You also want to let the health check be async, so instead of a bool, the health check can return a Task<bool>.

To allow the health check function to be injected, add a parameter to the MonitoringMiddleware constructor. Also, add a private field in which to store the health check function.

Listing 9.2   Monitoring middleware with a health check injected

```
public class MonitoringMiddleware
{
  private AppFunc next;
  private Func<Task<bool>> healthCheck;

  public MonitoringMiddleware(AppFunc next, Func<Task<bool>> healthCheck)
  {
    this.next = next;
    this.healthCheck = healthCheck;
  }
...
}
```

With the health check function available in MonitoringMiddleware, you're ready to implement the /_monitor/deep endpoint. You'll refactor the Invoke method on MonitoringMiddleware slightly to look for any path that starts with /_monitor instead of only the /_monitor/shallow path. A second check on the path distinguishes between the /_monitor/shallow and /_monitor/deep endpoints.

Listing 9.3   Monitoring endpoints and calling healthCheck

```
private static readonly PathString monitorPath =
  new PathString("/_monitor");
private static readonly PathString monitorShallowPath =
  new PathString("/_monitor/shallow");
private static readonly PathString monitorDeepPath =
  new PathString("/_monitor/deep");

public Task Invoke(IDictionary<string, object> env)
```

> All requests to monitoring
> endpoints are handled in
> this branch.

```
{
  var context = new OwinContext(env);
  if (context.Request.Path.StartsWithSegments(monitorPath))
    return HandleMonitorEndpoint(context);
  else
    return this.next(env);
}
```

> All other requests
> are passed on to
> the rest of the
> pipeline.

```
private Task HandleMonitorEndpoint(OwinContext context)
{
  if (context.Request.Path.StartsWithSegments(monitorShallowPath))
    return ShallowEndpoint(context);
  else if (context.Request.Path.StartsWithSegments(monitorDeepPath))
    return DeepEndpoint(context);
  return Task.FromResult(0);
}
```

> Returns Task even
> though nothing is
> explicitly returned
> because the method
> is async

```
private async Task DeepEndpoint(OwinContext context)
{
  if (await this.healthCheck())
    context.Response.StatusCode = 204;
  else
    context.Response.StatusCode = 503;
}
```

> The health check may
> be async, so you must
> await the result.

```
private Task ShallowEndpoint(OwinContext context)
{
  context.Response.StatusCode = 204;
  return Task.FromResult(0);
}
```

Now you have a piece of middleware that implements both monitoring endpoints and is independent of anything particular to the Shopping Cart microservice. The implementation of the health check function will be particular to Shopping Cart, but you've purposefully kept that out of the middleware.

With the middleware in place, it's time to implement the health check. Then you'll add `MonitoringMiddleware` to the microservice's OWIN pipeline.

As mentioned earlier, the health check queries the Shopping Cart database for the number of shopping carts and compares the count to a threshold. Recall that the microservice uses a SQL database and that you're using Dapper to query that database. Using Dapper again, the following code performs the health check.

Listing 9.4 Health check that looks at the number of shopping carts

```
private const string connectionString =
  @"Data Source=.\SQLEXPRESS;
  Initial Catalog=ShoppingCart;
```

> Connection string
> for the shopping
> cart database

```
                Integrated Security=True";

    private readonly int threshold = 1000;
                                                    Queries for how many shopping
    public async Task<bool> HealthCheck()              carts are in the database
    {
      using (var conn = new SqlConnection(connectionString))
      {
        var count =
          (await conn.QueryAsync<int>("select count(ID) from ShoppingCart"))  ◁─┘
          .Single();
        return count > this.threshold;         ◁─┐ Decides whether the query
      }                                           │ results indicate that the
    }                                             │ microservice is healthy
```

This code encapsulates something specific for the Shopping Cart microservice: a simple operation that checks whether the microservice is healthy. This check makes sure Shopping Cart has access to its database and that there are shopping carts in the database. It doesn't capture every imaginable failure mode, but it can give a good indication of the microservice's health.

9.3.3 Adding the monitoring middleware to the OWIN pipeline

The only bits remaining are to inject the health check into `MonitoringMiddleware` and to add the middleware to the OWIN pipeline. You do both things in the `Startup` class.

Until now, you've only used the `Startup` class to add Nancy to the pipeline. Now, you'll put the health check method into `Startup` and extend the pipeline, resulting in the following listing.

Listing 9.5 Adding `MonitoringMiddleware` to the OWIN pipeline in `Startup`

```
namespace ShoppingCart
{
  using System.Data.SqlClient;
  using System.Threading.Tasks;
  using Microsoft.AspNet.Builder;
  using System.Linq;
  using Dapper;
  using Nancy.Owin;
  using global::ShoppingCart.Infrastructure;

  public class Startup
  {
    public void Configure(IApplicationBuilder app)
    {                                                     Adds
      app.UseOwin(buildFunc =>                            MonitoringMiddleware
      {                                                   to the OWIN pipeline
        buildFunc(next =>                        ◁─┘
          new MonitoringMiddleware(next, HealthCheck).Invoke);
```

```
      buildFunc.UseNancy();
    });
  }

  private const string connectionString =
    @"Data Source=.\SQLEXPRESS;
    Initial Catalog=ShoppingCart;
    Integrated Security=True";
  private readonly int threshold = 1000;

  public async Task<bool> HealthCheck()            The same health check
  {                                         ◁──┐  you saw earlier
    using (var conn = new SqlConnection(connectionString))
    {
      var count =
        (await conn.QueryAsync<int>("select cound(ID) from ShoppingCart"))
        .Single();
      return count > this.threshold;
    }
  }
}
}
```

With this in place, you can run the Shopping Cart microservice with dotnet and test the monitoring endpoints. A request to the /_monitor/shallow endpoint looks like this:

```
GET /_monitor/shallow HTTP/1.1
Host: localhost:5000
Accept: application/json
```

A successful response is as follows:

```
HTTP/1.1 204 No Content
```

Here's a request to the /_monitor/deep endpoint:

```
GET /_monitor/deep HTTP/1.1
Host: localhost:5000
Accept: application/json
```

And this is a successful response:

```
HTTP/1.1 204 No Content
```

Finally, the following is a failure response:

```
HTTP/1.1 503 Service Unavailable
```

This concludes the implementation of the monitoring middleware. Because only the health check is specific to the Shopping Cart microservice, and because that's implemented outside of the middleware, the middleware lends itself well to reuse across microservices.

9.4   *Implementing the logging middleware*

Next, you'll implement three pieces of middleware that relate to logging:

- One that makes sure all log messages includes a correlation token. Along with this, you'll make sure all outgoing HTTP requests contain the correlation token.
- One that logs all requests and responses.
- One that times the handling of each request and logs the result.

As mentioned earlier, you'll use Serilog to write log messages. You'll configure Serilog to write the log messages to the console; but Serilog supports writing to lots of places, including Elasticsearch, which you can use to send messages to the Logging microservice.

In this and the following sections, you'll see how to do the following:

1 Install and configure Serilog, and create a Serilog logger.
2 Write a piece of middleware that ensures that all log messages include a correlation token. If the incoming request has a correlation token in a header, the middleware will use that token; otherwise, it will create a new token and use that.
3 Write the necessary configuration and factory code to make sure outgoing requests have the correlation token.
4 Write a piece of middleware that logs all requests as well as all responses.
5 Write a piece of middleware that times the handling of each request and logs each one.
6 Add all three pieces of middleware to the OWIN pipeline in the Shopping Cart microservice.

The first thing to do is install the `Serilog` and `Serilog.Sinks.ColoredConsole` NuGet packages. You do that by adding them to the project.json file:

```
"dependencies": {
    "Microsoft.AspNetCore.Server.IISIntegration": "1.0.0",
    "Microsoft.AspNetCore.Server.Kestrel": "1.0.0",
    "Microsoft.AspNetCore.Owin": "1.0.0",
    "Nancy": "2.0.0-barneyrubble",
    "Polly": "4.2.1",
    "Dapper": "1.50.0-rc2a",
    "LibOwin": "1.0.0",
    "Serilog": "2.0.0-rc-600",
    "Serilog.Sinks.ColoredConsole": "2.0.0-beta-1001"
}
```

Now, go to the Startup.cs file to configure Serilog and create a logger object. The logger object is an `ILogger`—an interface from Serilog—and is the object used to send out log messages. Add this method to the `Startup` class.

Listing 9.6 Configuring and creating a Serilog logger

The correlation token will be added to a log context. This enriches all log messages with it.

Sets up logging to the console with a format including the correlation token

```
private ILogger ConfigureLogger()
{
  return new LoggerConfiguration()
    .Enrich.FromLogContext()
    .WriteTo.ColoredConsole(
      LogEventLevel.Verbose,
      "{NewLine}{Timestamp:HH:mm:ss} [{Level}]
      ({CorrelationToken}) {Message}{NewLine}{Exception}")
    .CreateLogger();
}
```

The `LoggerConfiguration` type is the entry point to a fluent API for configuring Serilog. Here, you configure Serilog to write to the console and to include the correlation token in what is written out. Serilog lets you write log messages to several different places at the same time—you add more `WriteTo` segments to do so. Serilog also allows you to *enrich* log messages, which means adding extra properties to them. Enriching can be used to add a server name, an environment name (such as QA or production), the role of the user who initiated the request, or whatever else you're interested in putting in log messages that isn't readily available in the code where you write the messages. Here, you use enriching to add the correlation token. You add the token to the *log context*, which is a Serilog facility that allows you to add log properties to everything that goes on in a certain context. We'll return to what this means shortly.

You'll call the `ConfigureLogger` method in the `Configure` method in the `Startup` class. After you've written all three pieces of middleware, you'll send the logger into the ones that need it. Remember that the `Configure` method is called during startup by ASP.NET Core. For now, it looks like this.

Listing 9.7 Creating a logger in `Configure` by calling `ConfigureLogger`

```
public void Configure(IApplicationBuilder app)
{
  var log = ConfigureLogger();

  app.UseOwin(buildFunc =>
  {
    buildFunc(next => new MonitoringMiddleware(next, HealthCheck).Invoke);
    buildFunc.UseNancy();
  });
}
```

Now that you've configured and created a logger, let's add a correlation token to the log context.

9.4.1 *Adding correlation tokens to all log messages*

Recall from chapter 6 that log messages become more valuable if you can use them to trace how a user request moves through the microservice system. The user request probably won't be handled by a single microservice. It's more likely that several microservices will collaborate to fulfill the user request. Being able to trace user requests across all those collaborating microservices is useful—and that's what a correlation token can give you. A correlation token is a GUID that you attach to a request and then pass to all collaborators when you call them during handling of the request. You pass the correlation token from one microservice to another in a custom HTTP request header called `Correlation-Token`:

```
GET /shoppingcart/42 HTTP/1.1
Host: localhost:5000
Accept: application/json
Correlation-Token: 600580e6-90b6-47e7-a054-1f5d2731135f    ◁──┐ Contains a
                                                              correlation token
```

The piece of middleware you're about to write will look for a `Correlation-Token` request header and, if it finds one, add it to the log context. Otherwise, it will create a new token and add that to the log context. Let's look at the middleware and then talk about what the log context does.

Add a new LoggingMiddleware file to the Shopping Cart microservice. You'll implement all three pieces of middleware in this file, starting with the following, which adds a correlation token to the Serilog log context.

> **Listing 9.8 OWIN middleware implemented as a lambda**

```
namespace ShoppingCart.Infrastructure
{
  using System;
  using LibOwin;
  using Serilog;
  using Serilog.Context;

  public class CorrelationToken
  {
    public static AppFunc Middleware(AppFunc next)
    {
      return async env =>                          Tries to find a correlation
      {                                            token in the request header
        Guid correlationToken;
        var owinContext = new OwinContext(env);
        if (!(owinContext.Request.Headers["Correlation-Token"] != null
            && Guid.TryParse(owinContext.Request.Headers["Correlation-
            ➥ Token"],                                                    ◁──
                            out correlationToken)))
          correlationToken = Guid.NewGuid();
```

Saves the correlation token for later use

```
owinContext.Set("correlationToken", correlationToken.ToString());   ◄─┘
using (LogContext.PushProperty("CorrelationToken", correlationToken))  ◄─┐
  await next(env);
};
}
}
}
```

**Adds the correlation
token to the log context**

This is implemented as lambda-style OWIN middleware. It tries to read a `Correlation-Token` request header from the OWIN environment; if it finds one with a GUID as the value, it uses that GUID as the correlation token. The middleware adds the correlation token to Serilog's log context. When a logger is created, it can be configured to use the log context to enrich all log messages. That's how you configured the logger earlier, which means the log messages you send will be enriched with the properties in the context. The correlation token is in the log context for all code executed under the `using` statement: that is, everything executed in the line `await next(env)`, including the rest of the OWIN pipeline, any middleware you add after the correlation token middleware, and Nancy. All in all, this means all log message you send in those pieces of middleware, in Nancy modules, and further inside the code of the Shopping Cart microservice.

The correlation token middleware checks for a `Correlation-Token` header before creating a new correlation token. Once a correlation token is created, it should be attached to any requests to other microservices made as a result of processing this one. That way, operations can be traced across all microservices involved. That's why the middleware adds the correlation token to the OWIN environment. The next step is to make sure all outgoing requests have the correlation token set, and for that you'll pick the correlation token back out of the OWIN environment.

9.4.2 Adding a correlation token to all outgoing HTTP requests

The Shopping Cart microservice sometimes makes requests to the Product Catalog microservice. When it does, the request should contain a correlation token in a `Correlation-Token` request header. Recall that you use `HttpClient` to make HTTP requests and that until now you've created a new instance of `HttpClient` when you're about to make an HTTP request. Let's change that slightly: you'll use a factory to create `HttpClient` objects, instead, and in that factory you'll set up the `HttpClient` to put a `Correlation-Token` header on every request.

To create, set up, and use the `HttpClient` factory, you'll do the following:

1. Write an `HttpClientFactory` class that can create `HttpClient` objects set up to send the correct `Correlation-Token` header with each request.

2. Create a Nancy bootstrapper that picks the correlation token out of the OWIN environment, creates an `HttpClientFactory`, and registers it with Nancy's dependency injection container.

3 Take a dependency on the `HttpClientFactory` factory in the part of Shopping Cart that makes HTTP requests. Nancy will take care of injecting the instance of `HttpClientFactory` that you created in the bootstrapper.

First, add an HttpClientFactory.cs file in the Shopping Cart microservice, containing the following code.

Listing 9.9   Creating `HttpClient` objects to send correlation tokens

```csharp
namespace ShoppingCart
{
  using System;
  using System.Net.Http;

  public interface IHttpClientFactory
  {
    HttpClient Create(Uri uri);
  }

  public class HttpClientFactory : IHttpClientFactory
  {
    private readonly string correlationToken;

    public HttpClientFactory(string correlationToken)      // Gets a correlation token injected
    {
      this.correlationToken = correlationToken;
    }

    public HttpClient Create(Uri uri)
    {
      var client = new HttpClient() { BaseAddress = uri } ;
      client
        .DefaultRequestHeaders
        .Add("Correlation-Token", this.correlationToken);   // Adds the correlation token to each request
      return client;
    }
  }
}
```

You add both an implementation and an interface, so code that needs an `HttpClient` only has to depend on the interface.

The next step is to set up an `HttpClientFactory` in a Nancy bootstrapper that registers a logger and an `HttpClientFactory` in the dependency injection container. Add this bootstrapper code in a new Bootstrapper.cs file.

Listing 9.10   Nancy bootstrapper

```csharp
namespace ShoppingCart
{
  using Nancy;
```

```
using Nancy.Bootstrapper;
using Nancy.TinyIoc;
using Serilog;

public class Bootstrapper : DefaultNancyBootstrapper
{
  private readonly ILogger log;                              Injects the
                                                             Serilog logger
  public Bootstrapper(ILogger log)
  {
    this.log = log;
  }

  protected override void ApplicationStartup(
    TinyIoCContainer container, IPipelines pipelines)
  {                                                          Registers the
                                                             logger in Nancy's
    base.ApplicationStartup(container, pipelines);           container
    container.Register(this.log);
  }

  protected override void RequestStartup(
    TinyIoCContainer container,
    IPipelines pipelines,                      Gets the correlation token
    NancyContext context)                      from the OWIN environment
  {
    base.RequestStartup(container, pipelines, context);
    var correlationToken =
      context.GetOwinEnvironment()["correlationToken"] as string;
    container.Register<IHttpClientFactory>(
      new HttpClientFactory(correlationToken));        Injects the correlation token
  }                                                    in an HttpClientFactory, and
 }                                                     registers the factory in
}                                                      Nancy's container
```

This bootstrapper uses the RequestStartup method to create and register an Http-
ClientFactory per request. It must be one per request, because each request has its
own correlation token. In the correlation token middleware, you stored the correlation
token in the OWIN environment. Here, you pick it out of the environment and hand it
off to HttpClientFactory. You get the correlation token directly from the OWIN environment dictionary rather than by creating an OwinContext with LibOwin, because
correlationToken is your own custom key that LibOwin knows nothing about.

If you run Shopping Cart now, it will crash at startup because the bootstrapper
doesn't have a default constructor. You created it with a constructor that takes an
ILogger because you want the same ILogger created in the Startup class to be used
everywhere. That's why you inject it into the bootstrapper and register it in Nancy's
container. Nancy will inject the correct ILogger instance whenever a class takes a
dependency on ILogger.

To make the microservice run again, change the Configure method in Startup
slightly to create the bootstrapper and hand it to Nancy.

Listing 9.11   Giving Nancy a bootstrapper to use

```
public void Configure(IApplicationBuilder app)
{
  var log = ConfigureLogger();

  app.UseOwin(buildFunc =>
  {
    buildFunc(next => GlobalErrorLogging.Middleware(next, log));
    buildFunc(next => CorrelationToken.Middleware(next));
    buildFunc(next => RequestLogging.Middleware(next, log));
    buildFunc(next => PerformanceLogging.Middleware(next, log));
    buildFunc(next => new MonitoringMiddleware(next, HealthCheck).Invoke);
    buildFunc.UseNancy(opt => opt.Bootstrapper = new Bootstrapper(log));   ←
  });
}
```

Creates a bootstrapper
and gives it to Nancy

Now the microservice can start, but you're still not using `HttpClientFactory`. Recall from chapter 5 that Shopping Cart has a `ProductCatalogClient` class that handles sending requests to the Product Catalog microservice. Modify that class to take a dependency on `HttpClientFactory`, so the `HttpClientFactory` object is created per request in the bootstrapper injected into any object Nancy creates.

Listing 9.12   Creating an `HttpClientFactory` object per request

```
private readonly IHttpClientFactory httpClientFactory;

public ProductCatalogClient(
  ICache cache,
  IHttpClientFactory httpClientFactory)
{
  this.cache = cache;
  this.httpClientFactory = httpClientFactory;
}
```

Nancy injects the
HttpClientFactory
registered per request
in the bootstrapper.

Next, you can begin using `HttpClientFactory` to create `HttpClient` objects instead of creating them with new. The `RequestProductFromProductCatalogue` method contains this line of code:

```
var httpClient = new HttpClient(productCatalogBaseUrl);
```

Change that one line so it looks like this:

```
var httpClient =
        this.httpClientFactory.Create(new Uri(productCatalogBaseUrl));
```

Now, requests made from `ProductCatalogClient` will contain a `Correlation-Token` header containing the correct correlation token. If Product Catalog is well behaved, reads the correlation token from the header, and uses it in all log messages as it should, you'll be able to trace user requests to add an item to their shopping cart through the Shopping Cart microservice to the Product Catalog microservice. That's helpful when debugging production issues.

Next up, you'll implement the two pieces of middleware that log requests and log request performance.

9.4.3 *Logging requests and request performance*

You have two more pieces of middleware to write. The first will log each incoming request and each outgoing response. Because the correlation token is part of these log messages, you can correlate the request and the response. Add the following request-logging middleware code to the LoggingMiddleware.cs file.

> **Listing 9.13 Middleware that logs the request and response**

```
public class RequestLogging
{
  public static AppFunc Middleware(AppFunc next, ILogger log)
  {
    return async env =>
    {
      var owinContext = new OwinContext(env);
      log.Information(
        "Incoming request: {@Method}, {@Path}, {@Headers}",
        owinContext.Request.Method,
        owinContext.Request.Path,
        owinContext.Request.Headers);
      await next(env);
      log.Information(
        "Outgoing response: {@StatusCode}, {@Headers}",
        owinContext.Response.StatusCode,
        owinContext.Response.Headers);
    };
  }
}
```

Sends a log message with the request method, path, and headers

Sends the request through the rest of the pipeline

Sends a log message with the response status code and headers

This is lambda-style OWIN middleware that picks out the most important bits of the request and response and sends log messages with them.

Next, add the request-performance middleware to the LoggingMiddleware.cs file. The request-performance middleware uses the Stopwatch class, so add this using statement at the top the file:

```
using System.Diagnostics;
```

The middleware is as follows.

Listing 9.14   Middleware that times request execution and logs the result

```
public class PerformanceLogging
{
  public static AppFunc Middleware(AppFunc next, ILogger log)
  {
    return async env =>
    {
      var stopWatch = new Stopwatch();
      stopWatch.Start();                                    ◁── Starts and stops the stopwatch
      await next(env);                                          before and after executing the
      stopWatch.Stop();                                         rest of the pipeline
      var owinContext = new OwinContext(env);
      log.Information(                                      ◁────────────┐
        "Request: {@Method} {@Path} executed in {RequestTime:000} ms",
        owinContext.Request.Method, owinContext.Request.Path,
        stopWatch.ElapsedMilliseconds);
    };                                             Sends a log message with
  }                                            information about the request
}                                                 and the execution time
```

This piece of middleware measures the time it takes to execute the rest of the pipeline. If you place the middleware early in the pipeline, this means the time it takes to handle the request. When the rest of the pipeline is finished, the middleware logs the execution time.

9.4.4   *Configuring an OWIN pipeline with a correlation token and logging middleware*

You've written all three pieces of middleware, and you can now add them to the OWIN pipeline of the Shopping Cart microservice. You'll build a pipeline with the correlation token middleware first, followed by the request-logging middleware, the performance-logging middleware, the monitoring middleware, and finally Nancy. The OWIN pipeline is built in the `Configure` method in the `Startup` class. With all the middleware added, the `Configure` method is as shown next.

Listing 9.15   OWIN pipeline with middleware and Nancy

```
public void Configure(IApplicationBuilder app)
{
  var log = ConfigureLogger();

  app.UseOwin(buildFunc =>
  {
    buildFunc(next => CorrelationToken.Middleware(next));
    buildFunc(next => RequestLogging.Middleware(next, log));
    buildFunc(next => PerformanceLogging.Middleware(next, log));
    buildFunc(next => new MonitoringMiddleware(next, HealthCheck).Invoke);
    buildFunc.UseNancy();
  });
}
```

Once the pipeline is set up, you'll see request and performance log messages in the console when you run Shopping Cart and send requests to it. For instance, start the microservice with dotnet and then send this request-monitoring request to it:

```
GET /_monitor/shallow HTTP/1.1
Host: localhost:5000
Accept: application/json
```

You'll see the following output in the console:

```
PS> dotnet run
Hosting environment: Production
Now listening on: http://localhost:5000
Application started. Press Ctrl+C to shut down.

22:24:04 [Information] (1717b4c2-9734-4425-933f-7cf18f9b0bca) Incoming
➡ request: "GET", PathSt
ring { Value: "/_monitor/shallow", HasValue: True }, [KeyValuePair`2 {
➡ Key: "Cache-Control",
Value: ["no-cache"] }, KeyValuePair`2 { Key: "Connection", Value:
➡ ["keep-alive"] }, KeyValueP
air`2 { Key: "Content-Type", Value: ["application/json"] },
➡ KeyValuePair`2 { Key: "Accept", V
alue: ["application/json"] }, KeyValuePair`2 { Key: "Accept-Encoding",
➡ Value: ["gzip, deflate
, sdch"] }, KeyValuePair`2 { Key: "Accept-Language", Value:
➡ ["en-US,en;q=0.8,da;q=0.6,nb;q=0.
4,sv;q=0.2"] }, KeyValuePair`2 { Key: "Cookie", Value:
➡ ["__atuvc=4%7C37; todoUser=chr_horsdal
; _nc=xoP1b4VkX70TpRWvKVfanfyaAckK8L8pkaVJehq4pns%3di5jbH1%2fJPKfbgy99
➡ ZaaFUhSoZtmNTYZxuHm3NPr
3mIdyVccjbWCrKBtYCYZFbaknlwUTSbgMnEwjl8HkLi%2fI4XTsa4hzaEngPZ5wp8waBcO
➡ 7sOHeARlfeMhbMF6x11iwkT
HebV67sBTW8B7S8u2jCgVtSlrps%2bXx6s3W4MH1NGJjJK6wy48O4xFmauLJWBQ%2bvISV
➡ XpROXKu%2fM5QdeKwTNw%3d
%3d"] }, KeyValuePair`2 { Key: "Host", Value: ["localhost:5000"] },
➡ KeyValuePair`2 { Key: "Us
er-Agent", Value: ["Mozilla/5.0 (Windows NT 10.0; WOW64)
➡ AppleWebKit/537.36 (KHTML, like Geck
o) Chrome/47.0.2526.111 Safari/537.36"] }, KeyValuePair`2 { Key:
➡ "Location", Value: ["http://
www.google.com"] }, KeyValuePair`2 { Key: "Postman-Token", Value:
➡ ["e180f522-dea5-0c56-0e35-9
c2be0626112"] }]

22:24:04 [Information] (1717b4c2-9734-4425-933f-7cf18f9b0bca)
➡ Request: "GET" PathString { Val
ue: "/_monitor/shallow", HasValue: True } executed in 001 ms

22:24:04 [Information] (1717b4c2-9734-4425-933f-7cf18f9b0bca)
➡ Outgoing response: 200, [KeyVal
uePair`2 { Key: "Date", Value: ["Mon, 25 Jan 2016 21:24:04 GMT"] },
➡ KeyValuePair`2 { Key: "Se
rver", Value: ["Kestrel"] }]
```

This output contains three log messages: one with the request, one with the execution time of the request, and one with the response—just as expected. You may notice that because you're using structured logging, it's easy to include a lot of data in a log message. When you're looking at the messages in the console, they can seem overwhelming; but when the log messages are sent to a Logging microservice with good search capabilities and a good GUI—for instance, using Elasticsearch for storage and Kibana for the GUI—the added data isn't a problem. On the contrary, it's valuable information.

In this chapter, you've built four pieces of OWIN middleware in the Shopping Cart microservice, but none of them use any of the microservice's business logic. All four may as well have been written in any other microservice. In chapter 11, you'll extract the pieces of middleware from Shopping Cart and package them in NuGet packages, ready to be reused across many microservices.

9.5 Summary

- Microservice systems need monitoring and logging just like any other server-side systems.
- Every microservice should be monitored and should send log messages.
- Because of the number of microservices in a system, setting up monitoring and logging needs to be easy.
- Correlation tokens make it easier to trace a request across several microservices.
- You can use OWIN middleware to create two monitoring endpoints: one that responds 204 No Content to any request, and one that performs a health check first.
- Structured logging is a good way to include valuable information in log messages and make that data searchable.
- Serilog is a library for doing structured logging.
- You can use OWIN middleware and Serilog's log context to add correlation tokens to log messages.
- You can use OWIN middleware to implement request and response logging and log request-execution times.
- You can use the OWIN environment to carry the per-request correlation token from middleware into a Nancy bootstrapper.
- You can set up `HttpClient` to include a `Correlation-Token` header with every outgoing HTTP request.

Securing microservice-to-microservice communication

Up to this point in the book, we've ignored security; but for most systems, security is an important concern that needs careful attention. This chapter discusses how to address security concerns in a microservice system. In a monolith, the monolith does user authentication and authorization—there is, after all, only the monolith to do those things. In a microservice system, several microservices are involved in answering most user requests; the question is this: which ones are responsible for authentication, and which ones are responsibility for authorization? You must also ask how much the microservices can trust each other:

- If one microservice authenticates a user, can other microservices trust that user?
- Are all microservices allowed to call each other?

The answers vary from system to system. The first part of this chapter discusses how to address these questions, and the second part dives into an implementation of one set of answers.

10.1 Microservice security concerns

Security is an important concern for almost any server-side system. It's also a very broad topic, much of which is outside the scope of this book. We'll concentrate on two areas of security that are relevant to developers of microservice systems: *authentication* and *authorization*, and how to secure communication between microservices.

Most systems have some functionality that's only accessible to logged-in users. Think about the point-of-sale system discussed in earlier chapters. In chapters 3 and 4, we talked about adding a loyalty program that allows registered users to receive special offers via email, based on their interests. If users are interested in golf, they'll be notified about good deals on golf balls. If users want to edit their interests—they may have given up golf and taken up quilting, instead—they need to be logged in. Otherwise, one user could edit another user's interests, resulting in their being notified about the wrong offers. Making sure a user really is who they claim to be is a matter of *authentication*. Deciding what the user is allowed to do—for instance, that they can edit their own interests but not anyone else's—is a matter of *authorization*.

Authentication and authorization are concerns that your systems will probably have regardless of whether you build them with microservices. The difference is that the granular nature of a microservice system begs the question: which microservices handle authentication and authorization? The following two sections address that question.

> ### Data in motion vs. data at rest
>
> Systems handle data. That data is most often essential to the systems, but it's also often essential to users. The data may be sensitive, such as users' home addresses, credit card numbers, or medical records. Even if the data isn't sensitive, it can still be valuable to the system—the product catalog of an e-commerce site isn't sensitive, but it's worth a lot to the business behind the site. The data your systems handle is important and needs to be handled safely. Broadly speaking, we can place data handling in one of two categories:
>
> - *Data in motion*—When data is moved from one part of a system to another, it's said to be in motion. For instance, when collaborating microservices exchange data via commands, queries, or events, the data they exchange is in motion.
> - *Data at rest*—When data is stored for later use, it's said to be at rest. For instance, when the microservice that owns a piece of data stores it in its database, that piece of data is at rest.
>
> It's important that data be kept safe in both situations. This chapter concentrates on data in motion, because this is where a microservice system differs from systems with other architectures. The techniques for securing data at rest are the same in a microservice system as in a monolithic or traditional SOA system.

10.1.1 *Authenticating users at the edge*

Authentication is about verifying that users are who they claim to be. In the context of a microservice system, that means verifying that requests are made on behalf of the users they appear to be from. Let's look at the example in figure 10.1, which shows part of the point-of-sale system from chapters 3 and 4—the part centered around the Loyalty Program microservice.

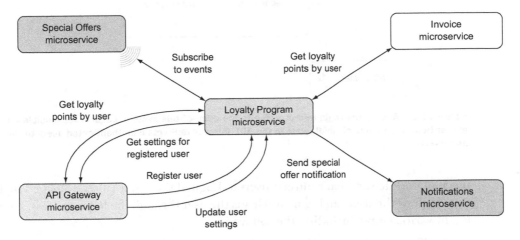

Figure 10.1   The Loyalty Program microservice in the point-of-sale system

If you add to the loyalty program a web frontend where registered users can edit their interests—for example, remove their interest in golf and add quilting, instead—you get something like figure 10.2. You only want users to be allowed to edit their own interests, not the interests of other users. Therefore, you require users to be logged in to be able to edit interests. In figure 10.2, you must authenticate the request to update user settings. The obvious place to perform the authentication is in the API Gateway microser-

vice, which is the microservice that receives the request to update the user settings from the client. That request is made on behalf of a user, and you must verify that clients are allowed to make requests on behalf of users. You do so by making sure the user is logged in.

Figure 10.3 adds a Login microservice to the system. The new microservice is responsible for handling the login process, but the API gateway is still responsible for making sure only requests from logged-in users are accepted. In the API gateway, authentication is handled by a

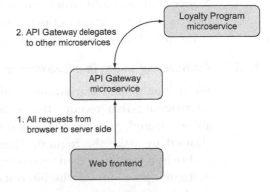

Figure 10.2 The web frontend for users of the loyalty program communicates only with the API gateway.

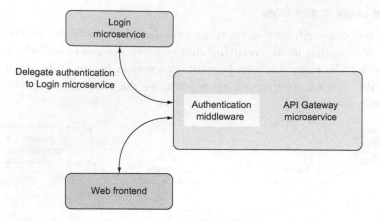

Figure 10.3   Adding the Login microservice to the point-of-sale system. Login is responsible for authentication; a piece of middleware in the API gateway redirects unauthenticated users to the microservice.

piece of middleware that redirects users to Login if they aren't already logged in. Login decides how the user can log in and leads the user through the login process. Users can log in various ways, including the following:

- With a username and password
- Via a two-factor login mechanism
- Via an external system, such as Active Directory
- Via social identity providers like Facebook, Twitter, Google, and so on

Whatever the login mechanism, the Login microservice handles the login and gives the API gateway proof of the user's identity in a form the API gateway can verify. There are standardized protocols to do this; the implementation half of this chapter uses the OpenId Connect protocol to achieve this separation.

Notice that user authentication is at the edge of the system—that is, it's done by the microservice that receives the request from the client. This is the general pattern: user authentication is done at the edge of the system.

10.1.2   *Authorizing users in microservices*

We've established that authentication is initiated at the edge of the system by the microservice that receives the request from the client. When the request has been authenticated, you know who the user is, but you don't know whether the user is allowed to make the request. That's a question of authorization. The user is only authorized to update their own interests. If a client sends a request on behalf of user A that attempts to update the interests of user B, the system should reject the request.

In a microservice system, the microservice at the edge—the one that initiates authentication—often isn't the microservice that performs the action the request is about. Figure 10.4 shows the loyalty program again. The API Gateway microservice

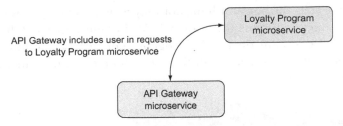

Figure 10.4   Authorization should be done as part of the business logic; the Loyalty Program microservice is responsible for authorizing updates to user settings.

gets requests from the client, but the Loyalty Program microservice is responsible for keeping track of user interests. Therefore, Loyalty Program updates users' interests.

Remember from chapter 3 that microservices are primarily scoped to business capabilities—a business capability is handled by one microservice. That includes authorization, because authorization is part of the capability's business rules. This is in line with letting the Loyalty Program microservice decide whether a user is allowed to update interests. For this to work, the user identity needs to be passed along from microservice to microservice. In the loyalty program, the API Gateway microservice must include the user identity in the requests it sends to Loyalty Program.

10.1.3 *How much should microservices trust each other?*

Microservices collaborate to deliver functionality to end users, assuming all microservices work toward delivering that end user functionality; but how can you be sure this is the case? Couldn't an attacker take control of a microservice and make it behave maliciously? Yes, that's possible. The question then becomes this: can one microservice trust another microservice? The answer to this question, unfortunately, is that it depends. It depends, for instance, on what threats the system faces and what the consequences of a successful attack would be. It can also depend on other factors, such as organizational structure and compliance with regulations.

At the highest level of trust between microservices, all microservices completely trust every request and every response from any other microservice. That is, implicitly, the level of trust among the microservices you've built so far in this book.

The principle of *defense in depth* suggests that this may not be a good idea. If an attacker can compromise just one microservice and have it make requests to other microservices, they will have full access to everything in the system. For a particular system, you may or may not be OK with that situation. If you aren't, you can limit which microservices can collaborate.

For instance, referring to figure 10.1, API Gateway, Special Offers, and Invoice are allowed to make calls to Loyalty Program, but Notifications isn't. On the other hand, only Loyalty Program is allowed to make calls to Notifications; the other microservices aren't. This limits the scope of what an attacker can do if they compromise one microservice.

You can take this a step further and limit not only which microservices can call each other, but also which endpoints they can call. For instance, Special Offers may only call the event feed endpoint on Loyalty Program, not the user administration endpoints. Conversely, API Gateway may call the user administration endpoints, but not the event feed.

> ### Some terminology
> We need to quickly define a bit of terminology:
>
> - *Scope*—An identifier for one or more endpoints that you want to protect. When a microservice wants to call any of those endpoints, it first needs permission to do so. That permission is given in the form of a token containing the scope. You can think of scopes as names for groups of endpoints you want to protect—for example, all endpoints that might alter product information may require the scope `product_information_write`.
> - *Access token*—A signed object that's used to allow access to resources. A microservice can request an access token for a given scope from the Login microservice. If Login will allow the microservice to access the scope, it returns an access token that can be passed along with requests to the endpoints the scope is for.
> - *OAuth and OpenId Connect*—Open standards that work together to allow authentication and authorization of both end users and microservices. You'll use these two protocols to perform authentication and authorization, but I won't go into detail about them because you'll rely on IdentityServer to implement them.

To enforce limitations on which microservices may collaborate, you create *scopes* in the Login microservice. When one microservice needs to call another, it will ask Login for permission by asking for a token that gives access to a particular scope. Login must authenticate the caller—for instance, by demanding that each service include a unique secret in its requests—and then decide whether to provide the token based on the permission you set up in Login. The microservice that receives the request can then inspect the token in a piece of middleware and verify that the required scope is present.

For instance, the Loyalty Program microservice can add a piece of middleware that requires a `loyalty_program_write` scope for all requests to endpoints that modify or register users. The API gateway then needs to ask the Login microservice for a token for the `loyalty_program_write` scope before making requests to Loyalty Program. Only if you've set up Login to allow calls from the API gateway to Loyalty Program will it provide the token. This setup ensures that Login is in charge of deciding which microservices can collaborate.

Even when you limit which microservices may collaborate and how they may collaborate, there's still an implicit trust that whatever one microservice sends to another is legitimate. If you use HTTPS instead of HTTP between microservices, you

> ### Defense in depth
>
> *Defense in depth* is an approach to security that uses several defense mechanisms in combination. The idea is to employ a layering strategy: if an attacker is able get past the first line of defense, they meet the next line of defense. For example, even though a microservice at the edge of a system may authenticate and authorize all incoming requests, it shouldn't have administrative rights to the server it runs on. Even if an attacker circumvents the authorization and tricks a microservice into executing uploaded code, the attacker still doesn't have full control over the server—they're limited by what the operating system allows the microservice to do.

get transport-level encryption and thereby some protection against an attacker tampering with requests going from one microservice to another. Even so, there's the question of whether the data sent with the request can be trusted. Of particular interest here is user identity, because you'll use that to perform authorization.

You saw in the last section that the API gateway should pass the user identity along with requests to Loyalty Program. If you want the microservice receiving a user identity in a request to be able to verify the identity, you need to pass the identity as an encrypted token and not as plain text.

As you can see, the level of trust between microservices will vary from system to system. You can choose from a range of trust levels. In the following sections, you'll implement a level of trust that follows the principles outlined so far in the chapter, but this isn't the only way to go about implementing these security principles.

10.2   *Implementing secure microservice-to-microservice communication*

For the remainder of this chapter, we'll dive into implementing security around the loyalty program. The security requirements are as follows:

- Authenticate users in the API gateway.
- Limit which microservices may collaborate.
- Allow microservices to verify user identities passed along from other microservices.

To fulfill the requirements, you'll rely on a few standards:

- OpenId Connect to authenticate users
- OAuth to limit which microservices may collaborate
- JSON Web Tokens (JWTs) for user identities

You'll also rely on an open source product called IdentityServer to play the role of the Login microservice. I'll introduce IdentityServer in the next section, and you'll get it up and running.

In the API gateway, you'll implement the setup illustrated in figure 10.5. The pipeline in the API gateway has an authentication middleware and Nancy. The authentication middleware checks whether users are authenticated and, if they aren't, redirects to the Login microservice.

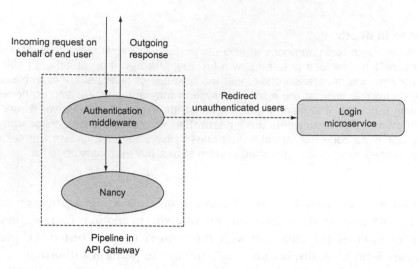

Figure 10.5   Use authentication middleware to redirect unauthenticated users to the Login microservice.

More terminology

Before we examine the implementation, you need to know some more terminology:

- *JSON Web Token (JWT)*—A standardized format for access tokens. JWTs can be cryptographically signed, which means a microservice receiving a JWT from another microservice can check the token's validity. If the token is valid, the contents can be trusted, and it's safe to rely on the JWT for authorization purposes.

- *Claims and* `ClaimsPrincipal`—Claims are key/value pairs used to provide information about an authenticated end user or microservice. In the case of an end user, claims can include the user ID, name, email address, and so on, as well as permissions the user has—such as write access to certain data. In the case of a microservice, claims can include a scope the microservice is allowed to access. .NET has built-in support for claims through the types in the `System.Security.Claims` namespace. In particular, you'll use `Claims-Principal`. A `ClaimsPrincipal` represents an authenticated user and provides access to inspect all of the user's claims.

- *Authorization HTTP request header*—A standardized HTTP request header that you'll use to send access tokens along with requests.

In the Loyalty Program microservice, you'll implement the pipeline shown in figure 10.6. There are two pieces of middleware in front of Nancy: one that ensures that all incoming requests have an access token for the scope needed to communicate with Loyalty Program, and one that reads the identity token that identifies the end user who originally initiated the request.

In the following sections, you'll implement these:

- A Login microservice for the point-of-sale system. It will be based entirely on IdentityServer.
- Middleware in the API gateway that initiates user authentication on incoming requests. If the user isn't logged in, they will be redirected to Login, where they can log in. The API gateway will use Login to verify that users are already logged in on subsequent requests.
- Secure communication between the API gateway and Loyalty Program. There are three parts to this:

  1 You'll set up a scope in Login and give the API gateway permission to call Loyalty Program.
  2 In the API gateway, you'll request a token from Login before each request to Loyalty Program. You'll put the token in the `Autho-rization` header of all requests to Loyalty Program.

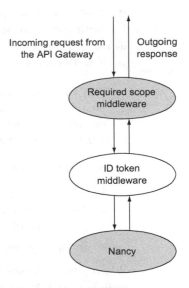

Incoming request from the API Gateway

Outgoing response

Required scope middleware

ID token middleware

Nancy

Figure 10.6 Use middleware to authorize requests and identify the end user.

  3 In Loyalty Program, you'll implement middleware that requires a token with the appropriate scope. If the scope isn't present, the middleware will short-circuit the pipeline and send a response with a 403 Forbidden status code back to the caller. If the scope is present, the request will be processed as usual.

- Transferring the user identity from the API gateway to Loyalty Program, and using it to perform authorization in your Nancy modules. To achieve this, you'll do the following:

  1 Add the user identity to a header in all requests from the API gateway to Loyalty Program.
  2 Read the user identity in a piece of middleware in Loyalty Program, and assign it to the user property on the Nancy context.
  3 Use the user from the Nancy context in the Nancy modules to perform authorization.

With all of these things in place, you'll have fulfilled the security requirements stated at the beginning of this section.

10.2.1 Meet IdentityServer

IdentityServer is an open source product that makes it easy to implement single sign-on and access control in web applications and HTTP APIs. It's .NET-based and designed to be a flexible framework that lets you set up an IdentityServer that suits your needs. In this example, you'll set up IdentityServer to play the role of the Login microservice in the point-of-sale system. You'll use hardcoded in-memory "databases" for both users and scopes, but IdentityServer supports a range of other options, such as using a relational database for users, or delegating login to another identity service such as Twitter, Google, Active Directory, or one of many others.

> **NOTE** You can find more information at https://identityserver.github.io/ Documentation, including thorough technical documentation demonstrating how to set up and use IdentityServer. This section doesn't go into detail and only shows how to do a simple setup.

Let's set up a simple Login microservice using IdentityServer. You'll do the following:

1 Create an empty ASP.NET Core project, just as you would for any other microservice.
2 Add the IdentityServer framework to the new microservice via NuGet.
3 Configure IdentityServer in the `Startup` class.
4 Set up a couple of hardcoded users and a scope for the Loyalty Program microservice.

When you're finished, you'll have a Login microservice with the components shown in figure 10.7. Note that almost all the microservice is implemented by IdentityServer.

Let's follow those steps. First, create a new empty ASP.NET Core project with Visual Studio or Yeoman, and call it `Login`. You've created many such projects in this book, so I won't repeat the details.

Next, add the IdentityServer NuGet package by adding `IdentityServer4` to the project.json file in the new microservice along with `Serilog` and some ASP.NET Core logging packages. The dependencies section in project.json should look like this:

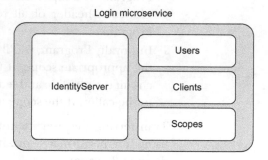

Figure 10.7 The Login microservice is built in IdentityServer.

```
"dependencies": {
    "Microsoft.NETCore.App": {
      "version": "1.0.0",
      "type": "platform"
    },
    "Microsoft.AspNetCore.Server.IISIntegration": "1.0.0",
    "Microsoft.AspNetCore.Server.Kestrel": "1.0.0",
    "Microsoft.AspNetCore.StaticFiles": "1.0.0",
    "Microsoft.AspNetCore.Mvc": "1.0.0",
    "Microsoft.Extensions.Logging.Console": "1.0.0",
    "Microsoft.Extensions.Logging.Debug": "1.0.0",
    "IdentityServer4": "1.0.0-beta5",
    "SeriLog": "2.0.0-rc-600"
  },
```

When you run `dotnet restore`, the IdentityServer framework will be added.

Let's make one more tweak to the new project to make sure the Login microservice runs on its own port. Change program.cs as follows, setting up the microservice to run on port 5001.

Listing 10.1 Configuring the port the Login microservice runs on

```
namespace Login
{
  using System.IO;
  using Microsoft.AspNetCore.Hosting;

  public class Program
  {
    public static void Main(string[] args)
    {
      var host = new WebHostBuilder()
        .UseKestrel()
        .UseContentRoot(Directory.GetCurrentDirectory())
        .UseIISIntegration()
        .UseStartup<Startup>()
        .UseUrls("http://localhost:5001")          ◁──┐  Configures ASP.NET Core
        .Build();                                      │  to listen on port 500I

      host.Run();
    }
  }
}
```

The third step is to configure IdentityServer. For the sake of simplicity, you'll use in-memory versions of everything IdentityServer needs. In a real situation, you'd most likely use another user login implementation and maybe other implementations for the other parts. The IdentityServer configuration is done in code using the Identity-Server API, in the `Startup` class. The following listing uses three classes—`Users`, `Claims`, and `Scoped`—that you'll write shortly.

Listing 10.2 Startup class with a simple IdentityServer configuration

```
namespace Login
{
  using System.IO;
  using Microsoft.AspNetCore.Builder;
  using Microsoft.AspNetCore.Hosting;
  using System.Security.Cryptography.X509Certificates;
  using Microsoft.AspNetCore.Http;
  using Microsoft.Extensions.Logging;
  using Microsoft.Extensions.DependencyInjection;

  using Configuration;

  public class Startup
```

```
{
  private readonly IHostingEnvironment environment;

  public Startup(IHostingEnvironment env)
  {
    this.environment = env;                    ◄──── ASP.NET Core can inject
  }                                                  dependencies into StartUp.

  public void ConfigureServices(IServiceCollection services)
  {
    var cert =
      new X509Certificate2(
        Path.Combine(
          this.environment.ContentRootPath,
          "idsrv3test.pfx"),
        "idsrv3test");

    services.AddSingleton<IHttpContextAccessor,
    ➥ HttpContextAccessor>();
    var builder = services
      .AddIdentityServer()                     ◄──── Configures
      .SetSigningCredential(cert);                    IdentityServer
    builder.AddInMemoryClients(Clients.Get());   ◄──── Sets up an in-memory
    builder.AddInMemoryScopes(Scopes.Get());            version of everything
    builder.AddInMemoryUsers(Users.Get());              IdentityServer needs

    services.AddMvc();
  }

  public void Configure(IApplicationBuilder app, ILoggerFactory
  ➥ loggerFactory)
  {
    loggerFactory.AddConsole(LogLevel.Trace);
    loggerFactory.AddDebug(LogLevel.Trace);

    app.UseCookieAuthentication(new CookieAuthenticationOptions   ◄──┐
    {
      AuthenticationScheme = "Temp",
      AutomaticAuthenticate = false,                    Adds authentication
      AutomaticChallenge = false                               middleware that
    });                                             IdentityServer relies on

    app.UseIdentityServer();

    app.UseStaticFiles();                           Adds routing that
    app.UseMvcWithDefaultRoute();         ◄──────── IdentityServer relies on
  }
}
}
```

ASP.NET Core configuration that IdentityServer depends on → (points to `services.AddSingleton<IHttpContextAccessor`)

Uses a certificate to sign tokens → (points to `builder` / `.SetSigningCredential(cert);`)

Starts IdentityServer → (points to `app.UseIdentityServer();`)

Now, you just need to add simple implementations of the Users, Clients, and Scopes classes. Let's start with Users.

Listing 10.3   Hardcoded definitions of `Users`

```
namespace IdentityServer.Configuration
{
    using System.Collections.Generic;
    using System.Security.Claims;
    using IdentityModel;
    using IdentityServer4.Services.InMemory;

    static class Users
    {
        public static List<InMemoryUser> Get()
            =>
            new List<InMemoryUser>
            {
                new InMemoryUser{
                    Subject = "818727", Username = "alice", Password = "alice",
                    Claims = new[]
                    {
                        new Claim(JwtClaimTypes.Name, "Alice Smith"),
                        new Claim(JwtClaimTypes.GivenName, "Alice"),
                        new Claim(JwtClaimTypes.FamilyName, "Smith"),
                        new Claim(JwtClaimTypes.Email, "AliceSmith@email.com"),
                        new Claim(JwtClaimTypes.EmailVerified,
                            "true", ClaimValueTypes.Boolean),
                        new Claim(JwtClaimTypes.Role, "User"),
                        new Claim(JwtClaimTypes.Id, "1", ClaimValueTypes.Integer64)
                    }
                },
                ...
            };
    }
}
```

Definition of user "alice" → points to the `new InMemoryUser{ Subject = "818727"...` line

List of claims for "alice" → points to the `Claims = new[]` line

More user definitions go here. → points to the `...` line

You add a number of users, such as Alice, that you'll be able to log in as later. This is somewhat unrealistic: the idea of the loyalty program is to get lots of users registered, so it doesn't make sense to hardcode them in the Login microservice. It would make much more sense to allow a range of social login options—Facebook, Twitter, Google, and so on—and let users authenticate using one of those when they want to register or change their profile. As I mentioned, IdentityServer supports these scenarios; all the information you need to implement them is in the IdentityServer documentation.

Next, you'll define a scope for the Loyalty Program microservice. Change Loyalty Program to only accepts calls that contain that scope in a token.

Listing 10.4   Hardcoded definitions of scopes

```
namespace IdentityServer.Configuration
{
    using System.Collections.Generic;
    using IdentityServer4.Core.Models;
```

```
public class Scopes
{
  public static IEnumerable<Scope> Get() =>
    new[]
    {
      // standard OpenID Connect scopes
      StandardScopes.OpenId,
      StandardScopes.ProfileAlwaysInclude,
      StandardScopes.EmailAlwaysInclude,
      new Scope
      {
        Name = "loyalty_program_write",
        DisplayName = "Loyalty Program write access",
        Type = ScopeType.Resource,
      }
    };
  }
}
```

Three standard scopes for end users decide what's included in identity tokens.

Definition of the scope of the endpoints in Loyalty Program

Unlike hardcoded users, having hardcoded scopes is realistic until the system reaches a certain size; there's nothing wrong with starting here. The downside is that whenever a new microservice is introduced, you'll need to change the code in the Login microservice and set up scopes for the new microservice. This can be OK for a while, but it gets out of hand when you reach a certain number of microservices.

Finally, you need to set up *clients*. Clients in this case are microservices that need to call other microservices. The client configuration tells IdentityServer which scopes to allow when a microservice requests a token.

Listing 10.5   Hardcoded definitions of clients

```
namespace IdentityServer.Configuration
{
  using System.Collections.Generic;
  using IdentityServer4.Models;

  public class Clients
  {
    public static IEnumerable<Client> Get() =>
      new List<Client>
      {
        new Client
        {
          ClientName = "API Gateway",
          ClientId = "api_gateway",
          ClientSecrets = new List<Secret>
          {
            new Secret("secret".Sha256())
          },
          AllowedScopes = new List<string>
          {
            "loyalty_program_write",
```

Configures the ID and secret the API gateway needs to request a token

Scopes to include in tokens for the API gateway

```
        },
        AllowedGrantTypes = GrantTypes.ClientCredentials
    },
    new Client                              ◁─────  Client that allows
    {                                               user logins through
     ClientName = "Web Client",                     a web frontend
     ClientId = "web",
     RedirectUris = new List<string>
     {
        "http://localhost:5003/signin-oidc",
     },
     PostLogoutRedirectUris = new List<string>
     {
        "http://localhost:5003/",
     },
     AllowedScopes = new List<string>
     {
                    "openid",
                    "email",
                    "profile",
     }
    }
  };
 }
}
```

This setup allows the API gateway to access the `loyalty_program_write` scope, which in practice means it can call endpoints at the Loyalty Program microservice. When the API gateway asks Login for permission to call Loyalty Program, it will be granted that permission.

This concludes the setup of the Login microservice. You can run it the usual way with dotnet.

10.2.2 *Implementing authentication with IdentityServer middleware*

In this section, you'll enable end users to log in. You'll assume that the API gateway provides users with some sort of web interface. This could be a JavaScript application that uses the endpoints in the API gateway and that's initially loaded from the API gateway. To use the JavaScript application, users need to log in.

Making the API gateway require users to log in is a matter of some setup at the ASP.NET Core level to have the application initiate authentication using the Identity-Server-based Login microservice. Before you write that setup code, you need to add the `Microsoft.AspNet.Authentication.Cookies` and `Microsoft.AspNet.Authentication.OpenIdConnect` NuGet packages to the API gateway. The dependencies section in the API gateway's project.json file should look like this:

```
"dependencies": {
    "Microsoft.AspNet.IISPlatformHandler": "1.0.0",
    "Microsoft.AspNet.Server.Kestrel": "1.0.0",
    "Microsoft.AspNet.Diagnostics":  "1.0.0",
```

```
"Microsoft.AspNet.Mvc": "6.0.0",
"Microsoft.AspNet.Authentication.Cookies": "1.0.0",
"Microsoft.AspNet.Authentication.OpenIdConnect": "1.0.0"
},
```

Once the packages have been added, change the Startup class in the API gateway to the following.

Listing 10.6   Authenticating via the Login microservice

```
public class Startup
{
  public void Configure(IApplicationBuilder app)
  {
    JwtSecurityTokenHandler.DefaultInboundClaimTypeMap.Clear();
    app.UseCookieAuthentication(new CookieAuthenticationOptions   ⟵──┐   Configures ASP.NET
    {                                                                    Core to read and
      AuthenticationScheme = "Cookies",                                 write a login cookie
      AutomaticAuthenticate = true
    });

    var oidcOptions = new OpenIdConnectOptions
    {
      AuthenticationScheme = "oidc",
      SignInScheme = "Cookies",
      Authority = "http://localhost:5001",    ⟵──┐  Points to the Login
      RequireHttpsMetadata = false,                 microservice as the
      ClientId = "web",                             authentication
      ResponseType = "id_token token",              authority
      GetClaimsFromUserInfoEndpoint = true,
      SaveTokens = true
    };
    oidcOptions.Scope.Clear();
    oidcOptions.Scope.Add("openid");
    oidcOptions.Scope.Add("profile");
    oidcOptions.Scope.Add("api1");

    app.UseOwin(buildFunc => buildFunc.UseNancy());
  }
}
```

Configures ASP.NET Core to use the OpenId Connect protocol (points to `var oidcOptions`)

Identifies this web client to the Login microservice (points to `ClientId = "web"`)

That's all it takes. Now users who aren't already logged in are redirected to a login page in the Login microservice that IdentityServer comes with out of the box. You can log in with the users you hardcoded, such as Alice. Once a user is logged in, subsequent requests will have a login cookie that the API gateway checks. As long as the cookie is valid, the API gateway will accept the requests; but as soon as it isn't, the user will be redirected to Login again.

10.2.3 *Implementing microservice-to-microservice authorization with IdentityServer and middleware*

With user authentication in place, the next thing to secure is communication between microservices. You'll use the Login microservice to make sure only microservices that are allowed to collaborate do so. To do that, you need to implement the communication shown in figure 10.8: the API gateway first requests an access token from the Login microservice and then includes that access token in the request to the Loyalty Program microservice.

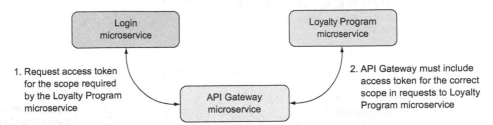

Figure 10.8 Using tokens to authorize requests between microservices

The Loyalty Program microservice checks that each request from the API gateway includes an access token and that the access token contains the required scope. The steps to implement this are as follows:

1. Modify the API gateway to request a token from Login before each request to Loyalty Program and to put the token in the `Authorization` header of all requests to Loyalty Program.
2. Modify Loyalty Program to require a token with the appropriate scope on each incoming request. You'll do this in middleware. If the scope isn't present, the middleware will short-circuit the pipeline and send a response with a 403 Forbidden status code back the to the caller. If the scope is present, the request will be processed as usual.

First, you need to request a token from the Login microservice. Because you want to put the token in every request you'll make to the Loyalty Program microservice, you'll request the token in the `HttpClientFactory` you created in chapter 8. Remember that `HttpClientFactory` is a small class that can create `HttpClient` objects ready to use to make requests, but with a standard configuration. In chapter 8, you used `HttpClient-Factory` to add correlation tokens to all requests; now you'll enhance `HttpClientFactory` to add access tokens to all requests, as shown next.

Listing 10.7 Adding access tokens and correlation tokens to requests

```
public interface IHttpClientFactory
{
    Task<HttpClient> Create(Uri uri, string scope);
```
← **Returns Task to allow the implementation to be async**

```
    }

    public class HttpClientFactory : IHttpClientFactory
    {
      private readonly TokenClient tokenClient;
      private readonly string correlationToken;

      public HttpClientFactory(string correlationToken)
      {
        this.correlationToken = correlationToken;          ◄─┐ Prepares to request an
        this.tokenClient = new TokenClient(                  │ access token from Login
          "http://localhost:5001/connect/token",
          "api_gateway",
          "secret");
      }

      public async Task<HttpClient> Create(Uri uri, string scope)
      {
        var response = await
          this.tokenClient
            .RequestClientCredentialsAsync(scope)          ◄─┐ Requests an access
            .ConfigureAwait(false);                          │ token from Login
        var client = new HttpClient() {BaseAddress = uri};
        client                                             ┌─ Adds the access
          .DefaultRequestHeaders                           │  token to outgoing
          .Authorization =                                 │  requests
            new AuthenticationHeaderValue("Bearer", response.AccessToken);  ◄─┘
        client
          .DefaultRequestHeaders
          .Add("Correlation-Token", this.correlationToken);
        return client;
      }
    }
```

With these enhancements to HttpClientFactory, you'll have access tokens on all outgoing requests as long as you remember to use HttpClientFactory to create HttpClients. In chapter 8, you also added HttpClientFactory to Nancy's DI container, so it's easy for any application code to take a dependency on HttpClientFactory and use it.

Now let's turn our attention to the Loyalty Program microservice, which needs to make sure only requests with a valid access token are accepted. Doing so only requires that you add LibOwin—as described in chapter 8—and the NuGet package Microsoft .AspNetCore.Authentication.JwtBearer to Loyalty Program. Then, you need to add a bit of configuration code to the Startup class in Loyalty Program and add a piece of middleware to the OWIN pipeline. Adding the configuration code changes the Startup class to the following.

Listing 10.8   Reading a bearer token from incoming requests

```
namespace LoyaltyProgram
{
  using System.Collections.Generic;
```

```
using System.IdentityModel.Tokens.Jwt;
using System.Threading.Tasks;
using LibOwin;
using Microsoft.AspNet.Builder;
using Nancy.Owin;

public class Startup
{
  public void Configure(IApplicationBuilder app)
  {
    JwtSecurityTokenHandler.DefaultInboundClaimTypeMap =
      new Dictionary<string, string>();

    app.UseJwtBearerAuthentication(options =>
    {
      options.Authority = "http://localhost:5001";
      options.RequireHttpsMetadata = false;
      options.Audience = "http://localhost:5001/resources";
      options.AutomaticAuthenticate = true;
    });

    app.UseOwin(buildFunc => buildFunc.UseNancy());
  }
}
}
```

> **Configures ASP.NET Core to read the bearer token on incoming requests and use Login to verify the token**

This tells ASP.NET Core to read the bearer token from the authorization header on incoming requests, which fits exactly with how you set it up in `HttpClientFactory` in the API gateway. ASP.NET Core will use the token to create a `ClaimsPrincipal` that you can access through the OWIN environment. The claims on that `ClaimsPrincipal` are the claims that the Login microservice sets when the API gateway requests an access token, which includes the scopes you allow for the API gateway.

The last piece involved in making sure Loyalty Program only accepts requests with the right scope is to add a piece of middleware that checks the principal for the required scope. Using the lambda style of OWIN middleware, extend the OWIN pipeline with a new piece of middleware as follows.

Listing 10.9 OWIN pipeline with middleware that requires a scope

```
app.UseOwin(buildFunc =>
{
  buildFunc(next => env =>
  {
    var ctx = new OwinContext(env);
    var principal = ctx.Request.User;
    if (principal.HasClaim("scope", "loyalty_program_write"))
      return next(env);
    ctx.Response.StatusCode = 403;
    return Task.FromResult(0);
  });
  buildFunc.UseNancy();
});
```

> **New piece of middleware**

> **Checks for the required scope**

> **If the scope is present, proceeds with the pipeline**

> **If the scope isn't present, responds with 403 Forbidden**

Now Loyalty Program will respond with a 403 Forbidden status code if a request comes in with an access token that doesn't contain the required scope. Putting this kind of setup in all of your microservices lets you control which microservices may collaborate.

10.2.4   Implementing user authorization in Nancy modules

Now that you've allowed users to log in and you have a setup for controlling which microservices can collaborate, you have only one more thing to implement: sending the user identity securely from one microservice to another, so you can do authorization in the correct microservice. The plan for implementing that is as follows:

1   In the API gateway, use `HttpClientFactory` to add another header, called `pos-end-user`, to all outgoing requests. It contains the user's identity.
2   In Loyalty Program, use a piece of middleware to read the user identity from the `pos-end-user` header.
3   In Loyalty Program, use the Nancy bootstrapper to assign the user's identity to the `CurrentUser` property on the Nancy context.

You'll implement these three steps in the following subsections.

ADDING THE USER'S IDENTITY TO REQUESTS

First, you want `HttpClientFactory` to add another header. You'll call the header `pos-end-user`, and it'll contain the end user's identity in the form of a token. That token is returned from the Login microservice when the user is authenticated and can be found as a claim called `id_token`. You already created an instance of `HttpClientFactory` on each request in the bootstrapper, but now you want to pass the ID token in to `HttpClientFactory` along with the correlation token it already gets.

Listing 10.10   Reading the ID token in the bootstrapper

```
using LibOwin;

public class Bootstrapper : DefaultNancyBootstrapper
{

  ...

  protected override void RequestStartup(
    TinyIoCContainer container,
    IPipelines pipelines,
    NancyContext context)
  {
    base.RequestStartup(container, pipelines, context);
    var correlationToken =
      context.GetOwinEnvironment()["correlationToken"] as string;
    var principal =
      context.GetOwinEnvironment()[OwinConstants.RequestUser]
      as ClaimsPrincipal;
```

Reads the user from the OWIN environment

```
    var idToken = principal.FindFirst("id_token");          ⟵── Reads the ID token
    container.Register<IHttpClientFactory>(
      new HttpClientFactory(idToken, correlationToken));         ⟵┐ Passes the ID
  }                                                               │ token to the
}                                                                 │ factory
```

This requires a change to `HttpClientFactory`, because it now needs to take in the ID token as a constructor argument. The updated `HttpClientFactory` is shown next.

> **Listing 10.11** `HttpClientFactory` that takes the ID token as a constructor argument

```
public class HttpClientFactory : IHttpClientFactory
{
  private readonly TokenClient tokenClient;
  private readonly string correlationToken;
  private readonly string idToken;

  public HttpClientFactory(
    string tokenUrl,
    string correlationToken,
    string idToken)
  {
    this.tokenClient = new TokenClient(tokenUrl, clientName, clientSecret);
    this.correlationToken = correlationToken;
    this.idToken = idToken;
    this.tokenClient = new TokenClient(
      "http://localhost:5001/connect/token",
      "api_gateway",
      "secret");
  }

  public async Task<HttpClient> Create(Uri uri)
  {
    var response = await
      this.tokenClient
        .RequestClientCredentialsAsync("loyalty_program_write")
        .ConfigureAwait(false);
    var client = new HttpClient() { BaseAddress = uri };
    client
      .DefaultRequestHeaders
      .Authorization =
        new AuthenticationHeaderValue("Bearer", response.AccessToken);
    client
      .DefaultRequestHeaders
      .Add("Correlation-Token", this.correlationToken);
    client
      .DefaultRequestHeaders
      .Add("pos-end-user", this.idToken);          ⟵┐ Adds the ID token
    return client;                                     │ to a header
  }
}
```

Now, all requests going out of the API gateway have a `pos-end-user` header containing the ID token.

READING THE USER'S IDENTITY FROM REQUESTS

The next step is for the Loyalty Program microservice to read the ID token from the header, which you'll do with a piece of middleware that you add to the OWIN pipeline in Loyalty Program.

Listing 10.12 Reading the ID token in a piece of middleware

```
public class Startup
{
  public void Configure(IApplicationBuilder app)
  {
    ...

    app.UseOwin(buildFunc =>
    {
      ...
      buildFunc(next => env =>                         Checks whether there's
      {                                                a pos-end-user header
        var ctx = new OwinContext(env);
        if (ctx.Request.Headers.ContainsKey("pos-end-user"))
        {
          var tokenHandler = new JwtSecurityTokenHandler();
          SecurityToken token;
          var userPrincipal =                          Reads and validates
            tokenHandler.ValidateToken(                the ID token
              ctx.Request.Headers["pos-end-user"],
              new TokenValidationParameters(),
              out token);
          ctx.Set("pos-end-user", userPrincipal);      Creates a user based
        }                                              on the ID token, and
        return next(env);                              adds it to the OWIN
      });                                              environment
    });
  }
}
```

This code reads the ID token from the request header, validates it, and, as a byproduct of that, creates a `ClaimsPrincipal` with all the claims in the ID token—that is, all the claims the Login microservice returned when the user logged in.

ASSIGNING THE USER'S IDENTITY TO NANCY'S CURRENTUSER

Once the `ClaimsPrincipal` object is in the OWIN environment, you can get it in the Loyalty Program bootstrapper and assign it to the `CurrentUser` on `NancyContext`, as follows.

Listing 10.13 Assigning the user created from the ID token to the Nancy context

```
public class Bootstrapper : DefaultNancyBootstrapper
{
    ...
    protected override void RequestStartup(          ← Called by Nancy on each
        TinyIoCContainer container,                     incoming request
        IPipelines pipelines,
        NancyContext context)                         Assigns the user from the ID token
    {                                                 in the custom HTTP header to the
        base.RequestStartup(container, pipelines, context);   user on the Nancy context
        context.CurrentUser =
            context.GetOwinEnvironment()["pos-end-user"] as ClaimsPrincipal;   ←
    }
}
```

Nancy offers some convenience methods you can use in your Nancy modules to do authorization. Suppose you want to only allow users with a certain claim to access the endpoints in a module. You can use `RequiresClaims`, like this:

```
public class UsersModule : NancyModule
{
    public SecuredModule() : base("/secret-stuff")
    {
        this.RequiresClaims("my claim");

        Get("/", ...);
        Post("/", ...);
    }
}
```

The `RequiresClaims` method can also be applied at the endpoint-handler level by calling it in a handler. In this case, you don't want to require any particular user claim in the module, but you do want to make sure users are changing their own interests. So, in the `Post` and `Put` handlers in `UserModule`, you check the identity of the user against the user ID provided in the request URL.

Listing 10.14 Check claims to make sure users are changing their own interests

```
public class UsersModule : NancyModule
{
    public SecuredModule() : base("/secret-stuff")
    {
        ...
        Put("/{userId:int}", parameters =>
        {
            int loggedInUserId;
```

```
int.TryParse(                                          Tries to read the id claim
  this.Context                                         from the user's identity
    .CurrentUser
    .Claims.FirstOrDefault(c => c.Type.StartsWith("id"))  ◄
    ?.Value.Split(':').Last() ?? "",
  out loggedInUserId);
int userId = parameters.userId;                        Compares the
if (loggedInUserId != userId)                      ◄   logged-in user to the
  return HttpStatusCode.Forbidden;                      user ID in the URL
var updatedUser = this.Bind<LoyaltyProgramUser>();
registeredUsers[userId] = updatedUser;
return updatedUser;
    });
  }
}
```

Now, users are only allowed to change their own interests.

This concludes the implementation of the security requirements. You've fulfilled these requirements by leaning on IdentityServer, which you used to implement a Login microservice. The API gateway uses Login to do authentication, and it's also Login that both authenticates and authorizes calls from the API gateway to Loyalty Program. Finally, you pass an ID token from microservice to microservice to share the identity of the logged-in user.

10.3 Summary

- Users should be authenticated at the edge of the system. That is, the microservice that first receives a user request should initiate authentication.

- Authorization should happen in the microservice system in the microservice that owns whatever data or action the request is for. The principle is that authorization is part of the business rules belonging to a business capability. Because microservices are—as you saw in chapter 3—designed around business capabilities, it follows that a microservice responsible for a business capability should also be responsible for any authorization related to that business capability.

- The principle of security in depth requires that you consider the level of trust you can accept between microservices. In some systems, it may be acceptable for microservices to trust requests from other microservices. In other systems, it may not.

- There's a trade-off between the convenience of having a high degree of trust between microservices and the security that follows from a lower degree of trust.

- You can introduce a Login microservice that's responsible for all authentication, including both end user authentication and authentication of calls from one microservice to another.

- You use the Login microservice to control which microservices may collaborate by configuring scopes and configuring which microservices receive which scopes.
- You can set up the Login microservice using IdentityServer.
- You can set up a microservice to use Login for end user authentication.
- You can make secure calls between microservices by including a token obtained from Login in each request and checking that the token contains the required scope in middleware in the microservice receiving the request.
- You can use an ID token obtained from Login to pass the user identity around in a more secure way than including a user ID in the request URL.
- You can read the ID token from incoming requests and assign it to the Nancy context, making it available to Nancy modules as a current user that can then be used for authorization purposes.

Building a reusable
microservice platform

11

This chapter covers

- Creating microservices more quickly with a reusable platform
- Components of a reusable platform
- Packaging reusable middleware with NuGet
- Building a reusable platform from several NuGet packages

A microservice system can include many microservices. You'll create new ones frequently, either because you're adding capabilities to the system or because you're replacing existing microservices. You want to able to create them quickly but include all the code that makes them behave well in production—that is, the infrastructure code you've created in the previous couple of chapters. In this chapter, you'll create a platform—consisting of NuGet packages—that enables you to quickly create new, well-behaved microservices.

11.1 Creating a new microservice should be quick and easy

In chapter 1, I listed a number of characteristics of microservices, including this one: *a microservice is responsible for a single capability.* I explained that this characteristic is a variation of the Single Responsibility Principle. Taking this seriously drives you toward having many microservices. And as the system evolves, you'll create new microservices fairly often when the system needs new end user functionality and as your understanding of the domain grows over time.

As discussed in chapter 3, you aren't likely to get the scoping of all microservices right the first time; and, when in doubt, you should create slightly bigger microservices. This also leads to the need to create new microservices along the way: when you gain a better understanding of the domain, the responsibilities of the different capabilities become clearer, and you'll sometimes discover that one microservice should be split in two.

Another characteristics of microservices from chapter 1 is as follows: *a microservice is replaceable.* The point is that a microservice can be completely rewritten quickly if its implementation becomes unsuitable. The code may get out of hand, or the design and technology choices you make early on may not be suitable for a growing load on the microservice; whatever the reason, you'll sometimes need to replace an existing microservice with a new one.

The bottom line is that when you work with a microservice system, you'll often need to create new microservices. If you don't, your system's services will slowly but surely become bigger, and its service boundaries will become less clear, meaning you'll lose the flexibility and speed of development that a microservice system provides. You need a way to make it both quick and easy to create new microservices so you won't be reluctant to do so.

11.2 Creating a reusable microservice platform

Chapters 8 and 9 explained that microservices must be well-behaved citizens in the production environment. They need to provide insight into their health through logging, they should allowing monitoring, and they need to follow the security standards you decide on for the system—for instance, authorizing microservice-to-microservice requests via scopes issued by a login microservice, as discussed and implemented in chapter 10. Thus, creating a new microservice involves more than just creating a new, empty project and adding Nancy NuGet to it.

That's why I recommend building a standard microservice platform to use across your .NET-based microservices in a microservices system. As shown in figure 11.1, the platform is installed in every microservice. In the second half of this chapter, you'll create such a platform, including the following:

- Monitoring- and logging-related middleware
- Security-related middleware
- Components that support sending HTTP requests according to the standards of your microservice system

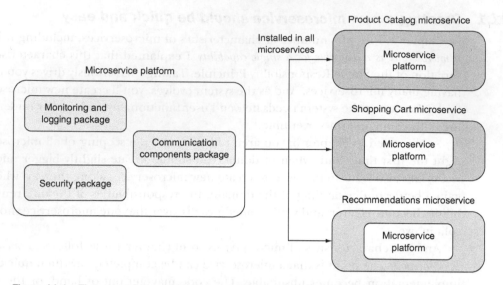

Figure 11.1   The microservice platform is a collection of packages implementing the technical concerns that cut across all microservices. The platform is installed in—and thus becomes part of—every microservice.

These are the platform areas I've chosen to cover for this book, but they aren't necessarily the things you'll need in a microservice platform for your system. I've tried to include common components. In particular, I think such platforms should include the monitoring, correlation token, request/response-logging, and performance-logging bits. They don't have to be in the exact form used in this book—you may, for instance, prefer a different correlation token format or another logging framework. Your authorization middleware will be tied to the approach you choose to use for security between microservices; but if you choose to put security measures in place around microservice collaboration, libraries supporting that should be included in your microservice platform.

The other side of the coin is this: should you include more in your microservice platform? There's no overarching answer, but you should be cautious about adding items: every time you include something in the platform, it becomes a little bigger and heavier. Furthermore, when you add something that all microservices are expected to include, what happens if they aren't running the same version of the platform? Can other microservices handle that? Can the infrastructure around your microservice system handle that? If the platform grows into something that must be in sync across all microservices, but it changes often, it becomes a serious bottleneck instead of an enabler. First, the platform must be updated in the code base of each microservice, and then each microservice must be deployed. If there are many microservices, that's a lot of work; and each time a new microservice is created, it becomes even more work.

Ideally, your microservice platform will hit the sweet spot of including only technical concerns that really do cut across microservices and that you can update incrementally—that is, in one microservice at a time over a period of time. This makes the barrier to creating a new microservice much lower: you need less-detailed knowledge about the cross-cutting technical concerns, and less effort is required.

11.3 Packaging and sharing middleware with NuGet

> ### Using NuGet for your platform
>
> NuGet is a package format as well as a group of tools for installing those packages. Until this point in the book, you've only installed existing NuGet packages; all of them have been publicly available in the package feed on nuget.org. But NuGet isn't limited to installing publicly available packages. As you'll see in section 11.3.3, you can install packages from your private package feed. And you can also create your own NuGet packages—as you'll also see in section 11.3.1—and put them in your private NuGet feed.

We'll now turn our attention to the code required to build a platform you can reuse across microservices. You've already built all the functionality that goes into the platform, but you've done so in one microservice at a time. Now, you'll extract the code from the microservices in which you created it and put it in packages that you can easily install and use in new microservices. You'll use NuGet because it will give you easy-to-create packages that your microservice can install and use. You're already using many NuGet packages in your microservices, so it's part of your workflow; the packages in the reusable microservice platform will fit right in.

You'll build the platform from the following pieces:

- The monitoring middleware from chapter 9
- The correlation-token middleware from chapter 9
- The request- and response-logging middleware from chapter 9
- The performance-logging middleware from chapter 9
- The authorization middleware from chapter 10 that checks a request token for a required scope
- The middleware from chapter 10 that reads the end user's identity token from incoming requests
- `HttpClientFactory` from chapters 9 and 10
- Automatic registration of `HttpClientFactory` in Nancy's container, which you'll build in section 11.3.3

As shown in figure 11.2, the platform will consist of the following NuGet packages:

- `MicroserviceNET.Logging`—Monitoring middleware, correlation token middleware, request- and response-logging middleware, and performance-logging middleware.

- MicroserviceNET.Auth—Authorization middleware and middleware that reads the end user's identity.
- MicroserviceNET.Platform—HttpClientFactory and automatic registration of HttpClientFactory in Nancy's container. This package depends on the other two.

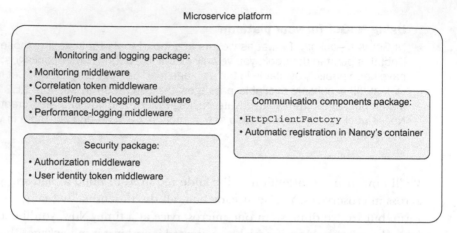

Figure 11.2   The microservice platform contains three packages, and each package contains code for a number of technical cross-cutting concerns.

Your microservices will only have to add the MicroserviceNET.Platform package and a little startup code to use and configure the microservice platform and get all the functionality it comes with. With the platform installed and configured, a microservice will have the pipeline shown in figure 11.3.

In the following sections, you'll create each of the three NuGet packages in turn.

11.3.1   *Creating a package with logging and monitoring middleware*

In this section, you'll create the MicroserviceNET.Logging NuGet package by doing the following:

1. Extract the monitoring, correlation token, request/response-logging, and performance-logging middleware created in chapter 9 from the Shopping Cart microservice to a class library called MicroserviceNET.Logging.
2. Add a convenience method that makes it easy to add the monitoring and logging middleware to an OWIN pipeline.
3. Create a NuGet package from the MicroserviceNET.Logging library.

The first step is to create a .NET Core class library and call it MicroserviceNET.Logging. You can do that with your IDE or with Yeoman. Then, add the monitoring and logging middleware pieces you developed in chapter 9 to the MicroserviceNET.Logging library. I'll repeat the middleware code here, but for an explanation of the code, refer to chapter 9.

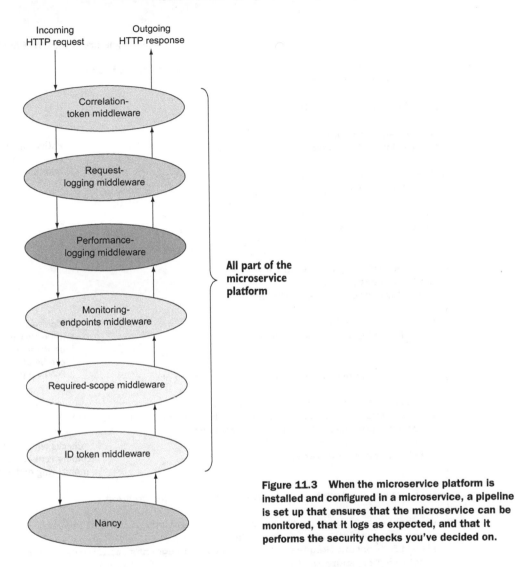

Figure 11.3 When the microservice platform is installed and configured in a microservice, a pipeline is set up that ensures that the microservice can be monitored, that it logs as expected, and that it performs the security checks you've decided on.

Add a MonitoringMiddleware.cs file to the `MicroserviceNET.Logging` project, and put the following code in it. It responds to requests to /_monitor/shallow and /_monitor/deep.

Listing 11.1   Monitoring middleware you developed in chapter 9

```
namespace MicroserviceNET.Logging
{
    using System;
    using System.Collections.Generic;
    using System.Threading.Tasks;
    using LibOwin;
```

```
using AppFunc =                              ◄─── Signature of the OWIN AppFunc
  System.Func<
    System.Collections.Generic.IDictionary<string, object>,
    System.Threading.Tasks.Task>;

public class MonitoringMiddleware
{
  private AppFunc next;
  private Func<Task<bool>> healthCheck;                    Paths you want to
                                                           respond to in this
  private static readonly PathString monitorPath =    ◄─┐ middleware
    new PathString("/_monitor");
  private static readonly PathString monitorShallowPath =
    new PathString("/_monitor/shallow");
  private static readonly PathString monitorDeepPath =
    new PathString("/_monitor/deep");

  public MonitoringMiddleware(
    AppFunc next,
    Func<Task<bool>> healthCheck)
  {                                                        Monitoring
    this.next = next;                                      middleware AppFunc
    this.healthCheck = healthCheck;                        implementation that
  }                                                        can be added to an
                                                       ◄─┘ OWIN pipeline
  public Task Invoke(IDictionary<string, object> env)  ◄─┘
  {
    var context = new OwinContext(env);
    if (context.Request.Path.StartsWithSegments(monitorPath))  ◄─┐
      return HandleMonitorEndpoint(context);
    else                                                Checks whether the
      return this.next(env);                            incoming request is for
  }                                                     a monitoring endpoint │

  private Task HandleMonitorEndpoint(OwinContext context)
  {
    if (context.Request.Path.StartsWithSegments(monitorShallowPath))
      return ShallowEndpoint(context);
    else if (context.Request.Path.StartsWithSegments(monitorDeepPath))
      return DeepEndpoint(context);
    return Task.FromResult(0);
  }

  private async Task DeepEndpoint(OwinContext context)
  {
    if (await this.healthCheck())                     Performs a microservice-
      context.Response.StatusCode = 204;              specific health check in the
    else                                              /_monitor/deep endpoint
      context.Response.StatusCode = 503;
  }

  private Task ShallowEndpoint(OwinContext context)
  {
```

```
          context.Response.StatusCode = 204;          ⟵──┐ Always responds with success in
          return Task.FromResult(0);                       │ the /_monitor/shallow endpoint
      }
    }
}
```

Next, add a LoggingMiddleware.cs file to the project. Put in it the following logging-related middleware from chapter 9: middleware for request and response logging, performance logging, global error logging, and creating and reading correlation tokens.

Listing 11.2 Logging-related middleware from chapter 9

```
namespace MicroserviceNET.Logging
{
  using System;
  using System.Diagnostics;
  using LibOwin;
  using Serilog;
  using Serilog.Context;
                                                Signature of the
                                                OWIN AppFunc
  using AppFunc =                        ⟵──┐
    System.Func<
      System.Collections.Generic.IDictionary<string, object>,
      System.Threading.Tasks.Task>;

  public class RequestLogging
  {
    public static AppFunc Middleware(AppFunc next, ILogger log)    ⟵──┐
    {
      return async env =>                          Middleware that logs requests
      {                                            and responses, implemented
        var owinContext = new OwinContext(env);    as lambda-style middleware
        log.Information(
          "Incoming request: {@Method}, {@Path}, {@Headers}",
          owinContext.Request.Method,
          owinContext.Request.Path,
          owinContext.Request.Headers);
        await next(env);
        log.Information(
          "Outgoing response: {@StatucCode}, {@Headers}",
          owinContext.Response.StatusCode,
          owinContext.Response.Headers);
      };
    }                                              Logs request times for all
  }                                                requests in a piece of
                                                   lambda-style middleware
  public class PerformanceLogging
  {
    public static AppFunc Middleware(AppFunc next, ILogger log)    ⟵──┐
    {
      return async env =>
```

```
            {
                var stopWatch = new Stopwatch();
                stopWatch.Start();
                await next(env);
                stopWatch.Stop();
                var owinContext = new OwinContext(env);
                log.Information(
                    "Request: {@Method} {@Path} executed in {RequestTime:000} ms",
                    owinContext.Request.Method, owinContext.Request.Path,
                    stopWatch.ElapsedMilliseconds);
            };
        }
    }
```

Middleware that sets a correlation token on the logging context for each request

```
    public class CorrelationToken
    {
        public static AppFunc Middleware(AppFunc next)
        {
            return async env =>
            {
                Guid correlationToken;
                var owinContext = new OwinContext(env);
                if (!(owinContext.Request.Headers["Correlation-Token"] != null
                    && Guid.TryParse(owinContext.Request.Headers["Correlation-
                        ➥ Token"],
                        out correlationToken)))
                    correlationToken = Guid.NewGuid();

                owinContext.Set("correlationToken", correlationToken.ToString());
                using (LogContext.PushProperty("CorrelationToken", correlationToken))
                    await next(env);
            };
        }
    }
```

Middleware that catches and logs all otherwise unhandled exceptions

```
    public class GlobalErrorLogging
    {
        public static AppFunc Middleware(AppFunc next, ILogger log)
        {
            return async env =>
            {
                try
                {
                    await next(env);
                }
                catch (Exception ex)
                {
                    log.Error(ex, "Unhandled exception");
                }
            };
        }
    }
}
```

You've now lifted all the monitoring and logging middleware code from the Shopping Cart microservice and put it in a class library. If you package this up, it will already be fairly easy to use in a microservice: just install the package and wire all the pieces of middleware into the OWIN pipeline. You did that in Shopping Cart, where it looked like the following.

Listing 11.3   OWIN pipeline set up in the Shopping Cart microservice

```
app.UseOwin(buildFunc =>
{
  buildFunc(next => GlobalErrorLogging.Middleware(next, log));
  buildFunc(next => CorrelationToken.Middleware(next));
  buildFunc(next => RequestLogging.Middleware(next, log));
  buildFunc(next => PerformanceLogging.Middleware(next, log));
  buildFunc(next => new MonitoringMiddleware(next, HealthCheck).Invoke);
  buildFunc.UseNancy(opt => opt.Bootstrapper = new Bootstrapper(log));
});
```

As you can see, to implement all the logging and monitoring, you need to add five pieces of middleware to the OWIN pipeline—and you must do so in the correct order. To make this easier, you'll create a convenience method that does it for you. Add a BuildFuncExtensions.cs file to the `MicroserviceNET.Logging` project, and put this code in it.

Listing 11.4   Adding the monitoring and logging middleware to the pipeline

```
namespace MicroserviceNET.Logging
{
  using System;
  using System.Threading.Tasks;
  using Serilog;                                              The rather scary
                                                              OWIN BuildFunc
  using BuildFunc = System.Action<System.Func<
    System.Func<
      System.Collections.Generic.IDictionary<string, object>,
      System.Threading.Tasks.Task>,
    System.Func<
      System.Collections.Generic.IDictionary<string, object>,
      System.Threading.Tasks.Task>
    >>;

  public static class BuildFuncExtensions                     Extension method
  {                                                           on BuildFunc
    public static BuildFunc UseMonitoringAndLogging(
      this BuildFunc buildFunc,
      ILogger log,
      Func<Task<bool>> healthCheck)
```

```
            {
        buildFunc(next => GlobalErrorLogging.Middleware(next, log));
        buildFunc(next => CorrelationToken.Middleware(next));
        buildFunc(next => RequestLogging.Middleware(next, log));
        buildFunc(next => PerformanceLogging.Middleware(next, log));
        buildFunc(next => new MonitoringMiddleware(next, healthCheck).Invoke);
        return buildFunc;
            }                                    ◁———  Returns BuildFunc to
        }                                              allow chaining of calls
    }                                                  to BuildFunc extensions
```

You add a extension method where each piece of middleware is added to the OWIN pipeline by using `BuildFunc`. The method takes two arguments, which the microservice using this is expected to provide. Now, to set up the monitoring and logging middleware, you can make a single call to the `UseMonitoringAndLogging` extension method in a microservice's `Startup` class, as shown next.

Listing 11.5 Using `UseMonitoringAndLogging` in a `Startup` class

```
public void Configure(IApplicationBuilder app)
{
    app.UseOwin(buildFunc =>                                    Adds the
    {                                                           monitoring and
        var log = ConfigureLogger();                            logging middleware
        buildFunc.UseMonitoringAndLogging(log, HealthCheck);  ◁ in the correct order
        buildFunc.UseNancy();
    }
}


private ILogger ConfigureLogger() {...}
public async Task<bool> HealthCheck() { ... }
```

This is all the code you need in the `MicroserviceNET.Logging` project. The only thing left to do is to create a NuGet package from the library, which you can do using dotnet. Go to the project folder—the one where project.json is located—in Power-Shell, and run this command:

```
PS> dotnet pack --configuration Release
```

This creates a NuGet package called `MicroserviceNET.Logging.1.0.0.nupkg` in bin/Release. Figure 11.4 shows `MicroserviceNET.Logging.1.0.0.nupkg` opened in NuGet Package Explorer. The package contains all the code of the `MicroserviceNET.Logging` project compiled to a DLL, plus an XML file containing the documentation comments from that code. You can also see that the package requires the Serilog library, which means that whenever this package is installed in a project, so is Serilog.

This package is ready to be installed and used in as many microservices as you want. At the end of this chapter, you'll return to installing this package from your local machine when you create a new microservice based on the platform you've built.

The dependencies

The contents of the package

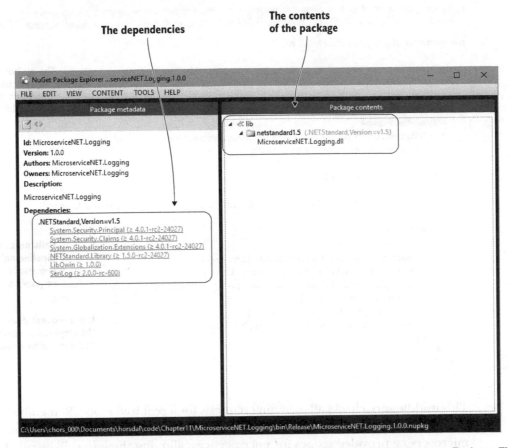

Figure 11.4 A peek inside `MicroserviceNET.Logging.nupkg` using **NuGet Package Explorer.** The package contains the logging and monitoring code compiled into a DLL. The package also indicates that it depends on Serilog.

11.3.2 *Creating a package with authorization middleware*

In this section, you'll build a `MicroserviceNET.Auth` NuGet package containing the authorization middleware you created in chapter 10. The steps are similar to those for creating the `MicroserviceNET.Logging` NuGet package:

1 Extract the authorization middleware from the Loyalty Program microservice in chapter 10 to a class library called MicroserviceNET.Auth.
2 Create a NuGet package from the MicroserviceNET.Auth library that includes all the code in the library.

Just as in the last section, you begin by creating a new class library. Call it Microservice-NET.Auth. Then, add an AuthorizationMiddleware.cs file to this new library, and add the following authorization middleware code from chapter 10.

Listing 11.6   Authorization middleware from the Loyalty Program microservice

```
namespace MicroserviceNET.Auth
{
  using System.Threading.Tasks;                          The authorization
  using LibOwin;                                          middleware uses the
                                                          lambda style of
  using AppFunc =                                         middleware.
    System.Func<
      System.Collections.Generic.IDictionary<string, object>,
      System.Threading.Tasks.Task>;

  public class Authorization
  {
    public AppFunc Middleware(AppFunc next, string requiredScope)
    {
      return env =>
      {                                                  Calls next in the
        var ctx = new OwinContext(env);                  pipeline only if the
        var principal = ctx.Request.User;                request has the
        if (principal.HasClaim("scope", requiredScope))  required scope
          return next(env);
        ctx.Response.StatusCode = 403;
        return Task.FromResult(0);                        If the request doesn't have
      };                                                  the required scope, gives a
    }                                                     403 Forbidden response
  }
}
```

This middleware checks all incoming requests for a required scope. Remember that in
chapter 10, you set up communication between microservices such that the Login
microservice provided scopes for microservices, allowing them to collaborate. Only if
Login allows it can two microservices collaborate. The scope is the proof that a
request is allowed by Login, which is why microservices must check incoming requests
for any and all required scopes.

In chapter 10, you also created middleware to read the end user's identity from a
header on requests between microservices. Extract that middleware, call it IdToken,
and put it in the MicroserviceNET.Auth library.

Listing 11.7   User identity middleware

```
using LibOwin;
using System.IdentityModel.Tokens;
using System.IdentityModel.Tokens.Jwt;

using AppFunc =
  System.Func<
    System.Collections.Generic.IDictionary<string, object>,
    System.Threading.Tasks.Task>;

public class IdToken
```

```
    {
      public static AppFunc Middleware(AppFunc next)     Checks for the header
      {                                                  that should contain
        return env =>                                    the end user's identity
        {
          var ctx = new OwinContext(env);
          if (ctx.Request.Headers.ContainsKey("microservice.NET-end-user"))  <──┘
          {
            var tokenHandler = new JwtSecurityTokenHandler();
            SecurityToken token;
            var userPrincipal =
              tokenHandler.ValidateToken(
                ctx.Request.Headers["microservice.NET-end-user"],
                new TokenValidationParameters(), out token);
          ctx.Set("microservice.NET-end-user", new User(userPrincipal));  <──┐
          }
          return next(env);                    Creates a user object based on the
        };                                         claims in the end user's identity,
      }                                           and adds it to the OWIN context
```

Reads and validates the end user's identity — (label pointing to ValidateToken block)

In chapter 10, you wrote some code in the Nancy bootstrapper to read the user object back out of the OWIN context and pass it on to Nancy, so Nancy knows about the user. You'll bring that functionality into the package, but in a slightly different way, using a Nancy interface you haven't seen before: IRequestStartup. Just as Nancy automatically picks up bootstrappers and Nancy modules, it also picks up implementations of IRequestStartup. Nancy will find all such implementations—including those in NuGet packages—at application startup time and hook them into the request pipeline. The IRequestStartup implementation reads the user from the OWIN environment and hands it over to Nancy, as follows:

```
public class SetUser : IRequestStartup                       Called on each request
{
  public void Initialize(IPipelines pipelines, NancyContext context) =>   <──┘
    context.CurrentUser =
      context.GetOwinEnvironment()["microservice.NET-end-user"]
        ➥ as ClaimsPrincipal;                    ┌─ Assigns the user to the user
}                                                 │  on the Nancy context
```

This little class makes the MicroserviceNET.Auth NuGet package easier to use, because this bit of functionality is automatically wired up. Unfortunately, the OWIN middleware pieces aren't wired up automatically; to make that part easy as well, create the following convenience method to add middleware to the OWIN pipeline.

Listing 11.8 Extension method to add authorization middleware

```
namespace MicroserviceNET.Auth                          Signature of the
{                                                        OWIN BuildFunc
  using BuildFunc = System.Action<System.Func<    <──┘
    System.Func<
```

```
      System.Collections.Generic.IDictionary<string, object>,
      System.Threading.Tasks.Task>,
    System.Func<
      System.Collections.Generic.IDictionary<string, object>,
      System.Threading.Tasks.Task>
    >>;

  public static class BuildFuncExtensions
  {
    public static BuildFunc UseAuthPlatform(
      this BuildFunc buildFunc, string requiredScope)
    {
      buildFunc(next => Authorization.Middleware(next, requiredScope));
      buildFunc(next => IdToken.Middleware(next));
      return buildFunc;
    }
  }
}
```

> Helper method for adding the authorization middleware and the identity token middleware

This is all the code you need to add to the `MicroserviceNET.Auth` package. Create the NuGet package with dotnet, like this:

```
PS> dotnet pack --configuration Release
```

The new package is called `MicroserviceNET.Auth.1.0.0.nupkg` and is found in the bin/release folder. Now you have two of the three NuGet packages that make up the microservice platform. In the next section, you'll build the last package.

11.3.3   *Creating a package with rest client factory*

The last package in the microservice platform will be called `MicroserviceNET.Platform` and will contain the `HttpClientFactory` you developed in chapters 9 and 10. It will depend on the other two packages, which means microservices will only have to install `MicroserviceNET.Platform` to get the entire platform.

The steps to create the `MicroserviceNET.Platform` package are as follows:

1 Create a new class library called MicroserviceNET.Platform.
2 Add the `MicroserviceNET.Logging` and `MicroserviceNET.Auth` NuGet packages you created previously.
3 Add the `RestSharp`, `IdentityModel`, and `Nancy` NuGet packages.
4 Add the LibOwin.cs file from http://mng.bz/8pRq, as described in chapter 8.
5 Add the `HttpClientFactory` code to `MicroserviceNET.Platform`.
6 Add a convenience method to `MicroserviceNET.Platform` that makes it easier to configure `HttpClientFactory` correctly and register it in the Nancy dependency injection (DI) container.

The first three steps are similar to what you've done many times. Once you've created the new `MicroserviceNET.Platform` project and added the NuGet packages, the dependencies section in the project.json file should look like this:

```
"dependencies": {
    "NETStandard.Library": "1.6.0",
    "MicroserviceNET.Auth": {
      "target": "project",
      "version": "1.0.0"
    },
    "MicroserviceNET.Logging": {
      "target": "project",
      "version": "1.0.0"
    },
    "Nancy": "2.0.0-barneyrubble",
    "IdentityModel": "2.0.0-beta5"
}
```

Setting up and using your own NuGet feed

The NuGet packages you build for the microservice platform are meant to be used only in your own microservice system. As such, they don't belong in the public NuGet feed on www.nuget.org. Fortunately, NuGet doesn't require much from a feed—a folder on your local disk or a shared folder on a network drive will do. You just need to configure NuGet to look for packages in that folder as well as on www.nuget.org.

First, you must decide on a folder in which to use your NuGet packages; in this case, use c:\nuget-packages\. Next, copy the NuGet packages to this folder. When the packages are created with `dotnet`, they're in the bin\Release folder under the project. Copy the package—that is, the .nupkg file—to c:\nuget-packages. Finally, configure NuGet to look for packages in the folder by adding the folder the list of feeds in the NuGet configuration file located under your user profile at ~AppData\Roaming\NuGet\NuGet.Config. For instance, my NuGet.Config looks like this:

```xml
<?xml version="1.0" encoding="utf-8"?>
<configuration>
  <packageSources>
    <add key="nuget.org" value="https://www.nuget.org/api/v2/" />
    <add key="test" value="c:\nuget-packages\" />
  </packageSources>
  <disabledPackageSources>
    <add key="NancyAsync" value="true" />
  </disabledPackageSources>
  <activePackageSource>
    <add key="nuget.org" value="https://www.nuget.org/api/v2/" />
  </activePackageSource>
</configuration>
```

Now, a call to `dotnet restore` will also look in c:\nuget-packages\ for NuGet packages, which enables you to install your own packages from that folder into various projects.

The next step is to add a new HttpClientFactory.cs file to the project and fill in the code for `HttpClientFactory`, which you wrote in chapters 9 and 10.

Listing 11.9 HttpClientFactory

```
namespace MicroserviceNET.Platform
{
  using System;
  using System.Net.Http;
  using System.Net.Http.Headers;
  using System.Threading.Tasks;
  using IdentityModel.Client;

  public interface IHttpClientFactory
  {
    Task<HttpClient> Create(Uri uri, string requestScope);
  }

  public class HttpClientFactory : IHttpClientFactory
  {
    private readonly TokenClient tokenClient;
    private readonly string correlationToken;
    private readonly string idToken;

    public HttpClientFactory(
      string tokenUrl,
      string clientName,
      string clientSecret,
      string correlationToken,
      string idToken)
    {
      this.tokenClient =
        new TokenClient(tokenUrl, clientName, clientSecret);
      this.correlationToken = correlationToken;
      this.idToken = idToken;
    }

    public async Task<HttpClient> Create(Uri uri, string requestScope)
    {
      var response = await
        this.tokenClient
          .RequestClientCredentialsAsync(requestScope)
          .ConfigureAwait(false);
      var client = new HttpClient() { BaseAddress = uri };
      client.DefaultRequestHeaders.Authorization =
        new AuthenticationHeaderValue("Bearer", response.AccessToken);
      client
        .DefaultRequestHeaders
        .Add("Correlation-Token", this.correlationToken);
      if (!string.IsNullOrEmpty(this.idToken))
        client
          .DefaultRequestHeaders
          .Add("microservice.NET-end-user", this.idToken);
      return client;
    }
  }
}
```

Annotations:
- **URL of the token endpoint in the Login microservice** → `string tokenUrl,`
- **Client name and secret used to obtain an access token from the token endpoint** → `string clientName,` / `string clientSecret,`
- **Per-request correlation token coming from a piece of middleware** → `string correlationToken,`
- **Token with the end user's identity** → `string idToken)`
- **Requests an authorization token from the Login microservice, allowing calls that require the scope in requestScope** → `.RequestClientCredentialsAsync(requestScope)`
- **Prepares the client to make requests to uri** → `var client = new HttpClient() { BaseAddress = uri };`
- **Adds the authorization token to a request header** → `new AuthenticationHeaderValue("Bearer", response.AccessToken);`
- **Adds the correlation token to a request header** → `.Add("Correlation-Token", this.correlationToken);`
- **Adds the end user's identity to a request header** → `.Add("microservice.NET-end-user", this.idToken);`

`HttpClientFactory` is responsible for creating `HttpClient` objects that can be used to make requests to other microservices. The factory makes sure the `HttpClient` objects are set up to only make requests that adhere to the rules of your microservice system. `HttpClientFactory` makes sure requests made with `HttpClients` it created have the following:

- *An authorization token for a scope*—The code that uses the `HttpClient` to make requests must specify which scope it wants on those requests, but `HttpClient-Factory` makes sure the authorization token is obtained and put on the requests.
- *A correlation token*—This can be used to trace a chain of requests through the microservice system. One of the pieces of middleware from the `MicroserviceNET.Logging` package makes sure correlation tokens on incoming requests are read. The token should be passed to `HttpClientFactory`, which makes sure the correlation token is also on any outgoing requests.
- *A token containing the end user's identity, if the request originates from an end user request*—A piece of middleware in the `MicroserviceNET.Auth` package handles reading the end user's identity from incoming requests. This token should be passed to `HttpClientFactory` so it can make sure the token is passed along with any outgoing requests.

You can see from listing 11.9 that `HttpClientFactory` takes no fewer than five constructor arguments. Two of these arguments—the correlation token and the identity token—come from middleware in the other packages in the microservice platform. These pieces of middleware add the correlation token and the identity token to the OWIN environment.

11.3.4 *Automatically registering an HTTP client factory in Nancy's container*

You want the platform to be easy to use when you're creating microservices with it. So, let's add a couple of methods to the `MicroserviceNET.Platform` package that simplify configuring the `HttpClientFactory`. These methods assume that microservices have added the middleware from the two other packages in the platform and that the correlation token and the identity token can be found in the OWIN environment.

Add a MicroservicePlatformHelper.cs file to the `MicroserviceNET.Platform` project. You'll add two methods to this file. The first will be called by microservices from the `Startup` class and will remember some static configuration: the token URL, the client name, and the client secret.

> **Listing 11.10 Storing static configuration required by `HttpClientFactory`**

```
namespace MicroserviceNET.Platform
{
  using System.Security.Claims;
  using Nancy;
```

```
using Nancy.Owin;
using Nancy.TinyIoc;
using LibOwin;

public static class MicroservicePlatform
{
  private static string TokenUrl;
  private static string ClientName;
  private static string ClientSecret;

  public static void Configure(
    string tokenUrl,
    string clientName,
     string clientSecret)
  {
    TokenUrl = tokenUrl;
    ClientName = clientName;
    ClientSecret = clientSecret;
  }
}
}
```

The second convenience method, shown in listing 11.11, is meant to be used from the Nancy bootstrapper, where it should be called at every request. It creates an `HttpClientFactory` based on that configuration and information from the OWIN environment and then registers it with the Nancy DI container, such that application code (Nancy modules, and so on) can take a dependency on `HttpClientFactory` and have it injected automatically.

Listing 11.11 Convenience method for registering `HttpClientFactory`

```
                    public static TinyIoCContainer UseHttpClientFactory(
                      this TinyIoCContainer self,
                      NancyContext context)
                    {
                      var correlationToken =
                        context.GetOwinEnvironment()?["correlationToken"] as string;
                      object key = null;
                      context
                        .GetOwinEnvironment()
                        ?.TryGetValue(OwinConstants.RequestUser, out key);
                      var principal = key as ClaimsPrincipal;
                      var idToken = principal?.FindFirst("id_token");
                      self.Register<IHttpClientFactory>(
                        new HttpClientFactory(
                          TokenUrl, ClientName,
                          ClientSecret,
                          correlationToken ?? "",
                          idToken?.Value));
                      return self;
                    }
```

Reads the correlation token from the OWIN environment

Reads the end user from the OWIN environment

Gets the end user's identity token from the user object

Creates an HttpClientFactory with all necessary information

Registers the HttpClientFactory as a per-request dependency in Nancy's container

This is all that goes in the `MicroserviceNET.Platform` package. All that remains is to build the NuGet package:

```
PS> dotnet pack --configuration Release
```

`MicroserviceNET.Platform` is built into bin/Release/ MicroserviceNET.Platform.1.0.0 .nupkg. Figure 11.5 shows the contents of that NuGet package, which is a DLL. The figure also shows that `MicroserviceNET.Platform` depends on the two other packages in the platform: `MicroserviceNET.Logging` and `MicroserviceNET.Auth`.

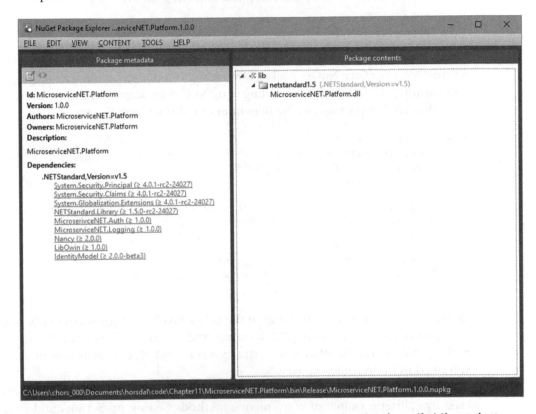

Figure 11.5 Looking in `MicroserviceNET.Platform.1.0.0.nupkg` **shows that the package depends on the other two packages in the platform—**`MicroserviceNET.Logging` **and** `MicroserviceNET.Auth`**—as well as a number of external packages.**

This concludes the implementation of your microservice platform. In the next section, you'll take the platform for a quick spin.

11.3.5 *Using the microservice platform*

You've built a platform that should make it easier to create new microservices that behave the way they should in your production environment. In this section, you'll create a small Hello World–style microservice, using the platform and Nancy. Because the microservice will be built using your microservice platform, it will have the platform's monitoring, logging, and security features.

Creating the microservice doesn't involve a lot of work. All you have to do is the following:

1 Create an empty web application called `HelloMicroservicePlatform`.
2 Add the `MicroserviceNET.Platform` NuGet package.
3 Configure the microservice platform in the `Startup` class.
4 Create a small Nancy bootstrapper, and configure the registration of `HttpClientFactory`.
5 Add a small Nancy module.

Begin by creating an empty web application with yo or Visual Studio. Add the `MicroserviceNET.Platform` NuGet package by adding it to the dependencies in project.json and running `dotnet restore`. Adding your NuGet package works the same as adding any other NuGet package, so the dependencies should look like this:

```
"dependencies": {
    "Microsoft.NETCore.App": {
      "version": "1.0.0-rc2-3002702",
      "type": "platform"
    },
    "Microsoft.AspNetCore.Server.IISIntegration": "1.0.0-rc2-final",
    "Microsoft.AspNetCore.Server.Kestrel": "1.0.0-rc2-final",
    "Microsoft.AspNetCore.Owin": "1.0.0-rc2-final",
    "Serilog": "2.0.0-rc-600",
    "MicroserviceNET.Platform": "1.0.0",
    "Serilog.Sinks.ColoredConsole": "2.0.0-beta-700"
  },
```

`MicroserviceNET.Platform` brings in the other two NuGet packages in the microservice platform—`MicroserviceNET.Logging` and `MicroserviceNET.Auth`—as well as Serilog and Nancy. In other words, `MicroserviceNET.Platform` brings in everything you need to build a microservice.

The next step is to configure the microservice platform. You do so in the `Startup` class by calling a couple of convenience methods, setting up Serilog, and creating a simple health check.

Listing 11.12 Configuring the microservice platform in the `Startup` class

```
public class Startup                                        Configures the
{                                                           monitoring and
    public void Configure(IApplicationBuilder app)          logging part of
    {                                                       the platform
      app.UseOwin()
        .UseMonitoringAndLogging(ConfigureLogger(), HealthCheck)  ⟵
        .UseAuthPlatform("test-scope")
        .UseNancy();
    }
}
```

Configures the authorization part of the platform ⟶

```
                 private ILogger ConfigureLogger()
                 {
                    ...
                 }

                 private static Task<bool> HealthCheck()
                 {
                    ...
                 }
            }
```

Now you have the monitoring endpoints, the request logging and performance logging are in place, and you're checking access tokens on incoming requests. The remaining parts of the platform are related to outgoing requests. To get these up and running, add the following Nancy bootstrapper to the microservice.

Listing 11.13 Registering `HttpClientFactory` in Nancy's container

```
public class Bootstrapper : DefaultNancyBootstrapper
{
  protected override void RequestStartup(          ⟵──┐  Called by Nancy for
    TinyIoCContainer container,                         │  each request
    IPipelines pipelines,
    NancyContext context)
  {
    base.RequestStartup(container, pipelines, context);
    container.UseHttpClientFactory(context);       ⟵──┐  Convenience method
  }                                                     │  that registers
}                                                       │  HttpClientFactory in
                                                        │  Nancy's container
```

With this done, the microservice platform is configured and ready to run. This is all it takes to create a new microservice—from here on, it's a matter of adding behavior. The last step in creating your Hello World microservice is to add a Nancy module with a single endpoint that makes a request to another microservice and sends the response back to the caller (see listing 11.14). This isn't much of a behavior for a microservice, but it serves as an illustration of how the microservice platform works with regard to outgoing requests: the request to the other microservice has both a correlation token and an access token added to it by the microservice platform.

Listing 11.14 Using `HttpClientFactory` to make well-behaved requests

```
public class Hello : NancyModule
{
  public Hello(IHttpClientFactory clientFactory)
  {
    Get("/", async (_, __) =>
    {
```

```
var client = await
clientFactory.Create(
  new Uri("http://otherservice/"),
  "scope_for_other_microservice");
var resp = await
  client.GetAsync("/some/path").ConfigureAwait(false);
return resp.StatusCode;
});
  }
}
```

Creates an HttpClient to make requests to another microservice

Sends request to the other microservice, including a correlation token and an access token, which are added by the microservice platform

Now the Hello World microservice is ready to be used. You start it the same way as any other microservice, using dotnet. If you had another microservice running at http://otherservice, the Hello World microservice would only accept requests with a valid access token for the scope test-scope; it would log all requests and responses, and it would return the status code of the response from the other microservice. The Hello World microservice also has monitoring endpoints, and it uses a correlation token.

11.4   Summary

- Because you'll often be building new microservices in a microservice system, you need to be able to quickly and easily build a new one from scratch.
- To meet cross-cutting requirements for monitoring, logging, and security, there are a number of things that all microservices in a system need to do. Which things, exactly, differ from system to system.
- You should develop a reusable microservice platform for your microservice system. With such a platform, it's simply to create new microservices that behave as they're supposed to in terms of logging, monitoring, and security.
- A reusable microservice platform should only address cross-cutting technical concerns such as monitoring, logging, and security.
- A reusable microservices platform shouldn't address domain logic, because this differs between microservices.
- NuGet is a good format for distributing a microservice platform.
- You can easily set up a local NuGet feed.
- You use the dotnet pack command to create a NuGet package.
- You can create NuGet packages to do the following:
  - Add monitoring endpoints to microservices
  - Add request/response logging to microservices
  - Add performance logging to microservices
  - Add correlation tokens to all log messages
  - Add correlation tokens to all outgoing requests
  - Only allow incoming requests with an access token for a required scope
  - Add an access token for scopes to all outgoing requests
- You can build NuGet packages from libraries.
- You can use custom NuGet packages in your microservices.

Part 4

Building applications

This part of the book adds a finishing touch to the picture: how to create applications for end users. You've learned how to break down a system into microservices and how to create those microservices. In chapter 12, you'll put a GUI on top of your microservices so end users can take full advantage of their functionality.

Creating applications over microservices

This chapter covers

- Building an end user application on top of a microservice system
- Understanding the composite application, API gateway, and the backend for frontend design patterns
- Using server-side and client-side rendering in web applications

So far, we've concentrated on implementing business capabilities in microservices and exposing those capabilities through HTTP APIs. But end users don't use HTTP APIs—they use web apps, mobile apps, desktop applications, smart TVs, VR glasses, and other applications on devices with interfaces geared to humans. To give end users access to all the capabilities of microservices, we need to implement applications on top of microservices. This chapter is about doing that: we'll move from looking at designing single microservices to bringing all the microservices together in an architecture that supports building applications for end users.

We'll start with a broad, nontechnical discussion of how to approach building applications on top of a microservice system. Then we'll go into three specific architectural patterns for implementing applications: The *composite application, API gateway,* and *backend for frontend* patterns.

12.1   End user applications for microservice systems: one or many applications?

There are several ways to go about building end user–oriented applications both from a user perspective and from a technical perspective. We'll begin with the user perspective and look at a range of ways to surface the functionality in your microservices to end users in applications: from general-purpose applications that provide all the functionality of the system to a collection of small, specialized applications, each of which offers only a few capabilities. These two ways of surfacing functionality represent each end of a spectrum, as illustrated in figure 12.1.

Figure 12.1   A wide spectrum of application types can be build on top of a microservice system, ranging from general-purpose applications to very specialized applications.

Between the two extremes lie many other options for building applications that cover bigger or smaller parts of the microservice system's functionality. Where on the spectrum the applications for a particular microservice system should fall depends on the context of that particular system: its end users, its functionality, and so on.

Both ends of the spectrum have merit. The next two sections discuss them, to give you a feel for the breadth of ways your microservice systems can provide functionality. The choice of where on the spectrum to land impacts how your application(s) should be built and which design pattern you should use.

12.1.1   General-purpose applications

A microservice system can provide a great deal of functionality. Consider, for instance, a line-of-business system for an insurance company. The system drives business processes including selling policies, setting prices, and handling claims made by customers. Users include the following:

- Salespeople who call and solicit potential customers
- Actuaries who set policy prices and evaluate business risks based on estimated future claims and income
- Appraisers who valuate goods that customers want to insure and about which customers make claims
- Claims adjusters who investigate and settle customer claims
- IT staff who oversee users and permissions

You implement all the different business capabilities of the insurance system in different microservices, but you may also decide to implement a common application that covers all functionality and is used by all users. This can be thought of as a *general-purpose application*. It can be any type of application—for example, a web application or a desktop application. The Facebook app for iOS or Android is an example of a general-purpose application: the app lets users do everything on Facebook, such as read their newsfeed, send messages, write on walls, manage settings, upload photos to albums, and more.

Various reasons may drive a decision to implement a general-purpose application that surfaces all functionality in the system. For example, some users in the insurance system may have more than one function, such as claims adjusters who also do appraisals. There also may be overlap between the functionalities needed by different types of users.

By managing their permissions, you can still limit what each user can do in a general-purpose application. But they all use the same application, and it provides all of the system's functionality.

12.1.2 Specialized applications

Another option for building applications on top of a microservices system is to build lots of small, specialized applications. This is in some ways the opposite of the general-purpose application approach: you have many highly specialized applications, each of which surfaces only a little of the functionality of the entire system. Continuing with the example of a line-of-business application for an insurance company, you may have separate specialized applications for the following:

- Browsing the catalog of policies offered by the company
- Creating offers for potential customers
- Creating an insurance policy for a customer
- Creating reports about currently active insurance policies
- Creating forecasts about the cost of future claims
- Registering and investigating claims
- Appraising insured goods
- Settling claims

With this approach, users must use more than one application. That may sound like a bad user experience at first, but is it really? If you choose to implement the applications as web apps, they can easily link to each other, creating a cohesive experience even though the functionality is spread over many small applications. And the philosophy of doing one thing and doing it well can lead to very good applications for each piece of functionality. For instance, Facebook has an Android app called Selfies for Messenger, which is for doing just one thing: taking selfies and sending them with Facebook Messenger. The app streamlines that single functionality.

Although I've only mentioned general-purpose applications and specialized applications, these aren't the only two possibilities. There's a spectrum of options (shown again in figure 12.2), ranging from one big application that provides all functionality in the system to a long list of single-capability applications. Other possibilities include

- Splitting the large, all-in-one application into two applications, with administrative functionalities in the first and all other functionality in the second
- Joining some of the single-capability applications into slightly larger applications that cover all the functionalities required by one type of user

Figure 12.2   To repeat: a wide spectrum of types of applications can be built on top of microservices.

In the case of the insurance company, one middle-ground approach would be to create an application for each type of user. Salespeople would get a sales application with all the functionality they need, from canvassing for leads to signing a deal. Likewise, actuaries, appraisers, claims adjusters, and IT staff would get applications tailored to their usage.

Although this approach avoids the complexities of big, general-purpose applications as well as those of a vast number of single-purpose applications, it does have its own issues: functionality will probably be duplicated between applications, some users play more than one role, and so on. There's no one right way; you need to decide where in the spectrum you fall, based on user-experience concerns rather than technical concerns.

Now, let's turn to the more technical side of things and look at three technical patterns for building applications on top of microservices.

12.2   *Patterns for building applications over microservices*

This section discusses the composite application, API gateway, and backend for frontend design patterns. I'll explain each pattern in turn and also discuss their pros and cons. Then I'll turn to the question of when to use each one.

12.2.1   *Composite applications: integrating at the frontend*

The first pattern for building applications over microservices is the *composite application.* A composite application is made up of functionality drawn from several places—in the case of microservices, from different microservices—by communicating with each one directly. Each microservice provides both functionality and a GUI for the functionality. Microservices may communicate with each other to perform their tasks; the composite application doesn't care.

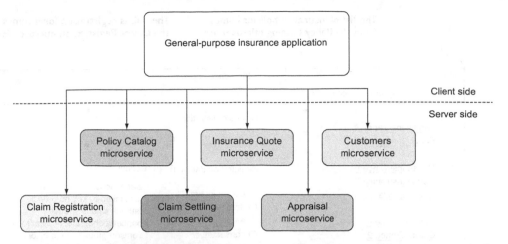

Figure 12.3 A composite general-purpose application uses many different microservices, each of which provides both functionality and a GUI for that functionality.

Figure 12.3 returns to the insurance example, with a general-purpose application that includes all of the system's functionality. The insurance system is built using microservices, so to provide all of the system's functionality through the application, the application needs to draw on the business capabilities of many microservices. There are more microservices in the system than are shown in the figure, and the application won't draw directly from all of them. The application composes these functionalities into one application—thus the term *composite application.*

When you build a general-purpose application in front of a microservice system as a composite application, the microservices provide functionality and also a GUI to go with the functionality. As a consequence, the GUI of the application is a composite of smaller GUIs drawn from different microservices. Figure 12.4 shows an example structure for the insurance application's GUI: it consists of four sections, each drawn from a microservice that provides both functionality and a GUI.

How GUI composition is achieved depends on the technology used to build the client. In the case of a desktop Windows Presentation Foundation (WPF) application (http:mng.bz/0YfW), you could, for instance, use a Managed Extensibility Framework (MEF, http://mng.bz/6NKA) to dynamically load components into the application, each of which could have its own piece of the GUI. In the case of a web application, the GUI can be built by loading HTML fragments and JavaScript bundles from the microservices into the main application and adding them to the DOM with JavaScript. In both cases, microservices provide both the functionality and the GUI.

Composite applications aren't all general-purpose applications; they can be smaller applications, as well. For instance, if the insurance application has one application per user type, each application must provide functionality that belongs to different business capabilities and therefore to different microservices. It follows that each per-user-type application can be built as a composite application.

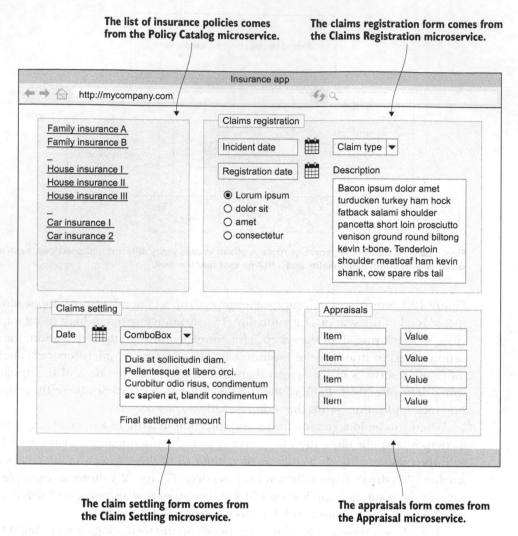

The list of insurance policies comes from the Policy Catalog microservice.

The claims registration form comes from the Claims Registration microservice.

The claim settling form comes from the Claim Settling microservice.

The appraisals form comes from the Appraisal microservice.

Figure 12.4   A composite application takes GUI components from different microservices and uses them to form a cohesive, composite GUI.

ADVANTAGES

When you're building composite applications, the GUI is split into smaller parts according to business capabilities, just as functionality is distributed across microservices following business capabilities. That means the GUI for each business capability is implemented close to the code for the capability and is deployed along with that code. Because the composite application draws the GUI for the capability from the microservice, the application is updated every time a microservice GUI is updated. This means the agility you gain by splitting the system into small, focused microservices applies to the application GUI, too.

DISADVANTAGES

A composite application is responsible for integrating all the functionality implemented throughout the system of microservices. This can be a complex task: there are potentially many business capabilities in a microservice system, and the application's GUI may not be split along quite the same lines, leading to pages that include UIs from several different microservices but that need to feel like a single screen to the end user.

This kind of complexity can mean that the composite application has intimate knowledge of how the microservices work and, in particular, how their UIs work. If the composite application begins to make too many assumptions about the microservices' UIs, it becomes sensitive to changes in each microservice, and thus the application as a whole may break because of GUI changes in a single microservice. If you wind up in that situation, you lose the agility that's one the major advantages of using a composite application.

In conclusion, composite applications can work very well—but only if you can avoid implementing complex integrations.

12.2.2 API gateway

The second pattern for building applications over microservices is the *API gateway*. An API gateway is a microservice with a public HTTP API that covers all of the system's functionality but doesn't implement any of the functionality itself. Instead, the API gateway delegates everything to other microservices. In effect, an API gateway acts like an adapter between applications and the system of microservices.

When you build applications in front of a microservice system that uses an API gateway, the applications are shielded from knowing anything about how the system functionality is split across microservices, or even that the system uses microservices. The application only needs to know about one microservice: the API gateway.

Throughout this book, you've seen the example of a shopping cart in an e-commerce system, including an API gateway. Figure 12.5 shows a request to add an item to a user's shopping cart coming in from the application to the API gateway, which delegates to other microservices to serve the request. The role of the API gateway in this case is to provide a single entry point for applications and thus simplify the system interface so that applications don't have to interact directly with several microservices.

You can build any kind of application in front of an API gateway, from a general-purpose application that uses everything the API gateway has to offer, to specialized, single-capability applications that use only a fraction of the API gateway, to everything in between.

ADVANTAGES

The main benefit of the API gateway pattern is that it decouples applications nicely from the way the system is decomposed into microservices. The API gateway hides that completely from applications.

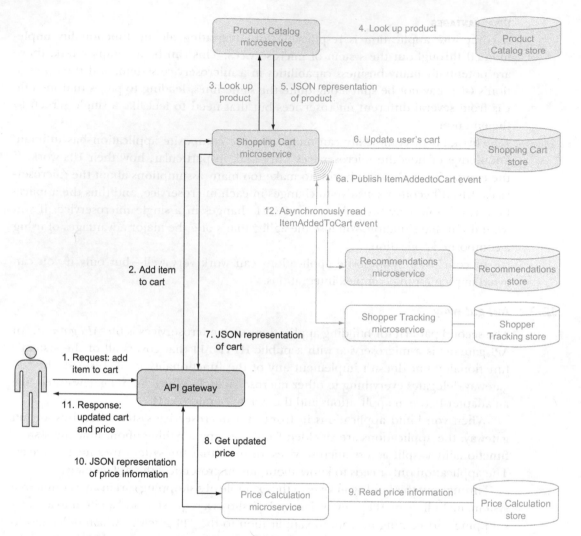

Figure 12.5   An API gateway is the single entry point for applications. Any request from an application goes to the API gateway, which delegates to the rest of the microservice system to fulfill the request.

In cases where several applications have overlapping functionality or where some applications are built by third parties, using the API gateway pattern facilitates the following:

- Maintaining a low barrier to entry for building applications
- Keeping the public API stable
- Keeping the public API backward compatible

Using an API gateway means application developers need to look at only one API in order to get started. You can concentrate on keeping the API stable and backward compatible while other microservices evolve.

DISADVANTAGES

The main disadvantage of the API gateway pattern is that the API gateway itself can grow into a large codebase and display all the disadvantages of a monolith. This is especially true if you succumb to the temptation to implement business logic in the API gateway. The API gateway may draw on many other microservices to serve a single request. Because it's combining the data from several microservices anyway, it's tempting to apply a few business rules to the data as well. Doing so may be quick in the short run, but it pushes the API gateway down the path toward becoming a monolith.

In conclusion, the API gateway pattern is very useful and often the right way to go. But keep a keen eye on the size of the API gateway, and be ready to react if it becomes so large that it's difficult to work with.

12.2.3 Backend for frontend (BFF) pattern

The third and final pattern for building applications over microservices that we'll look at is the *backend for frontend* (BFF) pattern. The BFF pattern is relevant when you need to build more than one application for a microservice system—for instance, the insurance system may have a web application for the most common functionality, an iOS app that appraisers can use on the road, and a specialized desktop application for actuarial tasks. A BFF is a microservice akin to an API gateway, but it's specialized for one application. If you use this pattern for the applications in the insurance system, you'll have a BFF for the web app, a BFF for the iOS app, and a BFF for the actuarial desktop application (see figure 12.6).

The point of a BFF is to support the single application built on top of it. That means the application and the BFF are tightly coupled: the BFF exposes the functionality the

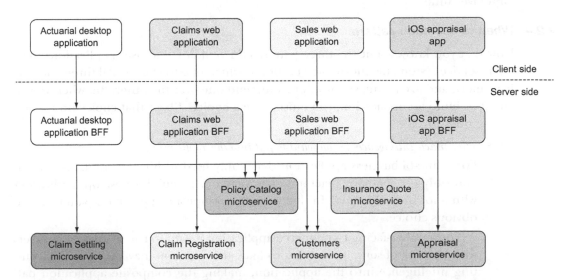

Figure 12.6   BFFs are used by a single application. The BFF is the only entry point for the application it's used by and therefore serves every request for that application. It answers requests by delegating to other microservices responsible for business capabilities.

application needs, and it does so in a way that makes writing the application as easy as possible.

ADVANTAGES

With the BFF pattern, each applications gets to use an API that's tailored exactly to its needs. With an API gateway, there's a risk of the API gateway becoming bloated as you add more and more functionality to it over time. With a BFF, this is less of a risk, because the BFF doesn't have to cover everything in the system: only the functionality needed by the application it serves.

It's fairly easy to know when something can be removed from a BFF: when no active version of the application it serves uses that functionality. Compare this to an API gateway with several applications in front: something can be removed from the API gateway only when no version of any of the applications uses it. All in all, BFFs offer a way to both simplify application development and keep the server side focused and well factored.

DISADVANTAGES

In cases where you have several applications that provide similar or overlapping functionality to end users—such as having both an iOS app and an Android app targeted at the same type of end user—the BFF pattern leads to duplicating code among several BFFs. This comes with the usual disadvantages of duplication: duplicated effort every time there are changes to the duplicated parts, and a tendency for the duplicated parts to drift away from each other over time and end up working slightly differently in different applications.

In conclusion, the BFF pattern can strike a good balance between placing the burden of integration on the application and creating an API gateway that may grow too large over time.

12.2.4 *When to use each pattern*

Now that you know about the three patterns for building end user applications for a microservice system, the inevitable question is which one to choose. All three patterns have merit and are useful, so I won't recommend one over the other. But when you're about to build an application, you must make a choice. I base that choice on the following questions:

- *How much intelligence do you want to put into the application?*
  For a line-of-business application that's only used within the company firewall and only on company machines, you may opt to build a desktop application with a lot of intelligence. In that case, the composite application pattern is the obvious choice.

  For a public-facing e-commerce application meant to run in any old browser, with the risk of somebody trying to hack the app, you may shy away from putting intelligence into the application, making the composite application pattern less attractive.

- *Is there more than one application? If so, how different are the applications?*

  If you haven't put much intelligence in the application, and if there's only one application, or if all applications provide similar functionality—maybe even in similar ways—an API gateway is probably a good choice.

  If there are several applications, and they provide different sets of functionality, the BFF pattern is a good option. With an API gateway or with BFFs, the intelligence is on the backend. The API gateway works well as long as it's cohesive—that is, as long as the set of all endpoints exposed by the API gateway has a certain consistency in terms of how applications should use them and how they're structured.

  If some endpoints follow a remote procedure call (RPC) style and others follow a representation state transfer (REST) style, they're inconsistent, and cohesion in the API gateway codebase will probably be low. In such cases, you should consider the BFF pattern. With BFFs, you can have some applications that work with an RPC-style API in one BFF and other apps that use a REST API in another BFF, without compromising cohesion. Each BFF can be cohesive and consistent by itself, but you don't need consistency among BFFs in terms of API style.

- *How big is the system?*

  With a large system—in terms of the amount of functionality it exposes—an API gateway can become an unmanageable codebase that exposes many of the disadvantages of monoliths. With large systems, using a number of BFFs is probably a better choice than one big API gateway. On the other hand, if the system isn't that big, an API gateway can be simpler than BFFs.

Finally, it's worth noting that you don't need to make the same choice for all applications. You may start with an API gateway and build a few applications on it, but then decide that a new application with an innovative approach to doing things doesn't fit the API gateway's way of doing things, and give the new application a BFF. Likewise, you may have internal-facing applications that use the composite application pattern, while at the same time having external-facing apps that go through an API gateway of BFFs.

12.2.5 Client-side or server-side rendering?

I've talked about three patterns for building applications over microservices: composite applications, API gateway, and BFF. If you build web apps using these patterns, there's another question to address: should you use server-side or client-side rendering? That is, should you generate ready-to-go HTML on the server—using, for instance, Razor (http://mng.bz/l73n)—or should you render the HTML in a JavaScript application, using one of the many JavaScript application frameworks such as Angular (https://angularjs.org), Ember (http://emberjs.com), Aurelia (http://aurelia.io), or React (https://facebook.github.io/react)?

This, again, is a question that doesn't have one clear answer but depends entirely on the application you want to build. How dynamic is the application? Is it more concerned with working with data or with showing and entering data? The more dynamic the app is, and the more its workflow is about working with and manipulating data, the more I lean toward client-side rendering; whereas the more static the app is, and the more the workflow is about viewing and entering data, the more I lean toward server-side rendering. The main point, though, is that the choice between client-side and server-side rendering is about the application you want to build, not the fact that you've chosen to use a microservice architecture on the server side.

All three patterns support both server-side and client-side rendering. More than that—they support mixing server-side and client-side rendering, such that some parts of an application are server-side rendered and others are client-side rendered. For instance, the catalog of policies in the insurance system is static and read-only in most situations; it probably makes sense to render it on the server side. On the other hand, the valuation calculator is a more dynamic component that lets users play around with parameters before saving a final result; it's probably well suited for client-side rendering in a JavaScript application. The two can coexist in the same application:

- If you're building a composite application, it can draw in the server-side-rendered catalog of policies as well as the JavaScript app for the valuation calculator. The microservice responsible for the policy catalog will provide the server-side-generated GUI for the policy catalog, whereas the microservice in charge of valuations will provide the valuation calculator JavaScript application.
- If you're using an API gateway, it can contain endpoints that return HTML and others that return data—for example, in the form of JSON. It can even contain endpoints that can return either HTML or JSON data, based on the `Accept` header in the request. So again, an app can contain a server-side-rendered policy catalog along with a client-side-rendered valuation calculator.
- If you're using BFFs, you have the same possibilities for having endpoints return HTML, data, or both. In addition, BFFs give you the opportunity to make different decisions for different applications: in one BFF, the policy catalog can be server-side rendered, but in another it may be client-side rendered.

The choice between server-side and client-side rendering of a web GUI isn't impacted by the fact that the server side uses microservices. All the patterns we've looked at for building applications over microservices support both server-side and client-side rendering.

12.3 *Example: a shopping cart and product list*

Let's look at a concrete example and see the code required to implement a couple of pieces of functionality in one application. This example uses one application pattern and doesn't show the other two in detail; it will show you how to bring together functionality from a number of different microservices in an application, which is also at the core of the other two patterns.

The remainder of this chapter picks up the example of the shopping cart on an e-commerce website from earlier chapters. First I'll recap the example, then I'll show you a small UI for the shopping cart and a product list, and finally you'll implement them.

On the e-commerce website, users can browse products and add them to the shopping cart. When a user adds a product to their cart, the process shown in figure 12.7 is triggered. A number of things happen:

1 The item is added to the shopping cart.
2 A new total is calculated for the contents of the cart.
3 The Recommendation microservice and Shopper Tracking microservice are notified of the change to the shopping cart through the event feed on the Shopping Cart microservice.

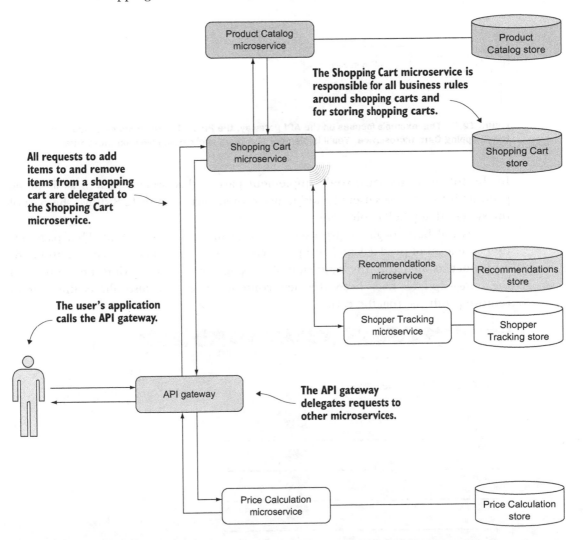

Figure 12.7 The Shopping Cart Microservice is responsible for storing and maintaining shopping carts on behalf of users, but the API gateway makes that functionality (along with other pieces of functionality) available to end users to use in a web app.

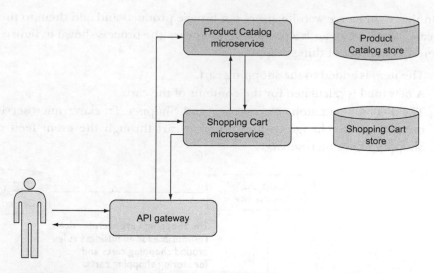

Figure 12.8   This example focuses on the API gateway, the Product Catalog microservice, and the Shopping Cart microservice. You'll implement part of an application based on those three.

In the following sections, you'll implement part of this process as well as a simple product list that allows users to add items to their carts. Figure 12.8 shows the part of the system that you'll implement.

This will be enough to give users the page shown in figure 12.9. That page lets users see a list of products and add products to their shopping cart. When a user adds a product to their cart, the right side of the page—the part showing the contents of the cart—updates and shows the new contents. The page also allows the user to remove products from the cart.

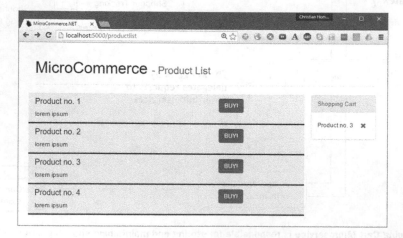

Figure 12.9   The part of the e-commerce application that you'll implement shows a list of products and lets users add and remove products from their shopping cart.

To implement this UI, you'll perform the following steps:

1 Reuse the Product Catalog microservice and Shopping Cart microservice from chapter 5.

2 Create an API gateway.

3 Create the product list from figure 12.9:
- Create an endpoint in the API gateway for fetching a page with the product list.
- Make the new endpoint read the list of products from Product Catalog.
- Create a view with the list of products, and return it from the new endpoint.

4 Add the shopping cart from figure 12.9 to the web page:
- Make the API gateway get the current state of the shopping cart from Shopping Cart.
- Add the shopping cart to the web page.

5 Create an endpoint in the API gateway for adding products to the shopping cart:
- Add a POST endpoint for adding products to the shopping cart in the API gateway.
- Call Shopping Cart from the API gateway to add the new product.
- Update the view the user sees to reflect that a product was added to the shopping cart.

6 Create an endpoint in the API gateway to remove products from the shopping cart.

You'll use the Product Catalog microservice and the Shopping Cart microservice from chapter 5 just as they are in the new API gateway. You could, at this point, add the microservice platform from chapter 11 to these microservices, but for the sake of brevity you'll skip that step. The only thing you'll do in these microservices is make sure they run on different ports so that they can run at the same time on your development machine. You specify these ports in the microservices' respective project.json files—I use 5100 for Product Catalog and port 5200 for Shopping Cart.

> **NOTE** To keep the scope of this example tenable, I've cut some corners. Most notably, you won't implement a login system. Instead, you'll hardcode the user ID. This means the application can only manage that single user's shopping cart. In chapter 10, you saw how to deal with security in general, including authenticating end users.

12.3.1 Creating an API gateway

Create a new project for the API gateway the same way you've created projects many times before. Call the new project ApiGateway. Then, add the microservice platform you developed in chapter 11 as a NuGet package to the new project. Remember that the platform pulls in a few other packages, such as Nancy; the list of dependencies in the project.json file should look like this.

Listing 12.1 Dependencies in the API gateway

```
"dependencies": {
    "Microsoft.NETCore.App": {
        "version": "1.0.0-rc2-3002702",
        "type": "platform"
    },
    "Microsoft.AspNetCore.Server.IISIntegration": "1.0.0",
    "Microsoft.AspNetCore.Server.Kestrel": "1.0.0",
    "Microsoft.AspNetCore.StaticFiles": "1.0.0",
    "Microsoft.AspNetCore.Owin": "1.0.0",
    "MicroserviceNET.Platform": "1.0.0",
    "Serilog.Sinks.ColoredConsole": "2.0.0-beta-700"
},
```

> The platform depends on Nancy, so this installs Nancy, too.

Next, change the Startup.cs file in this new project to do the same initialization of Nancy that you've seen before, as well as the initialization of the microservice platform.

Listing 12.2 Initializing Nancy and the microservice platform

```
public class Startup
{
    public void Configure(IApplicationBuilder app)
    {
        var logger = ConfigureLogger();
        app.UseStaticFiles();
        app.UseOwin()
            .UseMonitoringAndLogging(logger, HealthCheck)
            .UseNancy(opt => opt.Bootstrapper = new Bootstrapper(logger));
    }

    private ILogger ConfigureLogger()
    {
        MicroservicePlatform.Configure(
            tokenUrl: "http://localhost:5001/",
            clientName:"api_gateway",
            clientSecret: "secret");
        return new LoggerConfiguration()
            .Enrich.FromLogContext()
            .WriteTo.ColoredConsole(
                LogEventLevel.Verbose,
                "{NewLine}{Timestamp:HH:mm:ss} [{Level}] ({CorrelationToken})
            ➥ {Message}{NewLine}{Exception}")
            .CreateLogger();
    }

    private static Task<bool> HealthCheck()
    {
        return Task.FromResult(true);
    }
}
```

> Configures ASP.NET Core to serve JavaScript and CSS files from the file system

> Configures the monitoring middleware from the microservice platform

> Shares the logger between the microservice platform and Nancy by passing it into the bootstrapper

> Does the static configuration of the microservice platform

> Dummy health check

```
public class Bootstrapper : DefaultNancyBootstrapper
{
  private ILogger logger;
  public Bootstrapper(ILogger logger)
  {                                              Holds on to
    this.logger = logger;                        the logger
  }
  protected override void ApplicationStartup(
    TinyIoCContainer container,
    IPipelines pipelines)                        Shares the logger with
  {                                              any module that wants a
                                                 dependency on ILogger
    container.Register(logger);
    container.UseHttpClientFactory(new NancyContext());
  }

  protected override void RequestStartup(
    TinyIoCContainer container,
    IPipelines pipelines,
    NancyContext context)                        Configures
  {                                              HttpClientFactory,
                                                 and registers it in
    base.RequestStartup(container, pipelines, context);   the container
    container.UseHttpClientFactory(context);
  }
}
}
```

Now you have an empty project, ready for the implementation of the API gateway.

12.3.2 *Creating the product list GUI*

The next step is to create the part of the application that lists products. Add a new Nancy module called `GatewayModule` to the API gateway, and add a `/productlist` endpoint to that module. `GatewayModule` will contain all the endpoints that serve the application to end users: it will have endpoints that give end users a web GUI and also endpoints used by the JavaScript in that web GUI.

To keep it simple at first, let's begin with an endpoint that does nothing. Then you'll add a GUI based on a hardcoded list of products, and finally you'll retrieve the real list of products from the Product Catalog microservice.

`GatewayModule` will serve the web frontend to end users, but start with the following endpoint that always responds with an empty 501 Not Implemented.

Listing 12.3 Placeholder endpoint implementation in the API gateway

```
namespace ApiGateway
{
  using System;
  using System.Threading.Tasks;
  using Nancy;

  public class GatewayModule : NancyModule
  {
    public GatewayModule()
    {
```

```
      Get("/productlist", _ => 501);
    }
  }
}
```

The next step is to add a GUI that shows the product list. So far, throughout the book, you've returned data—for example, in the form of JSON—from all endpoints. Now, you'll return a GUI, in the form of server-side-generated HTML. Unsurprisingly, Nancy supports this very well. Out of the box, Nancy comes with its own view engine called the Super Simple View Engine (SSVE, http://mng.bz/ydy4), which you'll use for this example.

Nancy, SSVE, and Razor

Nancy lets you use several different view engines. Out of the box, Nancy comes with the Super Simple View Engine (SSVE); but if you'd rather use another view engine—Microsoft's Razor view engine, for instance—you can. Like everything else in Nancy, the view engine can be replaced or supplemented with another view engine. For instance, to use Razor with Nancy, you install the `Nancy.Viewengines.Razor` NuGet package. which contains the code needed to adapt Razor for Nancy and which also pulls in Razor itself.

In this chapter, you'll stick with SSVE. It really is a simple view engine, but it supports passing a model object into views and using that model object for basic templating such as `if` conditions, accessing properties on the model, and iterating over enumerable properties on the model; it also supports more-advanced features like partial views and master pages. The syntax for all features in SSVE is prefixed with @, as shown in the following example. First, you define a type for the model object used in this example:

```
public class MyModel
{
  public string Headline { get; set;}
  public bool SomeCondition { get; set; }
  public IEnumerable<string> SomeList { get; set; }
}
```

Now, use it in a view:

```
<html>
 <body>
   <h1>@Model.Headline</h1>
   @If.SomeCondition
      <p>the condition is true</p>
   @Endif
   <ol>
     @Each.SomeList
       <li>@Current</li>
     @EndEach
   </ol>
 </body>
</html>
```

(continued)
This view uses the `Headline` property from the model object as a headline, checks
the Boolean `SomeCondition`, renders a short paragraph only when `SomeCondition`
is `true`, and renders an ordered list with a bullet for each string in `SomeList`.

To make the /productlist endpoint return a view, change it as shown next. It returns a
view called `productlist` and passes a hardcoded list of products into the view as a
model object.

Listing 12.4   Hard-coded endpoint implementation in the API gateway

```
namespace ApiGateway
{
  using System;
  using System.Threading.Tasks;
  using Nancy;

  public class GatewayModule : NancyModule
  {
    public GatewayModule()
    {
      Get("/productlist", _ =>
      {                                          Hard-coded list
        var products = new[]                     of products
        {
          new Product {ProductId = 1, ProductName = "T-shirt"},
          new Product {ProductId = 2, ProductName = "Hoodie"},
          new Product {ProductId = 1, ProductName = "Trousers"},
        };
        return View["productlist", new { ProductList = products }];
      });
    }
  }
}
```

Returns a view called productlist and
passes the product list into the view. The
productlist view is shown in listing 12.5.

Listing 12.4 uses a Nancy feature you haven't used before: `View["productlist", new
{ ProductList = products }];`. This is how you return a view from a Nancy module.
The first argument is the name of the view, and the second is an optional model
object that will be passed to the view and that can be used while rendering the view.

To implement the `productlist` view, create a new file called productlist.sshtml
next to GatewayModule.cs, as shown in listing 12.5. The file extension .sshtml tells
Nancy that this a SSVE view. The productlist.sshtml file contains a simple view that iterates over the list of products in the model object and builds an HTML list from the
products. To give the page a bit of structure, you import the Bootstrap CSS framework
(http://getbootstrap.com), and add a few Bootstrap CSS classes here and there.

Listing 12.5   Simple product list view

```html
<!DOCTYPE html>
<html>
<head>
<link rel="stylesheet"                                              ← Imports Bootstrap and
 href="https://maxcdn.bootstrapcdn.com/bootstrap/3.3.6/css/bootstrap.min.css"    uses it for all styling
 >
 title>MicroCommerce.NET</title>
</head>
<body>
  <div class="container">
    <div class="page-header">
      <h1>MicroCommerce <small>- Product List</small></h1>       ← Adds a heading
    </div>                                                            to the page
      <div class="row">
        <div class="col-md-8">
          @Each.ProductList                                      ← Iterates over all products
          <div class="row"                                          in the product list
             style="background-color: #eee; border-bottom-style: solid">
           <div class="col-md-8">
             <h4>@Current.ProductName</h4>                       ← Writes out the name
             <p>lorem ipsum</p>                                     of each product
           </div>
           <div class="col-md-4">
             <p></p>
             <button class="btn btn-primary" type="button">BUY!</button>   ←
           </div>
          </div>
          @EndEach
        </div>
      </div>
    </div>
  </div>
</body>
</html>
```

Adds a row for each product →

End of the iteration over products →

Adds a placeholder BUY! button for each product. The button doesn't work yet.

This code renders a product list, but the products are hardcoded in the API gateway. They should be fetched from the Product Catalog microservice. To do that, change the /productlist endpoint in `GatewayModule` to make an HTTP request to Product Catalog to get the list of products.

Listing 12.6   Finished endpoint implementation in the API gateway

```
namespace ApiGateway
{
  using System;
  using System.Collections.Generic;
  using System.Linq;
  using System.Threading.Tasks;
  using MicroserviceNET.Platform;
  using Nancy;
```

```
using Nancy.ModelBinding;
using Newtonsoft.Json;
using RestSharp;
using Serilog;

public class GatewayModule : NancyModule
{
  public GatewayModule(IHttpClientFactory clientFactory, ILogger logger)    ◄─────  The HttpClientFactory
  {                                                                                  and ILogger set up in
    Get("/productlist", async _ =>                                                   Startup are injected.
    {
      var client = await
        clientFactory.Create(                                    ◄─────  Creates an HttpClient,
          new Uri("http://localhost:5100/"),                             and points it to Product
          "product_catalog_read");                                       Catalog at port 5100
      var response = await
        client.GetAsync("/products?productIds=1,2,3,4");       ◄─────  Sends an HTTP GET
      var content = await                                              request to Product
        response?.Content.ReadAsStringAsync();                         Catalog
      productList =
        JsonConvert
        .DeserializeObject<List<Product>>(content)
        .ToArray();
      logger.Information(productList);
      return View["productlist", new { ProductList = productList }];    ◄─────
    });
  }                                                                        Passes the list of
                                                                           products to the view
  public class Product
  {
    public string ProductName;
    public int ProductId;
  }
}
```

The label **Deserializes the list of products from Product Catalog** points to the `productList = JsonConvert.DeserializeObject<List<Product>>(content).ToArray();` lines.

Now that the list of products is fetched from the Product Catalog microservice, the view shows the correct products (see figure 12.10).

Figure 12.10 When you've fetched the list of products from the Product Catalog microservice, you can see them in the GUI.

12.3.3 Creating the shopping cart GUI

The next bit of GUI that you want to add is the contents of the shopping cart. To do this, first extend /productlist to call not only the Product Catalog microservice but also the Shopping Cart microservice.

Listing 12.7   Extending /productlist to fetch the shopping cart

```csharp
namespace ApiGateway
{
    using System;
    using System.Collections.Generic;
    using System.Linq;
    using System.Threading.Tasks;
    using System.Net.Http;
    using MicroserviceNET.Platform;
    using Nancy;
    using Nancy.ModelBinding;
    using Newtonsoft.Json;
    using Serilog;
    using static System.Text.Encoding;

    public class GatewayModule : NancyModule
    {
        public GatewayModule(IHttpClientFactory clientFactory, ILogger logger)
        {
            Get("/productlist", async parameters =>
            {
                var userId = (int)parameters.userid;

                var client = await
                    clientFactory.Create(
                        new Uri("http://localhost:5100/"),
                        "product_catalog_read");
                var response = await
                    client.GetAsync("/products?productIds=1,2,3,4");
                var content = await response?.Content.ReadAsStringAsync();    // ?. is the C# 6 null-conditional operator.
                logger.Information(content);
                productList =
                    JsonConvert
                    .DeserializeObject<List<Product>>(content)
                    .ToArray();

                client = await                                                 // Creates a new HttpClient for calling Shopping Cart
                    clientFactory.Create(new Uri(
                        "http://localhost:5200/"),
                        "shopping_cart_write");
                response = await client.GetAsync($"/shoppingcart/{userId}");    // Gets the shopping cart from Shopping Cart
                content = await response?.Content.ReadAsStringAsync();
                logger.Information(content);
                var basketProducts = GetBasketProductsFromResponse(content);

                return View["productlist",
```

```
              new
              {
                ProductList = productList,              ◁─────  Deserializes the response
                BasketProducts = basketProducts                 from Shopping Cart
              }];
          });

      private List<Product> GetBasketProductsFromResponse(string responseBody)
      {
        return
          JsonConvert
            .DeserializeObject<ShoppingCart>(responseBody)      ◁────  Transforms the
            .Items                                                     response from
            ?.Select(item =>                                          Shopping Cart into
              new Product                                             a view model
              {
                ProductName = item.ProductName,
                ProductId = item.ProductCatalogueId
              })
            ?.ToList() ?? new List<Product>();
      }
    }

    public class Product
    {
      public string ProductName;
      public int ProductId;
    }
                                          ┌──  API GatewayModule's
    public class ShoppingCart      ◁──────┘    model of a ShoppingCart
    {
      public IEnumerable<ShoppingCartItem> Items { get; set; }
    }

    public class ShoppingCartItem
    {
      public int ProductCatalogueId { get; set;}
      public string ProductName { get; set; }
    }
  }
}
```

Annotations:
- Passes the list of products in the shopping cart to the view → (points to `?.Select(item =>`)

Next, extend the view to render the contents of the shopping cart on the right side of the page.

Listing 12.8 Extending the view to include the shopping cart

```
<!DOCTYPE html>
<html>
<head>
<link rel="stylesheet"
 href="https://maxcdn.bootstrapcdn.com/bootstrap/3.3.6/css/bootstrap.min.css"
 integrity="sha384-1q8mTJOASx8j1Au+a5WDVnPi21kFfwwEAa8hDDdjZlpLegxhjVME1fgjWP
```

```
      ➡ Gmkzs7"
 crossorigin="anonymous">
<title>MicroCommerce.NET</title>
</head>
<body>
  <div class="container">
    <div class="page-header">
      <h1>MicroCommerce <small> - Product List</small></h1>
    </div>
      <div class="row">
        <div class="col-md-8">
          @Each.ProductList
          <div class="row"
              style="background-color: #eee; border-bottom-style: solid">
            <div class="col-md-8">
              <h4>@Current.ProductName</h4>
              <p>lorem ipsum</p>
            </div>
            <div class="col-md-4">
              <p></p>
              <button class="btn btn-primary" type="button">BUY!</button>
            </div>
          </div>
          @EndEach
        </div>
        <div class="col-md-4">
          <div class="panel panel-info">
            <div class="panel-heading">Basket</div>
            <div class="panel-body">
              @Each.BasketProducts
                <div>
                  @Current.ProductName
                  <button class="btn btn-link">
                    <span class="glyphicon glyphicon-remove"
                    aria-hidden="true"></span>
                  </button>
                </div>
              @EndEach
            </div>
          </div>
        </div>
      </div>
  </div>
</body>
</html>
```

Adds a column on the right for the shopping cart

Writes the name of each product

Iterates over the products in the shopping cart

Placeholder button that looks like an X. The button doesn't work yet.

This view iterates over the products in the shopping cart and shows them all. With both the product list and the shopping cart, the view looks as shown in figure 12.11.

You have the complete application GUI but no functionality. The BUY! buttons don't work, nor do the Xs in the shopping cart. You'll change this in the next two sections, where you'll add some behavior to the application.

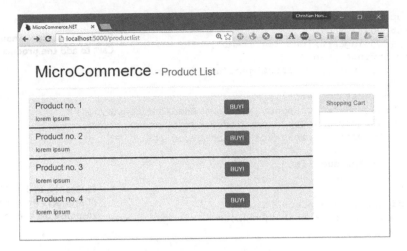

Figure 12.11 Now that you've built the first part of the application, it can show a list of products and an empty shopping cart.

12.3.4 *Letting users add products to the shopping cart*

The first piece of behavior you'll add will make the BUY! button in the product list work. You'll do two things:

1 Add an endpoint to `GatewayModule` that allows the application to add a product to the shopping cart. This endpoint in the API gateway is thin and delegates to the Shopping Cart microservice.

2 Add an `OnClick` function to the BUY! button that calls the new endpoint in `GatewayModule`.

The following listing shows the endpoint in `GatewayModule` that lets the application add a product to the shopping cart.

Listing 12.9 Endpoint to add a product to the shopping cart

```
public GatewayModule(IHttpClientFactory clientFactory, Ilogger logger)
{
  ...

  Post("/shoppingcart/{userid}", async parameters =>         New endpoint
  {
    var productId = this.Bind<int>();                        Reads a product ID from
    var userId = (int) parameters.userid;                    the body of the request

    var client = await
      clientFactory.Create(                                  Creates an HttpClient for
        new Uri("http://localhost:5200/"),                   calling Shopping Cart
        "shopping_cart_write");
```

```
var response =  await
  client.PostAsync(
    $"/shoppingcart/{userId}/items",                    ◄──┐ Sends a request to Shopping
    new StringContent(                                      │ Cart to add the product
      JsonConvert.SerializeObject(new[] { productId }),
      UTF8,
      "application/json"));
var content = await response?.Content.ReadAsStringAsync();
var basketProducts = GetBasketProductsFromResponse(content);
logger.Information("{@basket}", basketProducts);

return View["productlist",
  new
  {                                                         Passes the updated list
                                                            of products from the
    ProductList = productList,                              response back to the view
    BasketProducts = basketProducts               ◄──┘
  }];
});
}
```

This endpoint receives some data—a product ID—in the body of the POST request and delegates to the Shopping Cart microservice by sending it an HTTP POST request. Shopping Cart—as you've seen in earlier chapters—handles adding the product to the shopping cart, storing the updated shopping cart, and raising an event that notifies subscribers about the update.

To use this endpoint from the application, you need to add a bit of JavaScript to the view: a function that calls the new endpoint and replaces the current page with the page returned from the endpoint.

Listing 12.10 Calling the endpoint to add a product to the shopping cart

```
                  function buy(productId) {                              Function that's called
Checks              var xhttp = new XMLHttpRequest();                    when the request to the
whether the                                                              API gateway is completed
request was         xhttp.onreadystatechange = function() {      ◄──
successful   └─►      if (xhttp.readyState == 4 && xhttp.status == 200) {
                         document.write(xhttp.responseText);    ◄──┐
                         document.close();                         │ Prepares a POST request
Sends the            }                                             │ to the API gateway
POST               }
request      └─►  xhttp.open('POST', '/shoppingcart/123', true);
                  xhttp.setRequestHeader('Content-type', 'application/json');
                  xhttp.send( JSON.stringify(productId));          ◄──┐
                }
                                                            Replaces the contents of the current
                                                            page with the HTML in the response
                                                            from the POST request
```

This function adds a product to the shopping cart. It should be called whenever the user clicks one of the BUY! buttons. So, add an onclick handler to the BUY! button by changing the line in the view that renders the BUY! button for each product in the product list, as follows:

```html
<html>
...
            <button class="btn btn-primary" type="button"
             onclick="buy(@Current.ProductId);">
             BUY!
            </button>
...
</html>
```

> Calls the buy function with the product ID for the current product in the iteration over the list of products

That's all you need to do to make the BUY! buttons work.

12.3.5 *Letting users remove products from the shopping cart*

The last bit you need to implement will let users remove products from their shopping cart. Similar to the previous section, that means adding an endpoint to `GatewayModule` and adding an `onclick` handler to the X buttons in the shopping cart part of the application. Add a `DELETE` endpoint that again mainly delegates to the Shopping Cart microservice.

Listing 12.11   Endpoint to remove a product from the shopping cart

```
public GatewayModule(IHttpClientFactory clientFactory, Ilogger logger)
{
  ...

  Delete("/shoppingcart/{userid}", async parameters =>
  {
    var productId = this.Bind<int>();
    var userId = (int) parameters.userid;

    HttpClient client = await
      clientFactory.Create(
        new Uri("http://localhost:5200/"),
        "shopping_cart_write");
    var request =
      new HttpRequestMessage(
        HttpMethod.Delete,
        $"/shoppingcart/{userId}/items")
      {
        Content = new StringContent(
          JsonConvert.SerializeObject(new[] { productId }),
          UTF8, "application/json")
      };
    var response = await client.SendAsync(request);
    var content = await response?.Content.ReadAsStringAsync();
    var basketProducts = GetBasketProductsFromResponse(content);

    logger.Information("{@basket}", basketProducts);
```

> Prepares a DELETE request to remove a product from the shopping cart

> Sends the **DELETE** request to **Shopping Cart**

```
        return View["productlist",
          new
          {
            ProductList = productList,
            BasketProducts = basketProducts
          }];
      });
    }
```

To use this endpoint, add another JavaScript function to the view.

Listing 12.12   Calling the endpoint to remove a product from the shopping cart

```
function removeFromBasket(productId) {
  var xhttp = new XMLHttpRequest();
  xhttp.onreadystatechange = function() {
    if (xhttp.readyState == 4 && xhttp.status == 200) {
      document.write(xhttp.responseText);
      document.close();
    }
  }
  xhttp.open('DELETE', '/shoppingcart/123', true);          ◄─── Prepares to send a
  xhttp.setRequestHeader('Content-type', 'application/json');      DELETE request to
  xhttp.send(JSON.stringify(productId));                           the API gateway
}
```

Next, use this JavaScript function from the X button in the shopping cart part of the view:

```
<html>
...                                              Calls the removeFromBasket
                                                 function with the product ID
        <button class="btn btn-link"               for the current product
          onclick="removeFromBasket(@Current.ProductId);">    ◄───
            <span class="glyphicon glyphicon-remove"
             aria-hidden="true"></span>
        </button>
...
</html>
```

With this code in place, the example application works! The user can add products to and remove them from their shopping cart.

12.4   Summary

- There's a spectrum of possible kinds of applications to build on top of a microservice system, from general-purpose applications covering all the functionality in the system to small, single-capability applications.
- Applications over microservices can be built as composite applications that draw in functionality and GUI components from various microservices and compose them together to form a complete application.

- The composite application pattern allows microservices to stay decoupled, but the composite application itself can become complex.
- Applications over microservices can be built using the API gateway pattern, which puts one general-purpose API in front of all the microservices. That API gateway is the only microservice the application uses directly, but it delegates all requests to other microservices where the business capabilities are implemented.
- The API gateway pattern can simplify application development and decouple applications from the architecture of the server side.
- An API gateway can grow bigger over time because it needs to expose all functionality. This is especially true if several applications use the API gateway, because it needs to support all scenarios in all applications.
- Applications over microservices can be built with the backend for frontend (BFF) pattern. A BFF is a microservice that acts like an API gateway, but for only one application.
- BFFs are less prone to growing bigger than API gateways are.
- BFFs are tailored to the single application using them and should therefore make that application as simple to implement as possible.
- When you build web applications over microservices, you're free to use server-side rendering, client-side rendering, or a mix.
- All three patterns—composite application, API gateway, and BFF—support server-side rendering, client-side rendering, and mixes of the two.
- The implementation of an API gateway is very thin: all the endpoints you added to the example API gateway delegated to other microservices.
- Nancy supports returning server-side-rendered HTML using either the built-in Super Simple View Engine or Razor.

appendix A
Development
environment setup

This appendix describes how to set up a development environment for working with the code you write throughout this book. The development environment has five parts:

- *An IDE*—You can choose between using Visual Studio 2015 or newer, Visual Studio Code, ATOM, or JetBrains Rider. Visual Studio 2015 is Windows-only, whereas the other three work on Windows, OS X, and Linux.
- `dotnet`—You need the `dotnet` command-line tool.
- *Yeoman ASP.NET generator*—You need this to create ASP.NET Core projects. If you use Visual Studio, you can create projects through Visual Studio instead, but throughout this book you'll use Yeoman. Visual Studio and Yeoman project templates are similar, but not identical.
- *Postman*—You need a tool for making HTTP requests. There are many such tools, including cURL and Fiddler; but I recommend Postman, which I find easy to use and which works on Windows, OS X, and Linux.
- *SQL database*—On Windows, you can use SQL Server (which you'll do throughout the book); but if you prefer, you can use another SQL database, such as PostgreSQL.

I'll walk you through installing and getting up and running with the development environment in the following sections.

A.1   *Setting up an IDE*

There are four IDEs you can use with this book's code. Which one you choose is a matter of taste; all of them work fine with everything in the book. I, for one, have been switching back and forth among all four while developing the code for the book.

A.1.1   *Visual Studio 2015*

Visual Studio is the traditional choice for .NET development and has everything you'd expect from an IDE. Of relevance to the code in the book, Visual Studio gives you a good C# editor, IntelliSense in project.json files, NuGet package management, and launching and debugging of ASP.NET Core applications.

Visual Studio 2015 comes in a number of different editions. The free edition—Visual Studio 2015 Community—has everything you need to code along with the examples. To get Visual Studio 2015 Community, go to http://mng.bz/7i8F and choose Visual Studio Community. Doing so downloads an installer. Run it, and follow the instructions.

Once you have Visual Studio 2015 installed, you need to install the .NET Core plug-in for Visual Studio to get ASP.NET Core support in Visual Studio. You can find a link to the latest version of this plug-in at http://mng.bz/nvpd. It makes Visual Studio aware of ASP.NET Core and gives you project templates, project.json IntelliSense, automatic NuGet package restore when project.json is edited, and debugging of ASP.NET Core applications.

A.1.2   *Visual Studio Code*

Visual Studio Code is a lighter-weight, cross-platform alternative to Visual Studio 2015. It doesn't have the breadth of features Visual Studio has, but with the C# extension installed, it works well for the kinds of projects you write in this book: ASP.NET Core applications. Visual Studio Code provides a good C# editor, IntelliSense in project.json files, NuGet package management, and launching and debugging of ASP.NET Core applications.

You can get Visual Studio Code from https://code.visualstudio.com; click the Download button to access an installer suitable for your platform. Run the installer, and follow the instructions.

You also need the C# plug-in for Visual Studio Code. To install it, press Ctrl-P in Visual Studio Code to open the VS Code Quick Open bar. Then type `ext install csharp` and press Enter to install the C# extension.

A.1.3   *ATOM*

ATOM is a cross-platform, open source editor that's widely used across many different programming languages. To make ATOM work well with C#, you need to install the omnisharp-atom plugin that provides C# IntelliSense, refactorings, code fixes, IntelliSense in project.json files, automatic NuGet package restore, and launching of

ASP.NET Core applications. At the time of writing, there's no ASP.NET Core debugging capability in ATOM.

You can get ATOM from https://atom.io. Click the Download button, and follow the instructions. When ATOM is installed, you can get the omnisharp-atom plugin through ATOM's package manager: select File > Settings, choose Packages on the Settings page, and enter `omnisharp-atom` in the search box. The omnisharp-atom package should appear under Community Packages, and you can install it by clicking Install.

With the omnisharp-atom plugin installed, you can open a folder with a project.json file, and ATOM will recognize it as a .NET Core project and provide C#, NuGet, project.json, and `dotnet` support.

A.1.4 JetBrains Rider

At the time of writing, the Rider IDE from JetBrains is only available through the early access program, which you can apply for at www.jetbrains.com. Rider is a full-fledged, cross-platform C# IDE based on the IntelliJ IDE platform and the ReSharper Visual Studio plugin, both of which are tried-and-true JetBrains products. Rider, even in early access, provides very good C# code navigation, refactorings, code fixes, and IntelliSense. At the time of writing, Rider doesn't have good NuGet or debugging support for .NET Core, but the roadmap for Rider includes both of those, as well as an integrated test runner.

A.2 Setting up the dotnet command-line interface

You use the `dotnet` command-line tool throughout the book to run microservices, restore NuGet packages, create NuGet packages, and run tests. To install it, go to http://dot.net, click Download .NET Core, and follow the instructions for your preferred development platform.

A.3 Setting up Yeoman ASP.NET generator

Yeoman is a scaffolding tool based on Node.js. It's a versatile tool that can be used to generate ASP.NET Core projects as well as projects for many other stacks. To set up Yeoman to generate ASP.NET Core projects, you need Node.js, Yeoman, and the ASP.NET generator plugin.

To install Node.js using an installer or from a tarball, go to https://nodejs.org/en/download and follow the instructions. If you prefer to install it via a package manager such as `apt-get`, Homebrew, or Chocolatey, go to https://nodejs.org/en/download/package-manager, and follow the instructions.

Once you have Node.js installed, you also have npm—the package manager for Node. Let's use npm to install first Yeoman and then the ASP.NET generator. To install Yeoman, run this from a command line:

```
PS> npm install -g yo
```

You can now run Yeoman from the command line with the command yo. To install the ASP.NET generator plugin for Yeoman, run this from the command line:

```
PS> npm install -g generator-aspnet
```

You're now ready to generate ASP.NET Core projects by running the command yo aspnet from the command line.

A.4   *Setting up Postman*

Postman is a nice GUI tool for working with HTTP requests. It allows you to create any HTTP request and see all details of the response. This is useful when you're working with HTTP APIs, which you do a lot in this book. It also lets you test the HTTP APIs directly and see exactly what the response is in both success and failure scenarios.

You can get Postman from www.getpostman.com. Once it's installed, you can launch it and start making HTTP requests. Figure A.1, which also appears in chapter 1, illustrates how to create HTTP requests with Postman.

Now that you have an IDE, the dotnet command-line tool, and a tool for working with HTTP requests, you're all set to code along with the examples throughout the book.

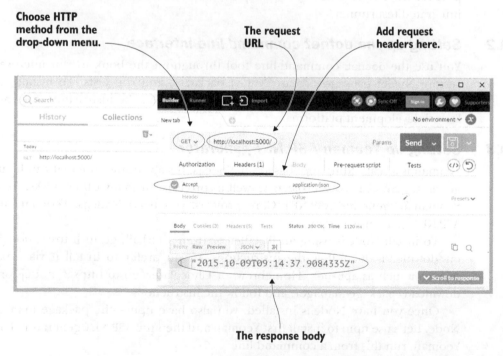

Figure A.1   Postman makes it easy to send HTTP requests while controlling the details of the request, such as the headers and the HTTP method.

A.5 *Installing SQL Server Express*

In chapter 5, you begin using a SQL Server database. You can get the installer for the free SQL Server Express database server from http://mng.bz/090m. Download the installer, run it, and follow the instructions.

If you aren't on Windows, I recommend using PostgreSQL. The Dapper library that you use in chapter 5 to talk to SQL Server can just as easily talk to PostgreSQL. To install PostgreSQL, follow the instructions for your OS at www.postgresql.org/download.

appendix B
Deploying to production

This appendix runs through the main options for running the microservices you develop throughout the book in a production environment. The main factor that affects where and how you can deploy the microservices is that they're based on .NET Core.

The microservices I discuss include two kinds of processes: HTTP APIs and event consumers. The HTTP APIs are based on ASP.NET Core and therefore run on top of Kestrel; the event consumers are .NET Core console applications.

Because .NET Core runs on both Windows and Linux, so can your microservices. Likewise, your microservices can run on your own servers or in the cloud—either Amazon or Azure.

B.1 Deploying HTTP APIs

All the HTTP APIs in this book's microservices are built in Nancy and run on top of ASP.NET Core. That means they run on top of the Kestrel web server. Kestrel isn't a full-featured web server; rather, it's a small, fast web server geared toward serving dynamic content from ASP.NET Core. The recommended way to use Kestrel in a production environment is to place it behind a reverse proxy. The reverse proxy can handle things that Kestrel isn't well suited for—like serving static files, SSL termination, and response compression. The setup is as shown in figure B.1 on Windows or Linux.

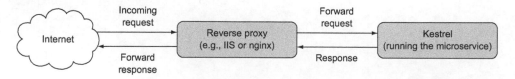

Figure B.1   Kestrel should run behind a reverse proxy.

B.1.1 Windows servers

To deploy the HTTP APIs of your microservices to a Windows server, you need to do the following:

1. Go into your microservice project, and create a deployment package with the command `dotnet publish`.
2. Install IIS on the server.
3. Install the .NET Core Windows Server Hosting Bundle into IIS.
4. Include a web.config file in the microservice project that configures `AspNet-CoreModule` to handle all requests. Such a web.config file is included in projects created with Yeoman.
5. Create a website in IIS that points to the deployment package and uses an application pool configured to use No Managed Code.

You can find detailed documentation for this setup at http://mng.bz/YA0j. It will work for your own Windows server as well as Windows cloud servers on Amazon and Azure.

B.1.2 Linux servers

To deploy the HTTP APIs of your microservices to a Linux server, follow these steps:

1. Alter the startup code in program.cs to make it listen on a Unix socket—for example, http://unix:/var/microservicenet/hello/kestrel.sock. This means adding a call to `UseUrls` on `IWebHostBuilder`. `IWebHostBuilder` is already created and otherwise configured in the program.cs file, so the `UseUrls` call is another in the existing chain of calls.
2. Go into your microservice project, and create a deployment package with the command `dotnet publish`.
3. Install nginx on the server.
4. Configure a site on nginx to forward all incoming requests to the Unix socket the microservice is listening on.
5. Configure the supervisor daemon to start up and supervise the microservice when the server boots.

You can find detailed documentation for this setup at http://mng.bz/ZWNh. It will work for your own Linux servers as well as Linux cloud servers on Amazon and Azure.

B.1.3 Azure Web Apps

Azure offers a PaaS–level option for running .NET Core web applications: Azure Web Apps. With this option, you don't have to handle the reverse proxy setup yourself—Azure does that. You just need to create a web app on Azure—for example, through the Azure portal. Then, you can deploy to the web app by creating a deployment package using `dotnet publish` and copying it to the web app via FTP or a number of other deployment options, including pushing to a Git repository. You can find detailed documentation for this setup at http://mng.bz/1ubQ.

B.1.4   *Azure Service Fabric*

Azure offers another PaaS-level option called Azure Service Fabric, which can also run your Nancy-based HTTP APIs. To do this, you have to start from a different project template than the one you use throughout the book; see the documentation at http://mng.bz/1WyY. Once you have a project ready to deploy to Azure Service Fabric, you can install Nancy and the other NuGet packages into it and do everything you do throughout the book using Nancy, Polly, and OWIN.

B.2   *Deploying event consumers*

The event consumers you write in chapters 4, 6, and 7 are .NET Core console applications that are ready to run as Windows services, so they only work on Windows. The event consumers are Windows-only because they're Windows services—but all the code for fetching events from a feed, keeping track of which events have already been handled, and handling events could just as well run on Linux. The only thing you'd need to implement differently to run on Linux is the implementation of Service-Base: the code that reacts to the start and stop signals from Windows when the Windows service starts and stops. The following sections outline some alternatives to using a Windows service to host the event consumer code.

B.2.1   *Windows servers*

On a Windows server, you can install the event consumer from chapter 4 as a Windows service, as described in that chapter. No modifications to the event consumer code are needed.

B.2.2   *Linux servers*

On Linux, you can run an event consumer with the supervisor daemon in much the same way you can run a Kestrel-hosted HTTP API on Linux. You need to change the code a little: instead of implementing ServiceBase and starting a timer in OnStart, the timer should be started at startup in the Main method.

To get ready to run the event consumer under the supervisor daemon, first run dotnet publish in the event consumer project. Then, write a supervisor configuration file for the event consumer in /etc/supervisor/conf.d/ with contents along the lines of the following:

```
[program:eventconsumer]
command=dotnet /var/microservicesnet/eventconsumer/eventconsumer.dll      ◁───┐
autostart=true                                                                │
autorestart=true                                                Path to the DLL created by
stderr_logfile=/var/log/eventconsumer.err.log                   the <data></data>dotnet
stdout_logfile=/var/log/eventconsumer.out.log                          publish command
environment=Hosting__Environment=Production
user=www-data
stopsignal=INT
```

Next, you need to restart the supervisor daemon, and it will pick up the new configuration and start the event consumer. These two commands restart the supervisor daemon:

```
sudo service supervisor stop
sudo service supervisor start
```

Now the event consumer runs under the supervision of the supervisor daemon.

B.2.3 Azure WebJobs

Azure WebJobs let you run console applications on Azure on a schedule (see http://mng.bz/R4m9). To do this, you should drop the implementation of `Service-Base` and do one batch of event handling whenever the console application is run. The Azure scheduler takes care of calling the event consumer on a schedule. When it runs, the event consumer can do whatever it needs to do, including polling an event feed, using a data store to keep track of handled events, and any business logic for handling events.

B.2.4 Azure Functions

Azure Functions is, in a sense, a lighter-weight version of Azure WebJobs, which is part of the wider Azure Service Fabric offering. Azure Functions also lets you run .NET code on a schedule handled by Azure. The documentation for setting up Azure Functions is at http://mng.bz/h7D9.

To run the event consumer as an Azure Function, you need to cut it back to the code to run a batch of event handling: the code to poll an event feed, the code to keep track of handled events, and the business logic to handle events. Azure takes care of calling the function on a schedule.

B.2.5 Amazon Lambda

Amazon Lambda is similar to Azure Functions. Again, you cut back the code for the event consumer to the code for running a batch of event handling. You can find the documentation for setting up Amazon Lambda to run C# code on a schedule at http://mng.bz/5wJd.

Further reading

Microservices

Cramon, Jeppe. "Microservices: It's not (only) the size that matters, it's (also) how you use them," parts 1–5. 2014–2015. http://mng.bz/zQ2a.

Fowler, Martin. "MicroservicePrerequisites." August 28, 2014. http://martinfowler.com/bliki/MicroservicePrerequisites.html.

———. "MonolithFirst." June 3, 2015. http://martinfowler.com/bliki/MonolithFirst.html.

Lewis, James and Martin Fowler. "Microservices." March 25,2014. http://martinfowler.com/articles/microservices.html.

Tilkov, Stefan. "Don't start with a monolith." June 9, 2015. http://martinfowler.com/articles/dont-start-monolith.html.

Newman, Sam. *Building Microservices: Designing Fine-Grained Systems.* O'Reilly Media, 2015.

———. "Pattern: Backends for Frontends." November 18, 2015. http://samnewman.io/patterns/architectural/bff.

Software design and architecture in general

Beck, Kent. *Test Driven Development: By Example.* Addison-Wesley Professional: 2002.

Conway, Melvin E. "How Do Committees Invent?" *Datamation* (April 1968). www.melconway.com/research/committees.html.

"Defense in Depth." *Open Web Application Security Project (OWASP).* www.owasp.org/index.php/Defense_in_depth.

Evans, Eric. *Domain-Driven Design: Tackling Complexity in the Heart of Software.* Addison-Wesley Professional: 2003.

Fowler, Martin. "TestPyramid." May 1, 2012. http://martinfowler.com/bliki/TestPyramid.html.

———. "IntegrationContractTest." January 12, 2011. http://martinfowler.com/bliki/IntegrationContractTest.html.

Freeman, Steve and Nat Pryce. *Growing Object-Oriented Software, Guided by Tests.* Addison-Wesley Professional: 2009.

Hohpe, Gregor and Bobby Woolf. *Enterprise Integration Patterns: Designing, Building, and Deploying Messaging Solutions.* Addison-Wesley Professional: 2003.

Humble, Jez and David Farley. *Continuous Delivery: Reliable Software Releases through Build, Test, and Deployment Automation.* Addison-Wesley Professional: 2010.

Martin, Robert C. "The Single Responsibility Principle." May 5, 2014. http://mng.bz/RZgU.

———. "SRP: The Single Responsibility Principle." http://mng.bz/zQyz.

Nygard, Michael T. *Release It!: Design and Deploy Production-Ready Software.* Pragmatic Programmers: 2007.

Vernon, Vaughn. *Implementing Domain-Driven Design.* Addison-Wesley Professional: 2013.

Technologies used

ASP.NET Core. www.asp.net/core. Dapper. http://mng.bz/7LHZ.
Elasticsearch. https://info.elastic.co/Getting-Started-ES.html.
Event Store. https://geteventstore.com.
IdentityServer. https://identityserver.github.io/Documentation.
Kibana. www.elastic.co/products/kibana. Nancy. http://nancyfx.org.
Nancy documentation. https://github.com/NancyFx/Nancy/wiki/Documentation.
Nancy samples. https://github.com/NancyFx/Nancy/tree/master/samples.
.NET Core. https://dotnet.github.io.
NuGet documentation. http://docs.nuget.org.
OAuth. http://oauth.net/2.
OpenID Connect. http://openid.net/connect.
OWIN standard. http://owin.org.
Polly documentation. https://github.com/App-vNext/Polly#polly.
Serilog. https://serilog.net.
xUnit. https://xunit.github.io.

index